The International Companion to James Macpherson and *The Poems of Ossian*

INTERNATIONAL COMPANIONS TO SCOTTISH LITERATURE

Series Editors: Ian Brown and Thomas Owen Clancy

Titles in the series include:

International Companion to Lewis Grassic Gibbon
Edited by Scott Lyall
ISBN 978-1-908980-13-7

International Companion to Edwin Morgan
Edited by Alan Riach
ISBN 978-1-908980-14-4

International Companion to Scottish Poetry
Edited by Carla Sassi
ISBN 978-1-908980-15-1

International Companion to James Macpherson and The Poems of Ossian
Edited by Dafydd Moore
ISBN 978-1-908980-19-9

The International Companion to James Macpherson and *The Poems of Ossian*

Edited by Dafydd Moore

Scottish Literature International

Published by
Scottish Literature International
Scottish Literature
7 University Gardens
University of Glasgow
Glasgow G12 8QH

Scottish Literature International is an imprint of
the Association for Scottish Literary Studies

www.asls.org.uk

ASLS is a registered charity no. SC006535

First published 2017

Text © ASLS and the individual contributors

All rights reserved. No part of this book may be
reproduced, stored in a retrieval system, or
transmitted in any form or means, electronic,
mechanical, photocopying, recording or otherwise,
without the prior permission of the
Association for Scottish Literary Studies.

A CIP catalogue for this title
is available from the British Library

ISBN 978-1-908980-19-9

Kingston
University
London

ASLS acknowledges the support of Kingston University
towards the publication of this book.

Contents

Series Editors' Preface vii
A Brief Biography of James Macpherson ix

Introduction 1
Dafydd Moore
1. The Correspondence of James Macpherson 14
Paul deGategno
2. Ossian and the Gaelic World 26
Lesa Ní Mhunghaile
3. Ossian and the State of Translation in the
   Scottish Enlightenment 39
Gauti Kristmannsson
4. Nostalgic Ossian and the Transcreation of the
   Scottish Nation 52
Cordula Lemke
5. Landscape and the Sense of Place in *The Poems of Ossian* . . . 65
Sebastian Mitchell
6. Ossian's Impact on the Discovery of Ancient
   Scandinavian Literature 76
Robert W. Rix
7. The Significance of James Macpherson's *Ossian* for
   Visual Artists 92
Murdo Macdonald
8. Macpherson's *Iliad* and the Logic of Literary Primitivism . . . 105
Dafydd Moore
9. Principles, Prejudices, and the Politics of James Macpherson's
   Historical Writing 119
Robert W. Jones

Endnotes 135
Further Reading 169
Notes on Contributors 173
Index 175

Series Editors' Preface

With the successful relaunch of the *Companions to Scottish Literature* series as the *International Companions*, under the aegis of the Association for Scottish Literary Studies, the series editors have decided to move from the former policy of publishing in annual tranches of two or three volumes to one of issuing volumes as and when they are ready. It is expected that this will still result in the publication of two or three volumes each year, but will offer more flexibility in terms of publication dates to allow for any unavoidable delays to individual volumes which might hold up the release of an annual tranche.

The publication of the first volumes under the aegis of the ASLS – on Lewis Grassic Gibbon, Edwin Morgan, and Scottish Poetry – has been well received and a number of volumes are now at various stages of preparation for future publication. The editors will continue their policy of publishing three kinds of volume: period, themed, and author volumes. This author volume on James Macpherson and the poems of Ossian has been developed under the meticulous editorship of Professor Dafydd Moore. It reflects a growing understanding of the Ossian phenomenon and sets it in the context of Macpherson's other work in a refreshing and insightful way. It is a timely and welcome addition to the *International Companions to Scottish Literature* series.

Ian Brown
Thomas Owen Clancy

A Brief Biography of James Macpherson

James Macpherson was born in Ruthven in Badenoch, Scotland, in 1736. He was educated at King's College and Marischal College, Aberdeen, where he would have come under the influence of the noted classicist Thomas Blackwell Jnr, whose *Enquiry into the Life and Writings of Homer* (1735) is taken to have been a key influence on *The Poems of Ossian*. He also studied at Edinburgh University, where he had a number of poems published, including two neoclassical epics on Highland themes, before gaining employment as a teacher and tutor, most notably to the son of Graham of Balgowan. It was in this capacity that he was visiting the border spa town of Moffat when he met the Edinburgh-based John Home, famous as the author of *Douglas* (1756), a meeting which would provide him with an introduction to the great and the good of the Scottish Enlightenment and the wherewithal to bring *The Poems of Ossian* to life.

The Ossianic phase of Macpherson's career was surprisingly short relative to its impact on Macpherson and, indeed, European literature. *Fragments of Ancient Poetry Collected in the Highlands of Scotland* appeared in 1760 followed by *Fingal: An Ancient Epic Poem in Six Books; Together with Several Other Poems, Composed by Ossian the Son of Fingal* in 1761/2 and *Temora: An Ancient Epic Poem in Eight Books; Together with Several Other Poems, Composed by Ossian the Son of Fingal* in 1763. These were collected together into the *Works of Ossian* in 1765 and were revised by Macpherson for a new edition nearly ten years later in 1773. 1773 also saw the publication of Macpherson's 'Ossianic' translation of Homer's *Iliad*.

Macpherson had an obvious flair for controversial historiography, and through the 1770s this was the major focus of his written output. His *Introduction to the History of Great Britain and Ireland* was published in 1771, but his attention soon turned to more contemporary matters.

1775 saw the *Papers Containing the Secret History of Great Britain* followed by *The History of Great Britain from the Restoration to the Accession of the House of Hanover.* His writing, which has always been politically loaded, took an ever more partisan turn. This can be seen in his *Rights of Great Britain asserted against the claims of America* (1776); the *Short History of the Opposition during the Last Session of Parliament* (1779); and *The History and Management of the East India Company* (also 1779). He also wrote extensively for the government in the pages of the *Private Advertiser.* From 1780 Macpherson was MP for Camelford in Cornwall (though he apparently never visited 'his' constituency or spoke in the Commons). He died in February 1796 at the Highland Estate he purchased through the proceeds of his eventful and lucrative career.

Introduction

Dafydd Moore

James Macpherson was born in 1736 in Ruthven and died sixty years later only a few miles down the road on his estate outside Kingussie. But the story of the son of a tenant farmer who ended his days at the house built for him by the Adams brothers and who was buried in Westminster Abbey at his own expense is as unusual as that trajectory suggests. As a child Macpherson may have witnessed the firing of Ruthven barracks by the Jacobite army in early 1746 and the final dispersal of the same after the catastrophe at Culloden later that spring. The Macphersons of Cluny were 'out' during the Rising of 1745 and suffered the indignities (and worse) of confiscation as the Government sought to break the power of the clans forever. Macpherson's uncle, Ewan Macpherson of Cluny, (Macpherson's father Andrew being an illegitimate son of the chief) was on the run in the Highlands for much of Macpherson's teenage years. His university education between 1752 and 1755 was marked by the necessity of moving from King's to Marischal College Aberdeen (the two institutions that would in the following century merge to form Aberdeen University), almost certainly as a result of changes in the length of the academic year that led to Marischal becoming cheaper to attend. Yet when he retired to the Highlands, he was able to restore the clan lands to the rightful heir (after he was himself offered them in return for his government service) and live himself the life of the beneficent laird on his own estate, supported by the proceeds of a lucrative career as a writer and, if not exactly politician, then political fixer. While some of the starker apparent paradoxes in this career (scion, albeit illegitimate, of a Jacobite clan who grows up to be Hanoverian political lackey) owe more to over-simplistic (and increasingly outdated) assumptions about the political and social landscape of the age than they do to genuinely insoluble contradictions within his character, nevertheless they do describe a remarkable path through eighteenth-century Britain and the British state as it emerges as a modern global power.

This volume gives an insight into all facets of Macpherson's career and, while considerations of *The Poems of Ossian* dominate the collection, it also seeks to cast light on those corners of it less frequently understood or even considered. This introduction sets the scene in three ways. Firstly, it offers a simple overview of Macpherson's career. Its Ossianic phase has garnered so much attention and been subject to so much discussion (at least relative to the rest of it) that it has had a tendency to overshadow what followed. The reception of (and storm about) *The Poems of Ossian* was, it goes without saying, a key determining factor in the future course of Macpherson's life, if only because it made his name (literally given that, following the fashion of the age, he was known as 'Fingal' Macpherson). On the other hand, there is much to be gained from laying out that course from beginning to end and appreciating the full contours of his career. Secondly, this introduction highlights the key features of Macpherson – by which it is soon clear one means *Ossian* – studies. It is not a literature survey (a synoptic bibliography of key texts is provided at the end) so much as an introduction to the key areas of debate and scholarly endeavour. Thirdly, the introduction sets the scene for the chapters that follow.

Macpherson: Life and Works

Macpherson was educated in Aberdeen and (for the clergy) Edinburgh University, though he seems to have left both, as was common at the time, without taking a degree. While in Edinburgh he tried his hand as a poet, having a number of pieces published in the *Edinburgh Review* (though not all the attributions are especially secure) and producing two epic poems, *The Hunter* and *The Highlander*, neither of which, it is safe to say, had the desired impact on the world of letters. He had a spell as a schoolmaster in Ruthven, but by 1758 was working as a family tutor to the son of Graham of Balgowan. In this capacity he met moral and social philosopher Adam Ferguson, who in turn provided him with an introduction to John Home, a fellow member of the Edinburgh literati, best known as the author of the play *Douglas* (1756), a neoclassical tragedy set in medieval Scotland in a not dissimilar milieu to Macpherson's *The Highlander*. Macpherson met Home in 1759 in the spa town of Moffat, and the encounter would change his life. Macpherson told Home of fragments of Gaelic poetry he had collected. Home persuaded an apparently reluctant Macpherson to show him some, and from there it was a short step to Edinburgh and the publication of seventeen *Fragments of*

Ancient Poetry Collected in the Highlands of Scotland and translated from the Galic or Erse Language. As Lesa Ní Mhunghaile's contribution to this volume recounts, this can be seen as some manner of culmination (at least of the first phase) of a growing interest in the possibility of an extant body of Gaelic poetry in Scotland. The preface, provided by Hugh Blair (soon to become Regius Professor of Rhetoric and Belles Lettres at Edinburgh in 1762) after conversations with Macpherson, spoke of the possibility of entire epics, even suggesting that one of the *Fragments* represented the opening of one such poem. Dinners were held, funds were raised, and Macpherson was packed off to the Highlands in search of such treasures. He made two trips, in August and September 1760 and between October 1760 and January 1761, collecting manuscripts and oral versions of ballads from a wide range of contacts. These activities resulted in two further volumes of poetry: *Fingal: An Ancient Epic Poem in Six Books; Together with Several Other Poems, Composed by Ossian the Son of Fingal* prepared for the press under Blair's watchful eye through 1761 and published in London in 1762; and *Temora: An Ancient Epic Poem in Eight Books; Together with* [...]. The first book of the epic *Temora* had appeared in the *Fingal* volume, though the complete volume was assembled and published (complete with a dedication to the Prime Minister Lord Bute) in London in 1763. In these volumes Macpherson claimed to have found not only an epic poem but an epic poet – Ossian – whose poems are in effect his reminiscences for the time of his father Fingal and a warrior society of which he is the last survivor. In all, the volumes use something in the region of sixteen or seventeen extant ballads in a variety of ways: plot lines, loose translations of passages, names or incidents. *Fingal* most closely corresponds to extant traditional ballads actually in Gaelic; *Temora* is furthest from the extant tradition.[1]

And that, from the point of view of *Ossian*, was substantially that. There was a complete works in 1765 and a second (in fact a third, counting the 1765 *Works*) edition in 1773. Scholars have demonstrated the detailed engagement with the text involved in these editions, but it remains the case that, despite the fears of those who suspected (given the repeated hints about further work yet to be brought to light) that any of the shorter poems might suddenly be revealed, *Temora*-like, to be a lost epic, Macpherson produced no further Ossian material. Equally, although he was involved in an ill-tempered exchange with Samuel Johnson at the height of the controversy about *Ossian*'s authenticity, he actually played a remarkably small direct role in the row over authenticity that rumbled on through the 1760s and 1770s. He may have left one thousand pounds in his will to aid the publication of the so-called originals, but as early as September 1763 David Hume was telling Blair that Macpherson 'has totally abandoned all care of [*Ossian*]', and he was as good as his word when he said in the preface to the new edition of 1773 that he now 'resigned them for ever to their fate'.[2] Even the bequest was merely the (belated) passing on of funds he had received from the Scottish community in India in 1784 to help him produce a Gaelic text and is therefore more striking as evidence of his lack of interest in the project during his lifetime than it is of a burning desire to provide the wherewithal for the venture as a gift to posterity.

By mid-1763, 'Fingal' Macpherson had swapped Edinburgh for London, was a drinking companion of Boswell and, by all accounts (or at least Boswell's), rather self-consciously a rake about town. In 1764 he travelled abroad as secretary to George Johnstone, governor of the newly acquired British colony of Florida. The trip was notable for an unfortunate, if convenient, episode during which Macpherson supposedly lost many of the original Ossianic manuscripts in a Florida swamp; and for the fact that this was his first contact with the government to whom he would provide his services for much of the rest of his career. He was back from Florida by 1766 (it is often assumed because he fell out with Johnstone, though Paul deGategno's contribution to this volume offers a corrective to this), though he retained his salary as a pension in return for his services as a political writer, at least until the loss by the British of their American colonies.

In presenting Ossian to the world, Macpherson had (with the help of others, Blair and Adam Ferguson most particularly) dressed him in all the scholarly finery that the Scottish Enlightenment could muster. Dissertations and footnotes pored over not only the (high) literary qualities of the poet but the wider social, political and sociological context for times and manners of Fingal, Ossian and their contemporaries. Ossian's translator and editor, the reader is directed to conclude from these volumes, is not only a man of literary taste and talent but a conjectural historian of substance. This material was eye-catchingly prominent, and indeed Fiona Stafford has argued that it is the claims made and positions adopted in this surrounding material (both for Ossian and Macpherson) that attracted the greatest controversy and ultimately 'brought Macpherson more abuse than praise'.[3] And it was to controversial conjectural history Macpherson turned next, with his *Introduction to the History of Great Britain and Ireland* (1771). In this, a work barely less fanciful than *Ossian*, he expands at substantial length on the theories of ethnic difference, conquest and division hinted at in the *Ossian* volumes (though strangely he makes only one passing and indeed rather hostile reference to the works of Ossian themselves within it) in order 'to show, what Macpherson unquestioningly believed, that most of [Britain's] early civilisation might be traced to [Celtic] institutions'.[4] Macpherson still had some literary ambitions to achieve – or perhaps scores to settle – and his final literary work, an Ossianic translation of Homer's *Iliad*, dates from this period in 1773, the year of his fully revised edition of *Ossian* itself.

Yet Macpherson's career was turning increasingly decisively away from the literary, though not from controversy. In 1775 he produced a collection of *Papers Containing the Secret History of Great Britain* followed by a work based upon these discoveries, *The History of Great Britain from the Restoration to the Accession of the House of Hanover*. This was conceived in fact as the concluding part of Hume's *History of England*. Hume disapproved of both the choice of author and the finished product, but it was a success, and Macpherson sold the copyright for three thousand pounds.[5] By this time he was also working on the Government's behalf as a surveyor of the press, and his career took a still more political turn over the course of the rest of the decade. By 1767 Macpherson was acquainted with John Macpherson (no relation), the son of John Macpherson of Sleat who had assisted him in his Ossianic researches. John Macpherson had returned from India to press the cause of Mohammed Ali, Nawab of Arcot, against the East India Company with the Ministry in London. James assisted John in his efforts, culminating in the production in 1779 of *The History and Management of the East India Company, from its origins in 1600 to the present time, Containing the Affairs of the Carnatic, in which the Rights of the Nabob are explained, and the injustice of the Company Proved*.[6] If the subtitle was not clear enough, then the observation contained in its preface that 'wading through the sink of East-India corruption and mismanagement is a task, which adds disgust to toil' cleared up any ambiguity. When John returned to India at the end of the decade (he would eventually succeed Warren Hastings as Governor-General in 1785), James became the Nawab of Arcot's London agent.

In 1780 he became the MP for Camelford in Cornwall, a seat in a rotten borough he occupied until his death, apparently without ever feeling the need to visit the constituency or speak in the House. He was also awarded a further secret pension in return for his services as a government writer. His *Rights of Great Britain asserted against the claims of America: Being an Answer to the Declaration of the General Congress* was a popular attempt (according to its advertisement) to 'extricate the contest now subsisting between Great Britain and her colonies from the errors of the ignorant, and the misrepresentations of designing men' and was published in 1776, going through five editions. His *Short History of the Opposition during the Last Session of Parliament* (1779), devoted to demonstrating that 'the most formidable foes of Great Britain were nursed in her own bosom' and acted 'not only against her interest, but her very existence as a great and independent kingdom', also found a ready audience. The Macphersons were formidable political writers, often through the pages of the *Private Advertiser*, with Macpherson's contribution to the cause ultimately acknowledged by Lord North to George III.

It was the proceeds amassed from these not always entirely reputable activities that allowed Macpherson to purchase an estate north of Kingussie and build his country retreat Balavil, or Belville (although he remained active in London for most of the year).[7] Even this apparently more straightforward part of his life has been dogged by some controversy (and not just over the spelling of the name of his house). He purchased land previously owned by Mackintosh of Borlum and removed the existing property to make room for his Adam-designed villa. Saunders, a Macpherson apologist on most matters, refers to Mackintosh as 'disgraced' and paints a picture of Macpherson as beneficent laird, eager to repay the debts of his youth and create, perhaps, the kind of Highland society the passing of which he laments in his dissertations on *Ossian*.[8] Others, however, have been less kind. In 1897, Charles Fraser-Mackintosh claimed in the second series of his *Antiquarian Notes* that Macpherson was an enthusiastic clearer and improver and sees the treatment of the previous property and its name Raitts as typical of his ruthlessness. In its own way this is a characteristically colourful and ambiguous final chapter to Macpherson's life, which ended at home at Balavil in February 1796.

Critical Afterlife

It is difficult to overstate the impact of *The Poems of Ossian* on the literature of Western Europe. They played a substantial role in the growth of interest in the native literatures of not only the British Isles but Northern Europe, sometimes by providing an uncomplicated inspiration for antiquarians and sometimes through spurring a desire to disprove or otherwise dispute their veracity. They were also key to the emerging literary discourse and aesthetic of Romanticism across Europe: Jerome MacGann considers that 'Ossian's influence on the literary scene of the late eighteenth century eclipsed all others', while Robert Crawford has suggested that Macpherson 'initiated and brought to fruition a tonal shift in Western writing'.[9] This being so, it is understandable that scholarship on Macpherson has been pretty exclusively devoted to *Ossian*, and within that organised until very recently around two dimensions of that impact: arguments about provenance and authenticity, and traces of influence.

Between 1760 and the end of the nineteenth century, the question of *Ossian*'s authenticity was seen in terms of the genuineness of Macpherson's claims, as various parties for various reasons cast doubt on the *Ossian* Macpherson presented. The most obvious were straightforward debates about forgery and fraud centred on the inherent unlikelihood of the survival of *Ossian* as it appeared over some fifteen centuries and most famously encapsulated by the feud between Samuel Johnson and Macpherson. Yet to see matters exclusively in these terms is to miss the point of much of the debate. It obscures, for example, the contributions of Irish antiquarians in highlighting the inadequacies, ignorance and worse of Macpherson's claims about Ireland, or a strand of debate concerned with appropriate generic designation.[10] To put it simply, whether it was Scottish, epic and/or fifteen hundred years old were as – if not more – pressing questions than straightforward accusations that Macpherson had made it all up, although popular culture to this day tends to see matters in these terms. For the record, as it were, D. S. Thomson's comprehensive *The Gaelic Sources of Macpherson's Ossian* (1952) spelled out, in terms that have been only slightly qualified and advanced in the intervening period, the reality of the relationship to the Gaelic milieu, as well as opened the door on the investigation of Macpherson's work in the context of Gaelic literature.

The work of Thomas Bailey Saunders and John Semple Smart either side of 1900 marked a change in scholarly emphasis, however. Both were less interested in debating the facts about *Ossian* than they were in interpreting the facts about the debate about *Ossian*.[11] Saunders is an apologist, Smart less indulgent, but both seek to place the controversy over *Ossian* within a wider context of (in Smart's case) a battle between neoclassical and historicist understandings of literature and (in Saunders's case) Anglo-Scottish cultural relations. The latter's emphasis on a war of ideas between Blair and Johnson, Scottish and English arbiters of taste, sounds on the one hand rather old-fashioned (at least in the emphasis on personality it implies), but on the other not so very far from the kind of construction likely to be placed on the episode by a twenty-first century 'four nations' critic seeking to demonstrate the dynamics of anglocentric canon formation.[12] While the question of Macpherson's relation to the authentic literature of the Gaelic world has remained an open one within Celtic and Irish studies, and indeed the place of Macpherson within the history of folklore fieldwork the subject of some discussion itself, commentary about the *Ossian* controversy has tended to follow Smart and Saunders's tack of explanation and interpretation, expanding and amplifying it to consider different dimensions of cultural politics, aesthetics, and the history of ideas to do with things such as property, the law, and the nature of creativity.[13]

The other great preoccupation of the critical reception of *Ossian* has been an interest in the popularity and influence the poems enjoyed. There is, of course, a crossover in the extent to which reinforcing, qualifying, rebutting, or emulating *Ossian* became a motivation for antiquarian scholarship across Europe, as Robert Rix's chapter in the current volume demonstrates. Yet it is also clear that *Ossian* enjoyed huge popularity amongst readers, writers, and artists who cared little for antiquarian exactitude or national pride. Poets, novelists, and painters across the anglophone world felt the power of Macpherson's vision, and, through some seminal translations, *Ossian* entered the cultural bloodstream of Europe, where particular emphasis has been laid on the importance of the poems in France, Germany, and Italy.[14] Indeed, it is Europe where large-scale attempts to reckon with Macpherson's role within national literary cultures have been attempted – notably Paul Van Teigham's two-volume *Ossian en France* (Paris, 1917) and Wolfgang Schmidt's four-volume *'Homer des Nordens' und 'Mutter der Romantik': James Macphersons 'Ossian' und seine Rezeption in der deutschsprachigen Literatur* (Berlin, 2003). The understanding of Macpherson's place within the literary culture of Britain and Ireland has been, by comparison, limited on the whole to bilateral considerations of *Ossian* and individual authors.[15] There are a number of reasons for this, including the fact that the current *Ossian* scholarship is by its nature suspicious of narratives that stress the influence of neglected figures on more recognised names by way of establishing their credentials. Such lines of argument can be interpreted as (or become) another version of the 'contributionist' argument about Scottish investment in the idea of Britain and, as such, work to reconfirm existing cultural power relations.[16] To put it another way, the 'four nations' or 'archipelagic' approach of the literature of Britain and Ireland to which much *Ossian* scholarship belongs is, on the whole, more invested in questioning the construction of the Romantic canon than it is in arguing Macpherson's place within it, and certainly not via asserting an influence that might only confirm a subsidiary or inferior status.

It has been this 'four nations' interest in eighteenth-century and Romantic literature that accounts for the range of interests in *Ossian* over the last thirty years. Indeed, John Kerrigan sees Macpherson as a major beneficiary of the approach.[17] This work has sought to understand literary culture in ways other than those previously determined by an anglocentric literary establishment; to highlight the competing models and locales of literary culture within the emergent British state; and bring fresh understanding of the period as one characterised by, in the words of Alan Rawes and Gerard Carruthers, 'negotiated dialogues where complicated questions of aesthetics, cultural politics and nation are asked, and answered in equally complex fashion'.[18] A key dimension of recent scholarship on *Ossian* has been the examination of the specific cultural politics of the text's interest in Scottish, and in particular Celtic, identity within the context of attempts to fashion and re-fashion a sense of Britishness. Some have seen Macpherson's evocation of a tearful and doomed Celtic heroism as an accommodation with, and indeed complicit within, the construction of an Anglo-British nation and culture, motivated by, in Fiona Stafford's words, a 'desire to render the Highlands safe forever'.[19] Though, as Stafford and Gaskill's introduction to their 1998 collection *From Gaelic to Romantic* makes clear, within all the lamenting and stoic resignation in the face of the inevitability of defeat, there remains a subversive, unreconciled and perhaps irreconcilable note of reproach. As Murray Pittock puts it, 'to the extent that [*Ossian*] was animated by a real expression not just of nostalgia but also of regret, Macpherson's epic offered a disturbing hint of injustice lingering amid its sentimental treatment of grief and loss.'[20] Equally, that *Ossian* proved so threatening and controversial should not be forgotten. The thought of a 'Northern Homer', a mythical point of origin and spokesman for many of the values held dearest by eighteenth-century English culture and society was a disturbing one and accounts for the vehemence of the response.

An increased awareness of *Ossian*'s centrality within the culture and aesthetic discourse of the eighteenth century has been another strong feature of the critical response to the poems over the last thirty years. Previously *Ossian* had really only been considered in relation to ideas of primitivism and the conception of the epic poet in studies that usually contrasted him with Homer.[21] However, from the mid-1980s attention turned to other dimensions of the poem and in particular its depiction of heroic virtue. Some, such as Luke Gibbons, see this in terms of the questions of cultural appropriation and assimilation discussed above, while others have seen *Ossian* as a crucial and telling case study for the preoccupations of Scottish Enlightenment thought.[22] Whatever the final inflection, however, this body of work has established *Ossian* as an important feature in the eighteenth century's interest in moral sentiment and its efforts to reconcile the values of politeness and sympathy with the more savage and antique values of public virtue.[23] This is but one of the ways in which the last three decades have seen significant changes, and in particular an increased sophistication, in our understanding of Macpherson's *Ossian*. Yet it is notable that the rest of Macpherson's career remains unconsidered in any serious way. If mentioned at all, it tends to be in somewhat hostile ways, as evidence of Macpherson's eye for the main chance and his eagerness to write and please for money, usually then reverse-engineered as a context for *Ossian* as the product of a profoundly cynical mind. Addressing this imbalance in qualitative, if not quantitative, terms is one of the key purposes of this Companion.

A Companion to Macpherson and Ossian

The chapters in this book respond to the critical fields outlined above and offer examples of the new thinking in the field from scholars across Europe and North America. The chapters on Macpherson are in different ways almost all interested in the notion of translation, between languages, cultures, even between disciplines and theoretical approaches. They also all share a determination to be non-judgmental in their grappling with the particularities of Macpherson. This effort to articulate Macpherson's career without resort to a rhetoric of the scoundrel is also shared by the chapters that seek to shed light on other aspects of Macpherson's career. One can, if one likes, make judgements of a moral nature about Macpherson and his activities (particularly perhaps those beyond the realm of the aesthetic), but they should at least be informed by and take account of the issues and features discussed here. The volume opens with Paul deGategno's account of key episodes in Macpherson's career as revealed through a selection of his correspondence, both published and unpublished. While not biographical as such, the chapter sheds light on a number of the more complicated and less examined of Macpherson's activities, and demonstrates how he used the letter as a means of political and personal advancement for himself and others.

The next six essays consider different aspects of Macpherson's most important and best known work *The Poems of Ossian*. In each case they offer arguments that fit into – and therefore provide case studies of the approaches adopted within – the critical landscape described above. They also complement each other, evolving a series of themes that allow the reader to develop a detailed and specific understanding of Macpherson's achievement. Lesa Ní Mhunghaile considers the relationship between *Ossian* and the Gaelic culture of Ireland and Scotland that gave it birth, identifying the differences but also some of the surprising congruencies between the Ossian of Gaelic culture and Macpherson's Anglophone invention. Ní Mhunghaile demonstrates a truth about Macpherson criticism that stretches back into the 1760s, that some of the most sensitive and considered assessments of Macpherson's achievement come from those with the ability to engage at first hand with the language and culture he is so often accused of travestying (so often by those without such an ability to engage directly in a linguistic sense).

Ní Mhunghaile's essay broaches questions of translation, and the following two essays consider different dimensions of the question of what the Ossian phenomenon tells us about, in the words of Gauti Kristmannsson, the 'state of translation'. Kristmannsson ambitiously and passionately places Macpherson within a long history of translation theory within Western Europe, arguing for his pivotal place in a fundamental shift in modes, and perceptions of modes, of translation. Kristmannsson's chapter, which stresses just how long-standing the assumptions and standards Macpherson was disrupting were, gives the reader a firm sense of the importance of *Ossian*. Cordula Lemke takes a different approach, considering how the notion of 'transcreation' within modern translation theory might provide a way of thinking through some of the issues within the critical debate between those that see *Ossian* as an act of resistance and renewal and those that perceive a nostalgic, false, and eventually damaging, consciousness at work. Lemke's chapter demonstrates the fertile ground that Macpherson represents for more theoretically informed critical approaches, but both chapters introduce new approaches from other fields to identify and argue specifics about Macpherson's achievement.

Lemke's chapter is interested in questions of landscape and nation, and similar ideas animate Sebastian Mitchell's detailed examination of the way that place is evoked in *Ossian*, questioning some prior assumptions about the vagueness and approximation of Macpherson's natural description (which can be traced at least as far back as to William Wordsworth in his 'Essay Supplementary to the Preface' to his *Poems* of 1815). He seeks a more nuanced understanding of how Macpherson's evocation of landscape could be effective for people and cultures at many removes from his Highland scene. Mitchell's chapter is also one of a number in this volume to demonstrate the ways in which the text of *Ossian* repays close consideration, and the sophistication of a prosody whose success in conveying an impression of spontaneous primitive sublimity still leads to assumptions about its lack of literary merit (at least when judged by its availability for conventional critical exegesis). Mitchell's essay usefully broaches questions of influence within the important contexts of national cultures, both literary and more broadly cultural. It provides a logical progression to the following pair of essays: Murdo Macdonald's broad consideration of *Ossian* within visual culture and writing about visual culture, and Robert Rix's analysis of *Ossian*'s influence upon the interest in Northern poetic traditions both within the United Kingdom and in Scandinavia. Rix shows the broad spectrum and complexity of approaches to Macpherson in relation to both national and sub-national cultures, and the ways in which he both inspired and infuriated others into print. Macdonald picks up the question of *Ossian* within the visual arts. He also places his analysis within the context of national politics both in the eighteenth century and more recently (wondering, for example, why no British or Scottish gallery has paid as much attention to Macpherson as ones abroad, or how an Ossian-inspired Turner painting might remain unacknowledged). His essay is a timely reminder of the cultural politics, and vested interests, at play within the *Ossian* story.

The volume concludes with two essays that cast light on other aspects of Macpherson's career, picking up, as it were, some of the clues offered in deGategno's opening essay. My own contribution seeks to consider afresh Macpherson's translation of the *Iliad*, questioning some of the more straightforward assumptions about Macpherson's motivations, the reasons for its less than spectacular success, and attempts to establish a more fruitful space for the consideration of the text within studies of the reception of classical literature in the eighteenth century in English. Macpherson's *Iliad* is little addressed, but, as compared with attention given to his work as a historian of British history since 1660, it is positively well-considered. Robert Jones begins the process of establishing Macpherson as a serious historian of rare polemical talent in his reading of Macpherson's abiding interest in the question of political opposition – both legitimate and, in his eyes at least, illegitimate – in relation to recent conceptualisations of enlightenment and sentimental historiography. Jones's chapter, which makes a compelling case for the reconsideration of Macpherson as a historian, provides an introduction to the field and a demonstration of the ways in which Macpherson scholarship in the round could develop over the next period. It provides a suitable conclusion to this volume, which has concerned itself with both summarising and articulating current centrally-held understandings, and advancing thinking in its own right.

CHAPTER ONE

The Correspondence of James Macpherson

Paul deGategno

James Macpherson's reputation as the poet of *Poems of Ossian* has undergone a judicious re-examination and analysis since the late twentieth century. This effort continues, for the most part, to show why dismissive and peremptory comments do not explain the poems, their influence, origin, or the man himself. This chapter focuses on Macpherson's letter writing and takes an initial, and admittedly selective, step toward understanding how he employed the letter in communicating with literary contacts, political friends and enemies, business associates, and family and friends. Though Bailey Saunders's 1894 biography presented a through-life portrait of Macpherson, we still lack the minute particulars of his multifarious roles as writer, government agent, journalist, Member of Parliament, and successful businessman. Discussion of the letters will follow four basic categories: literary connections, political, business, and personal interests involving about two hundred and fifty letters from the period 1760 to 1795. However, at least another three hundred letters exist in archives in Great Britain and the US, and this unseen and extant correspondence may provide further answers to unsolved problems. What emerges from this brief initial consideration of his correspondence is the rashness of any simple judgments about him. Yet a picture does start to emerge of Macpherson as a seasoned realist with a dualistic nature, who had the talent and capacity that permitted him to write as Ossian, and on the innocence of nature, and then set aside this falsetto voice, adopt another persona, and write polemical histories and pamphlets. Consideration of his letters offers us the opportunity to see this difference in action in a different forum and to gain a further insight into his multifarious activities through, as it were, his own words.

Of Macpherson's correspondence from the years 1760 to 1780, those letters that survive, or were thought most effective in explaining his motivation for translating and writing *The Poems of Ossian*, have been published in full or in part, or referenced, in Saunders, Stafford, the *Report of the Committee of the Highland Society,* and other recent publications.[1] However, other Ossianic letters do exist. For example, in the months leading to meeting the Edinburgh literati and the first significant recognition of his talent, Macpherson wrote a group of four letters, apparently unknown to Saunders, to the Rev. George Lawrie of Loudon.[2] These letters offer few personal details, but have the tone and effect of a writer already aware of the social and literary implications of his words. Equally, Macpherson's interior life seems close to the public image he would create.

On 27 February 1760 he wrote that 'I can however say in opposition to my countryman you speak of, that it is highly probable, if not absolutely certain, that my fragments are not of Irish extraction'. He also made the case for Scottish literature, claiming that 'I see no reason our writers have to make us a colony of Irish'. Given his position remained unequivocal and consistent through to the publication of *Fragments of Ancient Poetry* in June, this letter offers the earliest example we have of the Macpherson literary persona – the 'discoverer' of authentic Gaelic poetry who through his translation can present to his distinguished colleagues, John Home, the dramatist, and Hugh Blair, who became in 1762 Edinburgh University's first Regius Professor of Rhetoric and Belles Lettres: 'the inclosed [...] not as the best, but as it is clean writ out, and the readiest'. His modesty, linked to an aggressive enthusiasm, marks him as a young champion of Scotland: 'I hope that does not hinder us from having as great genius's [sic] as they [Irish] can boast of [...]. The Scots [...] have ever been a free people [...] their minds were as generous and free, as their hands were as alive in war.'

Less than three weeks later (18 March 1760), Macpherson wrote again from Balgowan, the estate where he continued as tutor to the future Lord Lynedoch. Again it offers a curious mixture of the familiar, self-effacing, and demanding, and it seems clear that he knew that Blair would read the letter. Blair had by this time already begun working with Macpherson on the *Fragments*, but the latter spurred on the fascination he had created with these small samples of English prose:

> I returned in less than three minutes to the cross, where I left you and your other friend with a promise to return in less than a quarter of an hour, but it would appear your walking to the meadow was indispensable. I had it much in my head to ask of you all the copies of the [...] fragments

you have, as I have not been at the pains of keeping a copy of them myself; nor so much as remember the subject of some them. [...] I made a sort of promise to Doctor Blair of sending more of our Highland Rhapsodies, I would rather chuse he would dispense with it upon several accounts.

But I am a man of my word, and accordingly have made preparations for satisfying his curiosity, if he does not easily pass from it. [...] These [translated fragments] will make up the dozen required. I would not make out more among my northern correspondents, tho they, say themselves, have been at pains to procure them. The truth is they think as little of them as I did myself [...]. I have so little esteem for my own abilities that I have no desire my translations should appear in publick.

Macpherson's anxieties, his fear that the general public would not appreciate or understand his fragments and his suspicions that writing 'notes or illustration on them' would be beyond his talent or at least interest, are ones he would repeat in public in the Preface and Dissertation within the *Fingal* volume. Robert Crawford has defined the Scottish Enlightenment as encapsulating 'the emerging tonality of Romanticism – lonely, agitated [...] "eyes full of tears for thy friends"' (p. 310), and this certainly captures Macpherson's feelings and doubts at this particular moment. Yet it is ultimately difficult to know whether this is genuine anxiety or part of an assumed persona adopted because of a genuine, albeit different, anxiety. When he told Lawrie that 'I will still fall short of my promise of the dozen [fragments] if you will not help me' (22 March 1760), it is difficult to tell whether this is genuine concern or the dramatisation of a jeopardy calculated to capture the alluring, exotic quality which the Select Society found so attractive. This young man of talent, who with the proper guidance and encouragement might carry off a magnificent feat of securing for the Scots a distinctive cultural identity, begged his friend not to 'readily expose' him if the fragments lacked beauty. He concluded, 'I am sorry I have no better subject [...] to merit your acquaintance with something more than a flimsy piece of poetry' (18 March 1760) and continued on the same theme: 'you see what trouble there is in having public spirit; if you had allowed the translator of the poems [to] lie concealed you would have none of this trouble' (22 March 1760).

These letters furnish the often intriguing inside story of his translations. First, he feared an insufficient number of fragments could be found, and then, once this problem was overcome, he remained unsettled whether the Edinburgh literati would support publication: 'The whole will make but a very small collection, but to give more, for some months at least, is beyond my power. I do not know whether I need give you a better opinion of them.' Doubting himself, he became defensive, arguing 'I am afraid [the scenery is] much more natural and beautiful to me who am brought up in the midst of wildness itself; than to a citizen;—you in town have no idea of the beautiful wildness of our hills' (22 March 1760). His letters in this early group are both expressive and revealing. They offer numerous examples of his loyalty to country, independence as a translator/author, generosity toward his supporters, but also obstinacy, anguish, false modesty, and perhaps even the first evidence of what will become the root of major criticism about the Ossian poems. After much posturing, Macpherson pointedly notes 'I am extremely obliged to Professor Ferguson for his promise of his correcting hand [...] I wish I was near him to show him the *originals*' (11 April 1760).

It is clear that from early on Macpherson sought a government position where his intellect and writing skills could help shape public affairs. In 1763 Macpherson's first taste of the world beyond the literary came when he accepted an invitation to travel to America and join George Johnstone, the new governor of the province of West Florida, as his secretary-general and unofficial minister of culture.[3] His party arrived in October of that year, and Macpherson immediately assumed extensive duties regulating the commerce, fees, and other regulations of the colony. Johnstone gave him carte blanche in managing the business of this new bureaucracy, and Macpherson also began applying himself to a conflict of interest he had acquired before leaving London of the sort that would characterise his career and provide a suggestive example of his organisational leadership, his ingenuity, his capacity for backstairs politics, and his ability to exploit the opportunities afford by the labyrinthine political and legal confusions of the growing British Empire.

Before leaving London, Macpherson had become agent and administrator for a colonial estate holder who had purchased land from its former Spanish owners. Despite being engaged in land distribution within the new colony, Macpherson petitioned the Governor's Council on behalf of his client. Unfortunately, his action was disallowed when the Council ruled it would not recognise earlier Spanish titles. Macpherson anticipated this development and proceeded, after careful review of the Council decree, to sell the land to an English settler and thus realise his client's investment in land he did not strictly own. Though no regular title would be provided to the new buyer, the Council did agree certain homes could be sold and granted 'an indulgence'. Macpherson's practice here and in another instance convinced Johnstone, who was having disagreements with his superiors in London as well as internal problems between the civil and military factions in the colony, that his secretary could best report in person on his effectiveness as governor and secure whatever advantages were necessary in maintaining Johnstone's administration. It is sometimes assumed that Macpherson's relatively short stay in America was a result of a falling-out between the two men, but there is no evidence for this, and indeed both James and John Macpherson would in 1782 strike an alliance with Johnstone in defending the East India Company against Government interference. Macpherson also kept the patents for the colonial offices he held, providing him with an annual salary, at least until the loss of the American colonies, the personal dimension of which national misfortune he was not slow to recognise in his correspondence. He was, he would tell Allan Macpherson on 21 January 1783 'completely dished up' by the loss of America, elaborating two days later that 'my office in that country, which would have been worth £1,000 a year [...] is gone forever. I am now, literally speaking, a very independent senator, as I have not derived a shilling from the crown, for more than two years.'[4]

On his arrival back in London in September 1765, Macpherson made his report to Henry S. Conway (1718–1794), Secretary of State for the southern department in the Rockingham ministry, and whose role as the chief enforcer of the Stamp Act would have later significance for Macpherson as controller of the press. Conway noted Macpherson's strengths as a writer and his forcefulness when he believed himself in the right. Conway offered Johnstone vague assurances of support while suggesting Macpherson had value: 'I have already seen Mr. Macpherson, and shall not fail to converse farther with him' (3 February 1766).[5]

Macpherson had in fact made meeting and knowing politicians of consequence a particular priority from his first arrival in London. Such connections were established in order to be beneficial to his future career, and those of friends and relatives. A case in point would be Charles Jenkinson, Under-Secretary of State and a protégé of Lord Bute. Macpherson saw in Jenkinson – a young, highly capable administrator who would for the time being align himself with George Grenville – a great commander in political affairs.[6] Grenville would be out of office by the time that Macpherson returned to England and, with Grenville's departure, Jenkinson left office as well. He did not return until 1766 through the efforts of the Chatham-Grafton ministry, becoming a lord of the Admiralty and then moving onto the Treasury. Macpherson maintained contact with him but found a more stable arrangement with

Frederick North (Lord North), who had served the Grenville ministry and was Chancellor of the Exchequer for the Chatham-Grafton administration in 1767. After much wrangling, North became Prime Minister in January 1770. Macpherson's activities now become perplexing, and one route toward understanding what he may have been doing besides preparing his study, *An Introduction to the History of Great Britain and Ireland* (1771), emerges from following the activities of his friend (but no relation) John Macpherson.[7]

John, eight years younger than James, was the son of the Rev. John Macpherson of Sleat, in Skye, who was a respected authority on 'Highland antiquities'. The two had first met in 1760 when James was on his 'Highland Tour' seeking Gaelic manuscripts and transcribing oral poetry for his Ossianic collection. John renewed his friendship with James in late 1766 when both were in London. John's uncle, Captain Alexander Macleod, convinced him to join his ship as purser on a voyage to India in March 1767. Before leaving, John persuaded James to shepherd the Rev. Macpherson's manuscript, *Critical Dissertations on the Origins, Antiquities, of the Caledonians* (1768), through the press. John would not return to England until November 1768, with a report for the ministry on the Royal Navy's capture of the Port of Mangalore on the Arabian Sea. His true intentions depended, however, on his meeting with Grafton and Jenkinson for whom he had more important information, at least from his perspective. In the short twenty months spent abroad, he had managed an introduction to Mohammed Ali Khan, the Nawab of Arcot and the Carnatic, who desperately needed a trusted agent who would speak to the government ministers in England concerning the East India Company's pressuring him for repayment of a significant debt. John Macpherson agreed on becoming his agent and carried money and jewels with him to England in hopes of offering various ministers bribes if they would intervene on behalf of the State against the Company. When his efforts failed with the government, he turned to James Macpherson for help.

A number of those who have concerned themselves with Macpherson's biography, often (though not exclusively) to blacken his name – Saunders, J. N. M. Maclean, Hugh Trevor-Roper, and George McElroy – believe James Macpherson had by now embarked on a career as a political journalist, receiving a government salary while writing what Maclean calls 'jets of venom' against Grafton's enemies in the daily *Public Advertiser*. Saunders believes, in more measured tones, that Macpherson was 'now engaged on behalf of the Government' in various journalistic activities though 'most of it is buried in obscurity' while even Maclean admits that 'no evidence has been found which throws light on [his] employment as a political journalist in 1766 and 1777' and 'insufficient evidence is available [...] to identify the "40 different Signatures" which John claimed he and James had used in 1769'. Nevertheless, Trevor-Roper claims that the Macphersons 'served the Duke of Grafton's government as hackwriters against its most formidable enemies, "Junius" and John Wilkes', while McElroy suggests that 'they were classic bad guy–good guy team of manipulators [...] attribut[ing] to Grafton the Ossianic virtues of firmness [...] and action'.[8] James Macpherson in all likelihood produced scores of letters for the *Private Advertiser,* but evidence, no matter how dramatically presented by these scholars, remains murky, uncertain, and dependent on so-called 'proveable pseudonyms'. Only Lord North in a memorandum to George III settles part of the question on Macpherson's journalistic role: '[He] has for many years been a most laborious and able writer in favour of the government [...] *The History of the Opposition,* the best defense of the American war, and almost all pamphlets on the side of Administration were the production of his pen'.[9]

However, evidence of James Macpherson's relationship with the editor of the *Private Advertiser,* H. S. Woodfall, does exist both in his correspondence and in a curious document known as the 'Resolution of Partners of the *London Packet*' (6 January 1770), in which he is one of ten individuals, some of whose names are immediately recognisable due to their reputations in the political, literary, and social world of London, to purchase 'a twentieth share' of the enterprise.[10] In its general substance, the account follows a joint stock contract wherein the proprietors establish and control the newspaper and manage the printer as well. William Strahan, an experienced journalist and publisher of the *London Chronicle,* agreed to take over printing the *London Packet.*[11] Other proprietors included Henry S. Woodfall; Henry Baldwin, proprietor of the *St. James's Chronicle*; Thomas Becket, publisher of *Fingal* and *Temora;* Caleb Whitefoord, a merchant involved in political journalism; and David Garrick, famous actor and manager of Drury Lane Theatre. All of them had personal or professional contact with James Macpherson.[12]

The Henry Woodfall and Macpherson correspondence depends on two later letters, both showing month and day but no year dates. Based on the letters' contents, they date from the period 1781 to 1783. On 13 June, Macpherson invites Woodfall and his brother William, former editor of the *London Packet* (1772–1774) who had left to manage the *Morning Chronicle,* to dinner at his home in Kensington Gate, and promises among the other guests will be Ralph Griffiths (1720–1803), founder and publisher of the *Monthly Review;* Colonel Allan Macpherson of Blairgowrie, cousin and business partner; and Thomas Becket. The letter is written in a friendly, forthcoming manner with an allusive style that nevertheless reveals some genuine concerns:

> You never sent me your acct. for the Advertisers of the years I was absent. Pray let me know it. You have been always the Constant Friend of my Black Prince. [… They] will suspect me as the No. l friend for all done or wrote on his side. Yet I am resolved to write nothing again. […] Let me have the Pleasure to see you and your Brother.[13]

'My Black Prince' presumably must refer to the Nawab of Arcot, and the veiled reference that follows is almost certainly to Macpherson's *History and Management of the East India Company,* which argued against the Company's treatment of the Nawab. As these elliptical (if casually racist) references might suggest, Macpherson never fully trusted the security of the mail, conjuring various spies who might gain advantage over him or those he served. In the 21 July letter to Henry Woodfall, which Saunders reprints as a facsimile version with little explanation, Macpherson alerts the printer to several juicy pieces of information he has about 'Old Paul', who is probably Paul Benfield whom both men knew well:[14] 'But what with the Porter and beef Steaks' he has consumed at a chop house; Macpherson cannot 'commit them to paper, without the aid of an amanuensis. […] look in upon me, within an hour, you will find me and do me a favour'. It is unclear whether the information he has about Benfield is of a piece with an evening that has left Macpherson too befuddled to write properly or whether it is of a more significant nature. However, he does urge Woodfall to come to dinner with his brother and 'carry Mrs. Woodfall', since Thomas Becket will bring his daughter, 'and I seriously wish to have two, rather than one woman. […] I have room and welcome you all'. Whether Macpherson simply enjoyed the company of the Woodfall brothers and Becket, where they could listen and review parliamentary intelligence, or whether he did have another motive for this social occasion remains a mystery.

This indeterminability is characteristic of Macpherson's correspondence as his activities in support of John Macpherson and the Nawab of Arcot became more intense. Macpherson's letters demonstrate a shrewd awareness of realpolitik and a lively persona, constantly re-inventing itself, and recalling Bruce Redford's comments on Samuel Johnson's correspondence: 'enlivening authority with ease and tempering ease with authority'. Six weeks after the *London Packet* meeting, on 20 February 1770, John Macpherson left for India a second time. James writes to him on 3 March 1770 and in two comments exhibits his penchant for secrecy and self-protection, edging over into artfulness, even evasiveness.

> I was with Lord N[orth]. It was an awkward meeting. [...] The Conversation was very general. [...] I am become much more indifferent since this interview [...] I will put an end to a state of very disagreeable Suspence [*sic*]. I believe many fictions have been told me. It is my business to convert them into real truth. [...] I speak enigmatically, under an uncertainty of your receiving this—but you'll understand me. Commission for me from China for a large parcel of R[ings]. The rougher they are, and the more like the battlements of a Castle, the Better.[15]

Maclean, in his hostile account of Macpherson's activities, believes the rings and the jewels are to bribe government officials within England. Yet the request (the rougher the better) seems hardly calculated to provide alluring bribes, and John Macpherson had not succeeded with such a plan earlier. No evidence exists to suggest that James attempted such a practice: rather he relied on the more sophisticated method of propaganda he had already mastered in the form of letters, pamphlets, histories, and newspaper articles. His letters during the period 1770 to 1783 confirm his role in a complex pattern of relationships between East India Company representatives, the Government, Members of Parliament, and the Indian administrative structure, in which each used each for their own purposes. As P. J. Marshall notes in relation to the Nawab of Arcot, 'through his borrowings and through other personal favors [*sic*] granted to the British at Madras, [he] was able to manipulate his protectors'.[16]

With the defeat in America, Lord North resigned in early 1782 and the divided Rockingham administration came to power in March (soon to be followed in July with the ineffective Shelburne cabinet, and then later the Fox–North Coalition). In April 1782 James Macpherson writes to Lord George Macartney, the Governor of Madras, alerting him to Parliament's 'total change' of policy toward the East India Company.[17] Macpherson was increasingly aware that once peace was negotiated with America the administration would turn upon the financial difficulties and desperate need for reform in India. This placed him in a potentially awkward position: an earlier advocate of reform to the Company (at least by implication) in so far as it was in the interests of the Nawab of Arcot, he was now alert to the fact that reform for different reasons could bring unintended consequences in the shape of new prominence for the placemen of a Whig administration he found unconducive (at least at that moment).

He sent his letter overland, a faster method than by ship around the Cape of Good Hope, but the risk remained high of its never reaching Macartney. 'I fear, that under a pretense of reformation, the needy dependents of those, now, in power, will be sent to occupy the great offices in the East.' Macpherson knew that Macartney had his own personal ambitions for wealth and power while in India and was keen to ensure that Macartney saw the best route to these in continued alliance with Warren Hastings, now the Governor-General. To guard against any change of alliance, Macpherson, a master of intrigue, writes that 'the system established here [London] is too violent to last long [...] but it will do a great deal of mischief'. He also states the true reason for his letter: 'tell the Nabob [sic][that] I cannot suppose that a proper settlement of his affairs will be entirely neglected. Besides, the tide may soon turn.' This letter conveys the flavour and substance of his correspondence with regards to India: an air of rising danger, an insistence that a line must be drawn somewhere, and a nod in the direction of the action that must be taken.

As regular and copious as his letters were to John Macpherson and many other Company figures, he does not write with posterity in mind. No elaborate process of editing, alteration, or thought of charting his life or career enters the correspondence. His focus remains on translating the information he has gained into useful intelligence, and he likes to take his stand on principle (his 'contract') and on common sense. Four days after writing to Macartney, he is more than usually explicit about his concerns regarding the Nawab, the contract/agreement he has made with him, and this curious difficulty whereby, having failed to get an earlier administration to intervene favourably in Indian affairs on the Nawab's part, they were confronted with an administration with an appetite to intervene, but not in a welcome manner.[18] Assuring the Nawab that 'under the disruption in Parliament [...] your affairs will acquire stability', he repeats what becomes a trope in these letters: 'the friends of your Highness will not however fail to exert themselves to render the new plan, as favourable as possible to your rights [...] founding them on the principles of political expediency and justice'. His agreement is reminiscent of what he has always believed as a bedrock of his entire career to date: 'the existing circumstances, will no doubt, give a temporary triumph to some of your Enemies but [...] their triumph will not be of long duration'.

Macpherson's optimism in the face of an aggressive effort in Parliament for a complete review of the East India Company's charter was based upon a scepticism that Parliament had the will and integrity to carry out substantial reform. He was proved right: even with the fall of the North ministry in 1782, Macpherson correctly projected two more years of debate before any reorganisation would actually occur. In the meantime Macpherson's ongoing tasks were two-fold: stabilise support for Hastings, whose energies began evaporating as the latter sensed his inevitable recall to England, and ensure all debts and obligations to his 'friends' (including himself in this calculation) had been settled whether the liability rested with the State, the Company, or the Nawab.

Macpherson seemed quite certain his years of effort in cultivating the friendship and support of Hastings would benefit 'all my friends. I believe him very sincere [do not] teaze or distrust him' (21 February 1781), and 'the conduct of Mr. H [...] will probably keep him, for some time, where he now remains. [...] That power will be exerted in favour of you [...] from the friendly assurances I have lately had from Mr. Hastings's own hand' (23 April 1781). Yet Macpherson also mentored his young nephew and colleague in India, Lieutenant Colonel John MacIntyre, on acting 'with prudence, modesty, and discretion' and urging him to 'take care that some factious people there may not play you off, as the engines of their own disappointment and resentment' (10 March 1781).[19] He advises his nephew, 'What man is safe, that has any enemies—and who is it, that has no enemies, if he deserves to have friends?' (18 June 1782).[20] The long struggle between the State and the Company would continue long past James Macpherson's active career, and his correspondence from 1781 to 1795 reflects continuous engagement with the issues through the change of Governor-Generals, including the remarkable opportunity presented when John Macpherson assumed the office on the resignation of Hastings in June 1785.

By the early 1780s, Macpherson's tireless efforts combined with those of his friends had begun to pay off in terms of his personal wealth. In July 1782 he writes to Allan Macpherson that '[t]here is nothing more flattering to me and to which I look forward with pleasing anxiety than our obtaining retreats, for the decline of life [...] in a pleasant country' (24 July 1782), and while he continues to rail against the loss of his Florida pension, the 'misfortunes which have deprived me of every shilling

I derived from the public', he reports that he has learnt of two small Highland estates, Raitts and Phoness, to be sold. After years of extolling the virtues of urban living, he expresses rapturously: 'I should love a romantic, extensive tract, in the highlands of Scotland [...] the exalted wildness of the highlands' (8 September 1783).[21] He commissions Allan's brother, (another) John Macpherson, as his agent in the Badenoch region, and over the following seven years a Robert Adam-designed mansion house is built surrounded by the assembled estates of nearly seven thousand acres, just outside of Kingussie – a short distance from his birthplace at Invertromie. Macpherson finds, 'I am much better lodged here than I expected. The truth is there is enough of the House finished, for me; and I shall not wait for better times, before I proceed, with the finishing of the principal story. As I think as little, as I can, on any business, I shall not enter upon the Subject, at present' (3 December 1792).[22] By the end of Macpherson's life, following the creation of his retreat, 'inspired with the love of nature and retirement', he could write on 20 March 1794 to his friend Caleb Whitefoord:

> It is somewhat hard, that a man, who has laboured the whole of the best part of the day, should not have some leisure and rest in the Evening of it; yet such is the case, with me—for my labour [...] being every year, more hurried, than the last: But as Diogenes said, when he was reading one of Cumberland's plays to a yawning Audience, and come to the 5th Act—"Courage, my friends, I see Land." [...] I believe, tomorrow or the next day, I may step on shore.[23]

In conclusion, Macpherson's letters illuminate various aspects of a rich and complicated life and career. They may not add a great deal to our understanding of Macpherson the poet, though they do in their own way demonstrate the ear of a poet in their cultivation of nuance, of the modulation in tone and voice as the occasion demands. They allow us to understand a man who was able to focus on the arrangements and intricacies in dealings with his political colleagues and business partners with an astonishing discipline. The letters discussed in this chapter, and the many others available in the archives, present a thoroughly personal, but cautious and sometimes hidden, image of the man who was Macpherson.

CHAPTER TWO

Ossian and the Gaelic World

Lesa Ní Mhunghaile

James Macpherson returned to his native Badenoch in 1756 to take up a post as a country schoolmaster. Once there:

> it is believed, he began to collect Gaelic poetry, without any other view at that time but to amuse himself in that solitude. That was no difficult task in the then state of Badenoch, when a number of old men were still alive who had a great mass of Gaelic poetry treasured up in their memory, which they used to recite to their countrymen when assembled beside a cheerful fire in the long winter nights.[1]

The poetry Macpherson collected primarily related to a vast corpus of Gaelic heroic literature that was hundreds of years old and had been preserved in the Scottish Highlands. This chapter will examine that corpus as a context for Macpherson's *Fragments of Ancient Poetry* (1760), *Fingal* (1761/2), and *Temora* (1763). It will begin by outlining the various interlinked strands of the heroic corpus, with a particular emphasis on the *Fiannaigheacht* ballad tradition (known in English as Fionn or Fenian ballads) that formed the basis of Macpherson's 'translations'. It will then discuss the relationship between the authentic Gaelic tradition and Macpherson's translations, drawing attention not only to differences but also to characteristics common to both.

The Heroic Gaelic Literature of Ireland and Scotland

Macpherson was following in the footsteps of a number of collectors, who, from the early eighteenth century, had been collecting Gaelic songs and poetry in the Highlands. Alexander Pope (*c.* 1706–1782), Minister of Reay, Caithness, made his collection around 1739, while Archibald Fletcher, a farmer in Auchalladar, Glenorchay, learned the poetry by heart and dictated it to local scribes in 1750. Jerome Stone (*c.* 1727–1756), a teacher in Dunkeld, made his collection around 1755, as did the Rev. Donald MacNicol (1735–1802), Minister of Lismore, Argyll.[2] Stone was responsible for publishing the first 'translation' of a Gaelic Fionn ballad, 'Bás Fhraoich' (Fraoch's Death), as 'Albin and the Daughter of Mey', in the *Scots Magazine* for January 1756.[3] His commentary highlighted the literary value of Gaelic poetry: 'those who have any tolerable acquaintance with the Irish language, must know, that there are a great number of poetical compositions in it [...] Several of these performances are to be met with, which for sublimity of sentiment, nervousness of expression, and high-spirited metaphors, are hardly to be equalled among the chief productions of the most cultivated nations.'[4]

Stone's publication drew attention to a literary tradition hitherto unknown outside the Highlands and almost certainly provided both an exemplar and the impetus for Macpherson's activities. Macpherson had grown up in a region in which the native Gaelic tradition, handed down orally from generation to generation, was still strong, and he would have been familiar with that tradition from childhood even if he was not strongly literate in Gaelic.[5] Some of that tradition had also been preserved in manuscripts created by and disseminated among the bardic order. Manuscript texts were written either in the Classical Gaelic standard language that had been employed by the learned classes in both Scotland and Ireland until the late seventeenth century or in the 'modified and distinctively Scottish form of Classical Gaelic' that emerged in the following century.[6]

Ireland and Scotland constituted a common linguistic area during the Middle Ages and shared a common literary heritage. Poets travelled between the two countries, and Scottish poets trained in Irish schools and vice versa.[7] As a result the same tales and ballads often circulated in both countries. An important component of this shared literary heritage is a corpus of heroic literature, central to which are two cycles of heroic tales known as the Fenian or Fionn cycle (*Fiannaigheacht, fian*-lore) and the Ulster cycle (*Rudhraigheacht*). Both comprise literary prose tales and narrative ballads in oral and manuscript form. The Fionn cycle was the most popular and widespread of all Gaelic narrative cycles. Traditionally situated in the third century, it relates the exploits of Fionn mac Cumhaill, his son Oisín and a band of warriors known as the *fianna*.[8] References to Fionn can be found in eighth-century texts written in Ireland where he is presented as a warrior and a seer. The key prose text is 'Agallamh na Seanórach' (*'The Colloquy of the Ancients'*), a number of narratives framed by a story in which the heroes Oisín and Caoilte mac Ronáin have survived long enough to relate the exploits of the *fianna* to St Patrick.[9] Other important texts in the cycle include 'Tóraigheacht Dhiarmada agus Ghráinne' ('*The Pursuit of Diarmaid and Gráinne*'), 'Cath Gabhra' ('*The Battle of Gabhra*'), and 'Cath Finntrágha' ('*The Battle of Ventry*').

The Ulster cycle, based on the Ulaidh, an ancient people from whom the province of Ulster got its name, is traditionally situated in the first century and centres on the king Conchobar mac Nessa, ruler of the Ulaid, and the hero Cú Chulainn. The longest and most important story is 'Táin Bó Cúailnge' ('*The Cattle Raid of Cooley*'). Also of note is 'Longes Mac nUislenn' ('*The Exile of the Sons of Uisneach*'), which tells the tale of Deirdre, destined at birth to cause slaughter and devastation in Ulster. Tales relating to the cycle are preserved in Irish-language manuscripts of the twelfth to fifteenth centuries, but the language of the earliest stories is dateable to the eighth century. In earlier tradition the Ulster and Fionn cycles were quite separate, but motifs from the Ulster cycle were gradually incorporated into the Fionn cycle, which over time took the place of the Ulster cycle in popular tradition. Distinction was preserved, however; though, as Thomson has noted, there were exceptions in Scotland such as 'Laoidh an Tailleoir' ('*The Ballad of the Tailor*').[10]

A discussion of the Fenian ballad (or lay) tradition is pertinent when considering the relationship between Macpherson and the Gaelic tradition.[11] The ballads or narrative poems, known as *laoi(dh)*, *dán* or *duan* in Irish and Scottish Gaelic respectively, are attributed in the tradition to Fenian heroes, particularly Oisín (Oiséan in Scotland). They are usually classified by subject matter by modern folklorists: *síodh*-ballads (ballads relating to the otherworld), *bruidhean*-ballads (ballads relating to battles), ballads of magical visitors, invader-ballads, ballads of internecine strife, pursuits and rescues, elopements, foreign expeditions, monster-slayings, and hunts.[12] The tradition contains a large number of narrative poems in addition to elegies and eulogies, poems about nature, and debate poems. Individual ballads may contain a number of different styles.[13] They are composed in loose forms of syllabic verse known as *óglachas*, and in the oral tradition they were chanted or sung.[14]

Although ballads are attested in Irish manuscripts from the time of the *Book of Leinster* (c. 1160), many of the ballads that are contained in surviving collections were composed during the period extending from the end of the twelfth century to the sixteenth century.[15] The oral and written lay tradition co-existed, each sustaining the other, although the written tradition was the stronger of the two until the seventeenth century. During that period there was no substantial alteration to the tradition with the important exception of a change in overall tone, which moved from heroic to romantic and started to find room for hints of the burlesque.[16] Around the sixteenth century, a number of ballads were collected together to form a new type of *Agallamh* known as *Agallamh Oisín agus Phádraig*.[17] Approximately one hundred and one complete copies of this text have been preserved in manuscripts, the earliest of which is found in the *Duanaire Finn* manuscript.[18] It is noteworthy that there was less interest in the debate between Oisín and Pádraig in the later Scottish tradition, perhaps due to the Reformation and the subsequent evangelical movements in the Highlands.[19] It is also important to note that after the sixteenth century the Scottish ballad tradition was primarily sustained by oral transmission, and it appears that the recitation of Fenian ballads survived in the repertoire of traditional singers longer in that country than in Ireland.[20]

There appears to have been greater variation in individual texts in Scotland during the later period than in Ireland, perhaps reflecting the stronger manuscript culture in Ireland, which had a tendency, relatively speaking, to stabilise texts, despite retaining a 'considerable variety of readings'.[21] In general, it is difficult to establish with certainty which ballads were composed in Scotland and which in Ireland. For example, the ballad 'Is fada anocht a n-Oil Finn' ('*Time passes wearily in Elphin tonight*'), in which Oisín laments the passing of the *fianna* and compares his present unhappiness to his former happiness, is common to the Irish and Scottish tradition, but, as it refers to Elphin in Co. Roscommon, it was most likely composed in Ireland and from there passed into the oral tradition in Scotland.[22] Certain ballads that were common to the two countries developed a distinct Scottish dimension as, for example, 'Eas Ruaidh' ('*Assaroe*') or 'Cath Ríogh na Sorcha' ('*The Battle with the King of Sorcha*'), while some ballads composed in Ireland, such as 'Laoidh Fhraoich', were accepted and localised in parts of Gaelic Scotland. Indeed, some ballads appear to have been preserved in Scotland only, such as 'Laoidh Fhraoich' and 'Laoidh Dhiarmaid', both of which were very popular in the Scottish tradition.[23] Scotland, therefore, played an important role in preserving ballads that had been lost in Ireland, and of course the converse may also be true.[24] It is important to emphasise this shared Gaelic literary heritage, particularly in light of Macpherson's claims that the Irish had appropriated 'Ossian and his heroes to their own country' and the ensuing reaction in Ireland to such claims.[25] As the evidence above demonstrates, it is too simplistic to claim that one country appropriated the literary tradition of the other.

The two most important collections of Early Modern Fionn ballads are contained in the Scottish manuscript *The Book of the Dean of Lismore*, and the Irish manuscript *Duanaire Finn* (*The Poem Book of Fionn*). The former was compiled in Perthshire by Sir James MacGregor, Dean of Lismore of Argyll, and his brother Duncan, mainly from the oral tradition between 1512 and 1542.[26] It is noteworthy for the distinctive orthography they employed. Scots-based and written in 'secretary hand', a style of European handwriting developed in the early sixteenth century for writing English, German, Welsh, and Gaelic, it conveyed 'an approximation of the Gaelic sounds' rather than an old Gaelic script or standard Classical Gaelic spelling.[27] Meek has noted that it 'represents what is perhaps the high point of meticulous recording of the Finn ballad texts within the medieval tradition'.[28] It contains around twenty poems belonging to the Fionn cycle.[29] The *Duanaire Finn* manuscript was written in Louvain and Ostende between 1626 and 1627 by Niall Gruama Ó Catháin and Aodh Ó Dochartaigh for their patron Captain Somhairle Mac Domhnaill of Antrim, an officer in the Spanish army of the Netherlands. It contains sixty-nine ballads from the Fionn cycle and a version of *Agallamh na Seanórach* omitting the poetry.[30] There are only four ballads common to *The Book of the Dean of Lismore* and *Duanaire Finn*. This is significant because it demonstrates that, despite the shared literary inheritance, the Scottish tradition was 'preserving if not actually creating' ballads that were not known in Ireland.[31]

In Ireland, the ballad tradition remained popular in both the manuscript and oral traditions during the eighteenth and nineteenth centuries. Ballads were regularly expanded, and a number of new Fionn ballads were composed during the eighteenth century. The first, 'Suirghe Ghuill', was composed by the poet and scribe Seán Ó Neachtain (c. 1640–1729) in Dublin in 1713. It was termed 'pseudo-Ossianic' or 'spurious Ossianic' by Standish Hayes O'Grady, who noted that 'the style and plot are mock heroic and burlesque'.[32] It tells of how Angliota, the king of Troy's daughter, visits Ireland in distress and requests the protection of the *fianna*. The second ballad, 'Laoi Oisín ar Thír na nÓg' ('*Oisín's lay concerning the Land of Youth*'), composed possibly around 1750, has been ascribed to Micheál Coimín (c. 1680–1760) of Co. Clare.[33] It recounts Oisín's journey to Tír na nÓg and his subsequent return three hundred years later. The theme was well known in the Gaelic literary tradition as it is found in the stories *Echtrae Chonnlai* and *Immram Brain*. Coimín displays a good knowledge of the *fiannaíocht* tradition, though the ballad displays the same weaknesses as other late compositions, suggesting that poets were constrained by the fetters of the ancient tradition and a genre that was exhausted by the eighteenth century. That said, had he not composed the ballad, the ancient story of Oisín in Tír na nÓg might have been lost to posterity.[34] Other late Fionn ballads include 'Laoi Mheargaigh' or 'Laoi Mhná Mheargaigh' (*'The Ballad of Meargach'* or *'The Ballad of Meargach's wife'*); 'Lá dhúinne ar Sliabh Fuaid' (*'One day on Sliabh Foy'*), which may have been composed by the Northern scribe Muiris Ó Gormáin; and 'Laoi Chab an Dosáin' (*'The Ballad of the Mouth of the Tuft'*), which has been termed 'one of the most obscene literary pieces in pre-modern Irish literature'.[35]

The Relationship Between Macpherson's Translations and the Authentic Gaelic Tradition

Macpherson claimed that the poems he had published were translations of the Gaelic-language material he had collected in the Highlands 'after a peregrination of six months.'[36] Although it appears that he had initially intended to replicate the poetic metre of the authentic tradition in the translations, they were eventually presented in rhythmical prose. It appears that Macpherson may have been heavily influenced by Hugh Blair in the decision to use this particular style and that it was most likely influenced by concerns regarding how Gaelic poetry could be best presented to an English-speaking audience.[37] Accusations of charlatanism and forgery abounded from the outset, but in recent decades scholars have come to a more nuanced understanding of Macpherson's treatment of Gaelic language material. It seems likely that Macpherson was not helped by being insufficiently conversant in literary Gaelic to fully understand his raw materials, and the 'confusion and vagueness' of some of his borrowings may be the result of him often having had only a general sense of the meaning of the texts he encountered.[38]

The first detailed attempt to deal with Macpherson's claims was an anonymous article entitled *Mémoire de M. de C. a Messieurs les Auteurs Du Journal des Sçavans*, probably penned by the Bishop of Cloyne John O'Brien (*c.* 1701–1769), published over five issues of the *Journal des Sçavans* in 1764.[39] A large part of the *Mémoire* consisted of a detailed attack on the historical structure that Macpherson had provided for his translations. In the final instalment, M. de C. argued that *Fingal* was composed of elements taken from the tales 'Cath Finntrágha' (*'The Battle of Ventry'*) and 'Bruidhean Chaorthainn' ('*The Rowan-tree Dwelling*') and was heavily dependent on a third tale written in verse, 'La guerre ou la descente de Dearg files de Diric Roi de Lochlin' ('*The war of the descent of Dearg, son of Diric, King of Lochlin*' [Scandanavia]). He claimed that 'Carthon' was also based on 'Bruidhean Chaorthainn' and noted the following:

> We shall never finish if we wish to enter here into a detailed examination of all his other poems: it suffices to note that they are all drawn from the same source, composed in the same spirit, and the originals have all been falsified with the same skill.[40]

The next serious attempt to examine the veracity of Macpherson's claims was an investigation by the Highland Society of Scotland in 1805. Its report concluded:

> [...] the Committee has not been able to obtain any one poem the same in title and tenor with the poems published by him. It is inclined to believe that he was in use to supply chasms, and to give connection, by inserting passages which he did not find, and to add what he conceived to be dignity and delicacy to the original composition, by striking out passages, by softening incidents, by refining the language, in short by changing what he considered as too simple or too rude for a modern ear, and elevating what in his opinion was below the standard of good poetry. To what degree, however, he exercised these liberties, it is impossible for the Committee to determine.[41]

The investigation compared *Ossian* with Fionn ballads collected by Duncan Kennedy and others and those published by Charlotte Brooke in *Reliques of Irish Poetry* (1789). One of the authentic ballads assessed in the *Report* was 'Laoidh an Mhoighre Bhoirb', also known in Scotland as 'Cath Rìgh na Sorcha' or 'Eas Ruaidh', the earliest version of which is found in *The Book of the Dean of Lismore*. The *Report* concluded that 'the simplicity and distinctness of narrative in the original ancient poem will be easily contrasted with the general and more ornamented expression of Macpherson's translation'.[42] However, it would be another ninety years before Ludwig Chr. Stern undertook a detailed study of Macpherson's poems and identified a number of the sources that Macpherson had employed.[43] He also examined Macpherson's Gaelic 'originals' as published posthumously in 1807 and was left in no doubt that they had been back-translated from the English texts.[44] Stern was scathing in his condemnation of *Ossian*: '[i]t may be conceded that Macpherson had to some small extent imbibed the spirit of Gaelic poetry, but he had so mixed it up with noxious sentimentality and religious unction that it became scarcely recognisable as a native product.'[45] Derick Thomson built on the foundation laid by Stern's work and demonstrated that Macpherson drew on sixteen or seventeen Gaelic ballads. He argues that Macpherson used the ballads in a number of different ways: 'sometimes adopting and adapting a plot, sometimes producing a loose translation of a sequence of lines or stanzas, and more often taking names or incidents or references from the Gaelic texts and reproducing variants of these.'[46]

Thomson found that the epic *Fingal* 'makes the most pervasive and detailed use of Gaelic ballads of any of Macpherson's books'.[47] Two ballads, 'Duan a' Ghairbh' and 'Laoidh Mhaghnuis', form the main outline of the plot, and the main episodes are based on three others: 'Fingal's visit to Norway', 'Duan na n-Inghinn' (*'The Ballad of the Maiden'*), and 'Suireadh Oisein air Eamhair Aluinn' (*'Oisín's Courtship'*). There were, however, other echoes. For example, Macpherson amalgamated versions of 'Moighre Borb' and 'An Ionmhuinn' (a seventeenth-century imitation of the former ballad) to create the 'Maid of Craca' episode in *Fingal*, Book III.[48] 'Moighre Borb' also formed the basis of Fragment VI. Macpherson also used other ballads in a more restricted manner elsewhere in the volume. These include 'Sliabh nam Ban Fionn', 'Ard Aigneach Goll' (*'The Praise of Goll'*), and possibly a ballad about Cú Chulainn's chariot.[49]

Macpherson's 'The Battle of Lora' has close affinities with the ballad 'Teanntachd Mhòr na Fèinne' (*'The Fian's great distress'*), following the same sequences of events contained in the Gaelic albeit laying emphasis in different places. St Patrick is transformed into a Culdee, the Fenian princess is given the name Bosmina, and a lengthy description of compensation in the Gaelic is greatly reduced.[50] Macpherson acknowledged that he used a version of the ballad he had received from James MacLagan but it appears that he also used a number of other versions of the ballad, namely those of Jerome Stone and a version similar to that of Archibald Fletcher.[51]

A version of 'Bás Chonlaoich' (*'The Death of Conlaoch'*) was used in the construction of 'Carthon', although Thomson describes Macpherson's treatment of the original as ruthless.[52] The Gaelic poem, a version of which is found in *The Book of the Dean of Lismore*, tells of how Cú Chulainn unwittingly kills his son Conlaoch. In 'Carthon', the heroes become Clessámmor and Carthon respectively and Macpherson reverses their roles. In 'Carthon' Clessámmor dies of grief, an addition to the

Gaelic ballad. As in all of Macpherson's adaptations of Gaelic works, the style he employs in 'Carthon' differs greatly from 'Bás Chonlaoich', which is 'told with economy and restraint'.[53]

A final example of Macpherson's adaptation of Gaelic ballads is found in his use of a ballad or prose story relating to the hero Ferdiad and the Ulster cycle tale 'Táin Bó Cúailnge' ('*The Cattle Raid of Cooley*'). Ulster cycle texts were in circulation in eighteenth-century Scotland, including among the works of Macpherson's contemporaries such as James MacLagan and Uilleam MacMhurchaidh. Thomson suggests that Macpherson may have obtained the ballad or story from oral sources or the historical works of Irish historians such as Geoffrey Keating and Roderick O'Flaherty.[54] It makes its appearance in *Fingal* (Bk. II) where Ferdiad is killed by Cuchullin. Macpherson's version provides a 'distorted summary' of the Irish tale and changes its atmosphere 'almost beyond recognition'.[55]

Donald Meek has also suggested that Macpherson was aware of the prose tale 'Cath Finntrágha', 'one of the tales most highly prized in the medieval Gaelic world', and that it may have influenced the storyline of *Fingal*.[56] The tale's main theme concerns an attack on Ireland by the Vikings, an important theme in Gaelic prose and ballads.[57] Meek has posited that Macpherson may have viewed the invasion theme as the major epic theme of medieval Gaelic literature and that he was trying to 'recapture the epic of invasion' in *Fingal*.[58] Macpherson's knowledge of prose as well as ballad tales is significant in another way too. After 1550 the distinction between prose and ballads became more fluid, particularly in the case of tales and ballads that shared a common theme. As a result, Macpherson may have found Gaelic ballads 'in a form which suggested that there was an easy exchange between prose and verse, and, in the final assessment, that there was no reason to distinguish the two forms'.[59]

Macpherson's translations omitted any references to Christianity although St Patrick played a prominent role in the authentic Gaelic ballad tradition.[60] Instead, the cleric is transformed into son of Alpin by Macpherson. A number of the Gaelic ballads tend to the anti-clerical and the comic tension between St Patrick and Oisín, who has great difficulty embracing Christian ideals of life, forms part of their appeal.[61] The absence of references to Christianity in the poetry was defended by Hugh Blair in his 'Critical Dissertation on the Poems of Ossian' (1763) and offered as proof of the antiquity of Ossian: 'the druidical superstition was, in the days of Ossian, on the point of its final extinction [...] whilst the Christian faith was not yet established.'[62] To sum up his treatment of his Gaelic sources on this point and others, in addition to taking inspiration from a number of prose tales, Macpherson used much of the detail of Gaelic ballads and tales but adapted and re-ordered them so as to re-fashion them into texts that would suit the tastes of Romantic readers and appeal to a non-Gaelic-speaking audience.

Characteristics Shared with the Authentic Gaelic Tradition

Yet, for all the differences with regard to the style and tone of Macpherson's translations and their relationship to the authentic Gaelic tradition, it is important to note that they share a number of characteristics in common with authentic Fionn ballads, characteristics that are key to the overall Ossianic affect.[63] Blair remarked that 'the two great characteristics of Ossian's poetry are tenderness and sublimity':

> Ossian is perhaps the only poet who never relaxes or lets himself down into the light and amusing strain […]. One keynote is struck at the beginning and supported to the end; nor is any ornament introduced, but what is perfectly concordant with the general tone or melody. The events recorded, are all serious and grave; the scenery throughout, wild and romantic […]. His poetry, more than that of any other writer, deserves to be styled, *The Poetry of the Heart*. It is a heart penetrated with noble sentiments, and with sublime and tender passions; a heart that glows, and kindles the fancy; a heart that is full, and pours itself forth.[64]

An elegiac theme is one of the distinguishing features of *Fragments*, and Meek has suggested that, in giving prominence to such themes, Macpherson was 'reflecting what became the dominant mood of the modern ballad corpus of Scotland'.[65] Ossian constantly compares his former and current condition unfavourably and, according to Blair, this contrast 'diffuses over his whole poetry a solemn pathetick air, which cannot fail to make impression on every heart.'[66] This is a comparison directly available to Macpherson from his Gaelic sources. In the following ballad, Oisín laments the fact that he has aged:

> Do bhádhusa úair fa folt buidhe cas
> is nach ffuil trem chenn acht fionnfadh gerr glas […]
> mfholt anocht is líath, ní bhía mar do bhá. (*Duanaire Finn* XXV)

> *Once I was yellow-haired, ringleted / Now my head puts forth only a short grey crop […] / Tonight my hair is hoar, it will not be as once it was.*

In 'Fragment II', Oisín presents himself as the last of his race: 'Yes, my fair, I return; but I am alone of my race. Thou shalt see them no more: their graves I raised on the plain'.[67] This can be compared with:

> Fada liom gach lá dha ttig
> ní mar sin fa cleachtadh dhúin
> mo bheith a ffegmais na fFían
> do cuir sin mo ciall ar ccúil (*Duanaire Finn*, LV)

Wearisome to me is each succeeding day: / It was not so we used to be: my being parted / from the Fianna has upset my wits.

Also common to both are the ways in which Ossian's nostalgia is evoked via features of the landscape:

> Guth gadhoir a gCnoc na Ríogh
> ionmhoin liom in síodh fo ffuil
> ba meinice leinn fulacht fían
> eidir in slíabh agus muir. (*Duanaire Finn*, XXXII)

The beagle's cry on the hill of kings! / The mound it circles is dear to me: / We often had a fian's hunting feast / between the moorland and the sea.

In 'Fragment VIII', Ossian is reminded of his father and son by the sound of the river:

> 'How hast thou fallen like an oak, with all thy branches round thee! Where is Fingal the King? where is Oscur my son? where are all my race? Alas! in the earth they lie. I feel their tombs with my hands. I hear the river below murmuring hoarsely over the stones. What dost thou, O river, to me? Thou bringest back the memory of the past.'[68]

There are many such examples of sentiment in the authentic tradition where feelings of love, sorrow, friendship, and nostalgia are expressed. A variety of emotions come to the fore in the first ballad in *Duanaire Finn*, 'Eól damh senchus Feine Finn', including jealousy, vengeance and guile, and pride.[69] In a ballad concerning Caoilte's sword, Oisín appears as a 'man of feeling' as he sheds tears, remembering the past escapades of the *fianna*:

> Nochan feadar créd do-dhén
> fil mo rosg ag sileadh dér
> cloidhiomh Caoilti ba caom gné
> is meabhair leamsa gurab é. (*Duanaire Finn* XLVII)

I know not what I shall do: / my eye is shedding tears: / I remember that this is comely Caoilte's sword.

In general, Macpherson's texts and the Gaelic ballads share an emphasis on the subjective experience and perspective of the individual, the creating consciousness of Oisín. Other characteristics in common include references to nature, hunting, life outdoors, and the honour code by which members of the *fianna* were bound. This latter characteristic was transformed into behaviour reminiscent of chivalry in Macpherson's epics, a feature that appealed to Blair in his commentary on 'Carric-thura' in 'Critical Dissertation': 'Lathmon is peculiarly distinguished, by high generosity of sentiment. This is carried so far, particularly in the refusal of Gaul, on one side, to take the advantage of a sleeping foe; and of Lathmon, on the other, to overpower by numbers the two young warriors, as to recall into one's mind the manners of Chivalry.'[70]

In conclusion, the relationship between James Macpherson's translations and the authentic Fionn tradition is complex. Although much work has been done by scholars such as Stern, Thomson, and Meek in identifying Macpherson's sources, there are still areas that would merit investigation, in particular his development of the overall framework for his Ossianic poems via Gaelic examples and his use of prose sources. As Meek suggests, his use of the ballad tradition might then merit a re-investigation in light of those aspects.[71] Equally, while there are significant differences between *Ossian* and its Gaelic inspiration, it is not true to say that all the features of the Ossianic are superimposed onto the Gaelic works. Rather, *Ossian* represents a heightening and emphasising of features of the Gaelic work in and through the language of eighteenth-century Sentimental writing in English.

In the final analysis, though, the most important dimension of the relationship between *Ossian* and the Gaelic world is the attention *Ossian* drew to the authentic Fionn cycle tradition in both Scotland and Ireland. In Scotland, the interest that was sparked in the tradition resulted in the collection of manuscripts and the bringing to light of collections that had already been made, while in Ireland the controversy Macpherson provoked with his allegations regarding the Scottish origin of the Fionn cycle led to the collection and publication of authentic material in order to refute his claims. The success of *Ossian* did indeed encourage a series of 'imaginary translations', 'pseudo-historical notes', and 're-fabricated Gaelic versions', but this does not detract from the fact that Macpherson's so-called 'translations' played an important role not only in the salvaging of a central component of the literary heritage of Ireland and Scotland but also in its elevation to a higher status throughout Europe.[72] Macpherson's *Ossian* and the imitations that followed it also acted as a stimulus to Gaelic poets and prose writers during the nineteenth century by offering them new ways to deal with Gaelic language and literature and 'fresh perspectives in which to view the Highlands, Islands, and even the Gaels themselves'.[73]

CHAPTER THREE

Ossian and the State of Translation in the Scottish Enlightenment

Gauti Kristmannsson

The Poems of Ossian are probably the most commonly used example in modern translation studies to illustrate the concept of pseudotranslation. In his seminal *Descriptive Translation Studies and beyond* Gideon Toury defines pseudotranslations thus: 'texts which have been presented as translations with no corresponding source texts in other languages ever having existed – hence no factual "transfer operations" and translation relationships – that go under the name of pseudotrans-lations, or fictitious translations'.[1] Such a concept did not exist in the eighteenth century, even if the idea may have, in practice. An example used by Toury is Horace Walpole's *The Castle of Otranto*, which was purportedly translated by one William Marshal of Gent. It is often considered the first Gothic novel, and as such an example of the innovative tendencies of pseudotranslation as they are used as a mechanism for introducing 'novelties while tying them to a hypothetical alien tradition'.[2] It is not certain that it is the pseudotranslations themselves that introduce the novelties, but rather translations which have appeared before and therefore serve as a model for the pseudotranslation, possibly because the literary system is not yet ready for such novelties from the hands of native authors.[3]

Toury's insistence on *Ossian* as the major example of pseudotranslation (and indeed André Lefevere's in *Constructing Cultures*) flies in the face of his own definition, since there existed certainly 'corresponding source texts' for *The Poems of Ossian* even if they were not 'directly' translated. This is apparent from Macpherson's own paratexts and significant subsequent scholarly endeavour, all of which had been published prior to the critical interventions by the translation scholars.[4] So it should have been at least clear that the matter was not black and white, as had actually been known from the beginning, even to Samuel Johnson, whose word appears to weigh more on the current debate than it deserves.[5]

Toury seems to be under Johnsonian influence, feeling compelled to add a footnote with a qualification to his previous definition later in his discussion:

> To be sure, to the extent that the source of a pseudotranslation can be pointed to, it would normally consist in a group of texts, even the model underlying that group, rather than any individual text. For instance, it is clear that the author of the *Book of Mormon* took advantage of a [certain part of] the tradition of Bible translation into English. In a similar vein, one possible way of settling the long dispute over the authenticity of Macpherson's Ossianic poetry as a translation is precisely to maintain that it is various elements of a *tradition* of oral poetry in Gaelic rather than a finite number of actual texts which underlie this body of texts. (The possibility that there may have been one source text for any one of his target texts has long been ruled out.)[6]

This might be said about the Bible and many other ancient and medieval texts too, texts that have been gathered from manifold sources and traditions, collated, and often translated into one text, sometimes even attributed to a single individual. It is just the *caveat* in the parenthesis that reads a little like Johnson's insistence, 'Where are the manuscripts?'[7] Johnson's rhetorical question, in view of what he actually knew very well about the *Poems of Ossian*, expresses in a nutshell the demands made to this one text, beyond many others of similar ilk, from both a textual critical perspective and the moral one.[8]

It is a remarkable phenomenon that a text, published more than two hundred and fifty years ago, is still being discussed controversially due to doubts about its provenance. It is scarcely an exaggeration to say that some modern scholars would only be satisfied by the existence of a Gaelic original of the *Poems of Ossian*, printed and published as one text with an ISBN number in the year AD 300. There are probably several reasons why the *Poems of Ossian* can still make some scholars foam at the mouth from fury and indignation. One is the 'Johnsonian factor'; admirers of Samuel Johnson see his personal dispute with James Macpherson as emblematic for the 'sturdy moralist' and have therefore taken 'his side' in the argument, even if there is evidence that he was himself not averse to some questionable methods of forgery and ghostwriting.[9] Another is the issue of nationalism and the position of Scotland in the United Kingdom, both then and now. The third is probably of moral nature, although it must be said that moral views have been instrumentalised in the debate from the beginning, and fundamental(istic) claims of an almost absolute truth have been expressed, even recently.[10] The fourth is the relatively recent notion of the author as an original creator, an idea that has been disputed at least since Barthes published his famous 'Death of the Author', but, judging from the Ossianic debate recently, it might have been about the death of the translator, James Macpherson.

Complex as the Ossianic controversies are, it should be borne in mind from the contemporary perspective that ideas of authorship, on translation, literary property, and textual criticism were considerably different around the middle of the eighteenth century, and, furthermore, the case may be argued that this highly influential and hotly debated text had a significant influence on ideas of authorship, translation, and editing as we see it. The absurdity of the fact that the matter has not been 'settled' yet is proof positive that exactly this text was pivotal in the understanding of these issues at the time and, when they become muddied again through new ideas and the deconstruction of the prevailing discourse, the *Poems of Ossian* suddenly gain relevance again and come under attack of those who are alarmed by changes, be they literary or political.

This chapter will seek to re-establish Macpherson's place as a translator within the Western literary tradition. It will trace the long history of the central ideas of literary translation and the ways in which Macpherson intervenes within them. It will argue that the challenge he offered was radical and that literary history has taken its revenge, attempting to kick over the traces of his endeavours and relegating him to convenient categories such as 'pseudotranslation' as a way of avoiding the implications of his achievement.

Translation theory was not the most important issue of the medieval period, things having been settled with St Jerome's definitive translation of the Bible, the *Vulgate*, and Latin serving as the *lingua franca* of educated Europe. But it had been prior to that period, among the Romans when they were incorporating Greek culture through various methods of translation, all the way from the word to the form alone.[11] Figures such as Cicero and Horace had been very influential in defining the parameters of translation, and they were cited for centuries afterwards, especially in the Renaissance and the following period. And it is during the Renaissance and especially the Reformation that what we might call the mother tongue movement took off. Some refer to this as the vernacularisation of Europe, but this term implies that it happened almost incidentally, or as Marshall McLuhan claims: 'print, in turning the vernaculars into mass media, or closed systems, created the uniform, centralizing process of modern nationalism.'[12] However, the process began before the introduction of print, although it certainly took off with that invention. In Ireland translation into the vernacular began very early in the Middle Ages, possibly because Christianity was introduced there peacefully as Michael Cronin has noted.[13] Gaelic vernacular 'high literary' texts were prevalent from at least the seventh century, and in Ireland the Gaelic language was clearly held on par with Latin as a high-register language throughout the early Middle Ages. This included translations and adaptations of classical texts into Gaelic, particularly in the tenth to twelfth centuries. Elsewhere the mother tongues of Europe were taking hold among the troubadours in France and their contemporaries elsewhere in Europe in the twelfth century, a development that may have induced Dante to write his *De vulgari eloquentia*. This represents a kind of manifesto for writing poetry in the mother tongue, and not only as 'a verbal invention composed according to the rules of rhetoric and music', but also as 'the great poets, that is, those who obey the rules [...]'.[14] The rules are Horace's, as he notes a few lines later, and the 'speech act' is to raise vernacular poetry to a new higher level, 'equivalent' to the ancients.

Vernacularisation of what may be termed 'popular poetry', for want of a better definition (that is poetry in the mother tongue created by wandering troubadours, minstrels, and such), therefore, came into being from the less educated. However, Dante's treatise directs how to apply the rules of the ancients to create 'great' poetry, which he himself went on to do. He had many 'followers' who may or may not have known of his treatise, but the idea spread around, even to those such as Petrarch who claimed not to have read him. Later Gian Giorgio Trissino, who wrote both an epic in Italian and a version of Sophocles' *Sofonisba* in the early sixteenth century, published an Italian version of Dante's *De vulgari*.[15] All over Europe tracts appeared in the same vein: Joachim du Bellay, one of the Pléiade poets in France, and Martin Opitz in the German speaking area to name only two. There was certainly a will behind the mother tongue movement, and one can speculate on how that will was reflected by the insistence of the protestants from Wycliffe onwards to translate and produce a mother tongue Bible.

The widespread use of the mother tongues in Europe for 'great' poetry and indeed drama resulted in an avalanche of translation, especially in those countries which had a shorter tradition because they were on the periphery geographically and/or culturally. In Renaissance England and Scotland we see hectic translational activity, although a little different from what was going on elsewhere in Europe:

In an Italian or French literary context, the term 'Renaissance' would refer to a rediscovery of classical and Biblical letters in the ancient languages of Greek and Latin. The principal result would be new texts and editions in those languages, accompanied by new commentaries. In sixteenth-century England virtually no classical and Biblical learning of this primary kind was produced. For the majority of educated people, ancient letters were rediscovered by means of a comparative process of ongoing translations between Latin and a group of European vernaculars.[16]

Correct as this may be regarding England, recent research in Italian Renaissance translation underlines that it took off there too in the sixteenth century.[17] Translation and rewriting of many kinds in the form of imitations and indeed commentaries was the main method of appropriating the foreign classics, both concretely and discursively. This took on a wide spectrum of translational activity, from the foreign form without the text to exact translations of texts and forms.

The latter was, however, more the exception as Boutcher notes: 'The problem may be that if we read these works as "translations" in the modern sense they will inevitably disappoint, because good modern translations will almost always be found to be more faithful, more fluent, more sensitive to literary texture.'[18] This is one of the key points when discussing translation either side of Macpherson's *Ossian*: translation as text production was seen differently after *Ossian* appeared on the scene, especially regarding the genre of imitations, which almost disappeared and has not resurfaced in any major way since. The 'liberal' method of translating was continued, indeed, throughout the seventeenth and eighteenth centuries.[19] It was also underscored theoretically by figures such as John Denham, Abraham Cowley, Wentworth Dillon, and most importantly John Dryden, whose threefold theory is perhaps the best indication of how authors and translators saw literary re-production at the end of the seventeenth century:

> First, that of metaphrase, or turning an author word by word, and line by line, from one language into another. [...] The second way is that of paraphrase, or translation with latitude, where the author is kept in view by the translator, so as never to be lost, but his words are not so strictly followed as his sense; [...]. The third way is that of imitation, where the translator (if now he has not lost that name) assumes the liberty, not only to vary from the words and sense, but to forsake them both as he sees occasion; and taking only general hints from the original, to run division on the groundwork as he pleases.[20]

This is perhaps the most sophisticated model of translation to have appeared by that time, and it exemplifies the unease with which Dryden and many before him and after dealt with rewriting and recreating what they considered to be 'great poetry', which could only be achieved in the mother tongue through, as it were, the agency of an ancient, canonical poet. These imitations, and indeed translations, were an attempt to incorporate ancient poetry into an English national context: they are cultural hybrids of content on a spectrum described by Dryden above. The translators rarely went for Dryden's first method (even if they claimed to), but used the second and third. In this they may well have been under the influence of Horace, whose condemnation of *fidus interpres* in his *Ars poetica* they most certainly knew, not least from Dillon's translation of that text.[21]

Lawrence Venuti points out in the opening of his chapter on Neoclassicism and Enlightenment in the *Oxford Guide to Literature in English Translation*:

> This period witnessed the decisive emergence of *fluency* as the most prevalent strategy for rendering foreign poetry and prose, both ancient and modern. Translators aimed for a stylistic refinement that usually involved a significant rewriting of the foreign text, but that at the same time worked to mask this rewriting.[22]

So imitation was an attempt to become an author, while rewriting 'great poetry' was one of the major strands in the construction of national literatures in Europe. Another was the translation of poetic forms without the texts themselves, thus masking fully the translational component while retaining the 'grandeur' of the ancient 'great poetry'.[23] This does not necessarily mean that the forms were taken directly from the Greek or Latin, but some sort of an equivalent was used as a surrogate which was supposed to have the same 'noble' characteristics as the ancient form embodied. The story of the heroic couplet or the ode in English would be cases in point. The poets often allude to their imitations as odes, since the original was an ode, but in English the form varies significantly.[24]

Translations, or what was then understood as such, were of course also part of the literary production, especially works of the ancient greats whose texts were not only 'imitated' but, to an extent, 'translated'. This meant very often a struggle in choosing the right form to replace the unwieldy ancient metres. In the case of Homer the struggle to attain an equivalent poetic form probably reaches its zenith in Pope's translation, and at the same time it shows the limitations of the heroic couplet. Even a poet of Pope's calibre was unable to realise the necessary fluency, or 'easy poetry' as Johnson called it in an article in the *Idler* in 1759 where he criticises Pope:

> The first lines of *Pope's* Iliad afford examples of many licences which an easy writer must decline:
>
> > *Achilles' wrath,* to Greece the *direful spring*
> > Of woes unnumber'd, *heav'nly* Goddess, sing,
> > The wrath which *hurl'd* to Pluto's *gloomy reign*
> > The souls of *mighty* chiefs untimely slain,
>
> In the first couplet the language is distorted by inversions, clogged with superfluities, and clouded by a harsh metaphor, and in the second there are two words used in an uncommon sense, and two epithets inserted only to lengthen the line; all these practices may in a long work be easily pardoned, but they always produce some degree of obscurity and ruggedness.[25]

Johnson is not often seen as much of a theorist of translation, but in fact he deserves to be in that club too, for he was both avid practitioner of the art himself and, as here, astute observer and critic of translation. Indeed, in modern readers of translation theory he is included along with Denham, Cowley, Dryden, and Roscommon, all of whom he himself treated in the *Lives of the Poets*.[26] First and foremost, Johnson was a translator himself; that he and many of his admirers and critics probably did or do not see it that way is a reflection of the elusive genre of imitation. Johnson himself defined imitation in his *Dictionary of the English Language* as 'a method of translating looser than paraphrase, in which modern examples and illustrations are used for ancient, or domestick [sic] for foreign'.[27] This is the third definition after two which refer to copying. He follows up with the quotation from Dryden cited above but without the afterthought in parentheses. It may be assumed then that he sees imitations as a type of translation, and, in fact, Johnson's profile as a writer is one of a translator, rewriter, and essayist, in addition to being a biographer and lexicographer. He began his career with a translation into Latin of a part of Pope's *Messiah* (1728), and most of his literary works are rewritings or translations of some sort: *A Voyage to Abyssinia* (1735) was translated by dictation from an abridged French translation of the Portugese text,[28]

London (1738) is an imitation of Juvenal's *Third Satire*, *The Vanity of Human Wishes* (1749) is an imitation of of Juvenal's *Tenth Satire*,[29] and Johnson's tragedy *Irene* (1749) was also based on previously published material. It is, therefore, reasonable to count him as an important theorist and translator of the period.

Johnson's importance and responsibility as a theorist and translator is thus even greater than often can be read in the secondary literature, both specifically on his life and works and also in the context of his dispute with James Macpherson. This dispute has often been cast as an argument about 'truth' and 'deception' and certainly it was, on the surface. The underlying argument about different views of translation and aesthetics has rarely been discussed in this context, but it may provide a new angle to the dispute about the 'dispute'.

Lawrence Venuti has discussed the hegemony of fluency or domestication in English literary translation in detail in his *The Translator's Invisibility*, wherein he delineates the few 'revolts' against that hegemony, most notably in Francis Newman's translation of the *Iliad* of Homer.[30] He discusses the stern response by Matthew Arnold, who, in Venuti's interpretation, solidly reaffirmed the domesticating tradition of English translation, especially that of the ancients. It is indicative of the distortion of literary history that has been achieved in the matter of Macpherson that he is not even credited with a 'hoax' in this 'history of translation' as the subtitle goes. Distortion it is, since Macpherson (and Hugh Blair) discussed translation in the paratexts to Ossian, and the former not only translated the *Iliad* himself, but also wrote a preface that may well be read as a 'revolt' against imitations and the domesticating dogma of English translation culture. In addition, the Ossianic texts were read and translated by huge audiences at the time, and, through the controversy, not only rocked the canon to its foundations, but also triggered a debate on translation and editing that lasted a century.[31]

The issue is complex, however, and it is necessary to examine briefly the 'translational' history of *Ossian* and some of the responses to *Ossian* before moving on to Macpherson's translation of the *Iliad*. The anonymous preface of the *Fragments*, written by Hugh Blair, was very blunt in its description of the translation method:[32] 'The translation is extremely literal. Even the arrangement of the words in the original has been imitated; to which must be imputed some inversions in the style, that otherwise would not have been chosen.'[33] Macpherson's own description of the translation in the 'Dissertation' before *Fingal* is very similar: '[A]ll that can be said of the translation, is, that it is literal, and simplicity is studied. The arrangement of the words in original is imitated, and the inversions of the style observed.'[34] Even if this is not taken at face value, neither statement is an observation of the domesticating dogma, quite the opposite. And in the preface to the 1773 edition, Macpherson, who by then had published his *Introduction to the History of Great Britain and Ireland* (1771), which went into its third edition the same year,[35] and was finishing his own translation of the *Iliad*, was bold enough to remind his opponents of his successes abroad as well as reiterating his translational approach:

> Through the medium of version upon version, they retain, in foreign languages, their native character of simplicity and energy. Genuine poetry, like gold, loses little, when properly transfused; but when a composition cannot bear the test of a literal version, it is a counterfeit which ought not to pass current. The operation must, however, be performed with skilful hands. A translator, who cannot equal his original, is incapable of expressing its beauties.[36]

The constant insistence on the originals is new, and it may be due to the fact that Macpherson spoke at least some Gaelic and that he was representing a culture that had been repressed by the victors of Culloden. It may also be an aesthetic and translational stance, and the best evidence for this is his translation of the *Iliad*, a text also neglected due to the 'sturdy morals' of literary critics who, with perhaps one or two exceptions, have been able to ignore its significance. This is despite the fact that it was not only the first major translation in English since Pope, but, in effect, did away with the heroic couplet in Homeric translation. The main exception is William Sotheby's translation of 1831, but if the stage is viewed chronologically it becomes apparent that Macpherson's translation represents a shift.[37] Steiner, the editor of *Homer in English*, says in his introductory note to Macpherson's translation excerpt:

> An *Iliad* by the immensely celebrated and suspect begetter of *Ossian*. Severely received on publication, it has lapsed into oblivion. None the less, the cadenced, monumental prose, with its scriptural touches, is not without a certain aura. And it anticipates not only Victorian tactics of 'archaic nobility' but also Doughty and T. E. Lawrence.[38]

The severity may well have to do with the revolutionary poetics this translation represented. *The Poems of Ossian* were also greeted with poetic indignation, as it were, and as Sebastian Mitchell puts it, 'Macpherson's prose *was* the problem. John Wodrow, Richard Hole, and Ewen Cameron all set *Fingal* in heroic couplets, in 1771, 1772, and 1776 respectively'.[39] Such a drastic conservative reaction to a text is rare, even rarer amongst a group of writers professing their admiration for that which they are reacting against. The rewriting or the intralingual translation into a dominant poetics must indicate a literary system shocked and responding with repeated reproduction within the 'acceptable' parameters. Mitchell adds that 'Cameron's version dramatically altered the overall tone of the poem, highlighting its melodrama at the expense of its fatalism. One might wonder why any writer would wish to verify the poem in this form, given that couplets seem so poorly suited to convey the poetry's distinctive rhythmic plangency'.[40] One answer might be that behind it was not only poetical urgency, but also a political one. The changes Cameron made also smuggled in allusions to contemporary political events, as I have argued elsewhere.[41]

But if *Ossian* in prose threatened at least the 'poetical order' of British culture at the time, a prose Homer was probably even worse, and as Mitchell delineates, Macpherson had to produce another revised edition within weeks, due to the furious critical reception, especially one 'considered account of the translation'.[42] This anonymous critique in the *Critical Review* attacked the major premise of Macpherson's translation according to his own preface: literalism.[43]

Macpherson's preface can perhaps be read as an attempt to justify the form of his Ossianic translations, but also like a manifesto for more exact and literal translations. His opening of the preface is characteristically self-confident, to say the least. In the modern jargon, it is clear that he sees that the canonisation of Homer as a construct that has not only to do with the quality of the work but also the parameters it set, which are seen as the 'rules' of poetry and are, therefore, always imitated. These imitations 'could never approach to the excellence of their original'.[44] With these words, Macpherson is, in effect, dismissing a centuries-old tradition of 'imitations', and that well before the Romantics.

Moving on to translations of Homer in the modern languages of Europe, he is also very critical and comes to the conclusion that '[t]hese versions were rather paraphrases, than faithful translations'.[45] Macpherson believes this is due to the 'fetters, which the prevailing taste of modern Europe, has imposed on poetry', and that it 'may well be admitted, as an excuse, for man of the best genius, for not succeeding in the characteristical simplicity of Homer'.[46] The argument relative to Homer is obvious, and that against his predecessors is a classic 'annihilation' in order to make space for his own version: 'The best translators have not, in short, occupied the whole ground. The simplicity, the gravity, the characteristical diction, and, perhaps, a great part of the dignity of Homer, are left untouched. They have rendered the father of poetry, in a great measure, their own.'[47] The rejection of previous translations may be an echo from another famous translator of Homer, albeit into French, Mme Anne Dacier, who also justified her prose translation (1699) with similar arguments.[48] Her preface was translated into English in 1712, and Pope refers to her in the preface to his translation of the *Iliad*, so her views were certainly well known in Britain.[49] But both her own countrymen and Pope considered her method to be inferior to verse translations.

Macpherson introduces his own translation with a story in which a friend, known for his good taste, encourages him to do the translation. This of course he does, but first he begs the 'Public [...] their indulgence, for a moment. He will, he owns, be much disappointed, if his readers will take the following version for MERE PROSE.'[50] In other words, Macpherson wants to use his innovation of cadenced prose in the Ossianic poetry to translate Homer, in order to achieve the sublimity and simplicity of the ancient bard. He is careful, however, not to align this method with some sort of 'fluency' and seems to be practising a studied distance from the English tradition: 'Though he has avoided, with great attention, to fall into the cadence of English heroic verse, a fault scarce ever separated from poetical prose, [the translator] has measured the whole in his ear: Which he finds has been, in some degree, guided by the sound of the original Greek.'[51] Not only is the Augustan verse discarded, but also its cadence, in favour of the sound of the foreign language. It is certainly a declaration of literalism or foreignisation in translation, if there ever was. After toying then with a wish that he apparently had to present the translation in blank verse, he simply goes all the way and declares:

> To do all the justice, in his power, to his Author, as well, as to render his version useful to such, as may wish to study the original, through an English medium, he has translated the Greek VERBATIM: Even to a minute attention to the very arrangement of the words, where the different idioms of the two languages required not a freedom of expression, to preserve the strength and elegance of the thought.[52]

It should not be forgotten that these words were not uttered by an unknown minion at the time, but one of the best-known men of letters in Britain, regardless of the Ossianic controversies. His fame went well beyond domestic borders, and he was about to take over from David Hume as a kind of historian of the kingdom in a project that made him astoundingly rich. Such considerations confirm not only his political connections, but also his cultural capital.

For all that, Macpherson had overstepped the line with something akin to *hubris*. The claims he makes on behalf of his translation are unattainable in any translation and he could, therefore, easily be attacked on exactly the premise he himself sets up. The reviewer in *The Critical Review* was well aware of that, and he carefully dismantles Macpherson's translation by applying Macpherson's own hasty, indeed haughty, statements, as to how he translated one of the best-known texts on the planet. After recounting Macpherson's 'promises', quoted above, he continues: 'First we will examine how far the translation is *literal*; then, how far it is *smooth* and *simple*; in what degree it is *various* and *harmonious*; and lastly, how much it gives of the *fire*, and *vigour*, and *sound* of the original.'[53] It goes without saying that any critic, with the necessary knowledge, could destroy a translation using these criteria, and Macpherson had provided these criteria himself. It is not beyond belief to speculate that the anonymous critic was Johnson: the author uses, for example, the opening of the poem, just as Johnson had done when criticising Pope in *The Idler*, as quoted above. Johnson certainly had a longer history in the Ossianic controversies than he has most often been credited with.[54] Interestingly, he also attacks Macpherson for his Homer translation in the famous letter to the 'Ruffian': 'Your abilities, since your Homer, are not so formidable [...]', as if this was the watershed in the Ossianic controversies.[55]

It probably was a watershed, in a sense, but it was a pyrrhic victory for Johnson. What he was most fiercely defending was the poetics and aesthetics he felt were threatened by the 'upstart' translator from the North. And Johnson's love of his Augustan poetics should not be underestimated, if Boswell is to be believed:

> He enlarged very convincingly upon the excellence of rhyme over blank verse in English poetry. I mentioned to him that Dr. Adam Smith, in his lectures upon composition, when I studied under him in the College of Glasgow, had maintained the same opinion strenuously, and I repeated some of his arguments. JOHNSON. 'Sir, I was once in company with Smith, and we did not take to each other; but had I known that he loved rhyme as much as you tell me he does, I should have HUGGED him.'[56]

Macpherson may have lost the battle and even his reputation, but the era of Augustan poetics was certainly over. Translation as imitation also mostly disappeared from the scene as well. And even if the battle for foreignising translation was probably also lost too – for 'fluency' and 'domestication' remained the translational dogma of English literature – there was from now on a clear demarcation between imitations and translations, which had not been there before. For example, the Scotsman Alexander Fraser Tytler, in his seminal *Essay on the Principles of Translation*, published in 1791, criticises Macpherson for the lack of fluency, although he considers the translation solid: 'Thus, Mr. Macpherson, in his translation of Homer, (a work otherwise valuable, as containing a most perfect transfusion of the sense of his author), has generally adopted an inverted construction, which is incompatible with the genius of the English language.'[57]

Tytler's essay does not mention the Ossianic poems – possibly because he did not know Gaelic, for his method is to compare originals with translations. It is, as Venuti notes, certainly 'a key document in the canonization of fluency',[58] but even if it toys with some of the translational productions of imitative poetics, its general principles do not fit them, as may be deducted from the three general rules regarding translation: '1) A translation should give a complete transcript of the ideas of the original work; 2) The style and manner of writing a translation should be of the same character with that of the original; 3) A translation should have all the ease of original composition'.[59] If followed, these rules exclude the kind of imitation Dryden and Johnson defined and practised.

It is, on the other hand, an irony of literary history that the translator who certainly applied both imitative and literal translational approaches, who perhaps first in the English language propagated foreignising translation, even if he failed at it, has become lambasted as a 'pseudotranslator' without any real research into his ideas of translation or his work as a translator. He was in his time one of the most important literary figures in British letters and his influence on other authors, native and foreign, is monumental by any measure. It is perhaps one of the greatest injustices of literary history to deny him his rightful place within it regardless of his moral character, a trait which after all has nothing to do with the history of literature and aesthetics. Never mind 'pseudotranslation', the literary history we have been taught on Macpherson and his period is, without him and his work, truly 'pseudohistory'.

CHAPTER FOUR

Nostalgic Ossian and the Transcreation of the Scottish Nation

Cordula Lemke

Transcreating a Nation

It has often been noted that James Macpherson's *Poems of Ossian* have a distinct postcolonial agenda. They were published at a time when a body of opinion existed that there was a need to counter supposedly English traits of character with features that were perceived as being typically Scottish. The motivation for this assertion of identity was to fend off an English cultural hegemony that threatened to turn the Union of Parliaments of 1707 into a colonial enterprise. When Macpherson's collection of Highland ballads attracted the attention of the intellectual scene in Edinburgh, the Edinburgh Literati saw the text as an opportunity to employ poetry for their nationalist, though not separatist, aims. Anything Scottish was deemed worth noticing, but they had the highest regard for the supposedly ur-Scottish phenomenon of Gaelic culture. Thus, James Macpherson, with a working knowledge of Gaelic and an antiquarian zeal for the collection of Gaelic ballads, was seen as an ideal mediator.

As is well known, Macpherson's Ossianic poetry was soon declared a fraud, yet it remained firmly in place as a European bestseller. Still, it triggered a debate about authenticity and forgery, which keeps researchers busy up until today. By now, an agreement has been reached that Macpherson's poems cannot be wholly ascribed to either side. Macpherson did indeed translate ballads he discovered in the Highlands, but his claims of having found a complete epic poem of a bard called Ossian can only be attributed to his own 'creativity'.[1] In a manner typical of the Enlightenment thinkers' obsession with unity, he created a harmonious entity out of the diverse ballads he encountered, and declared one of their characters, Ossian, to be their author.[2] Although the accusation of forgery makes the question of national identity more problematic than it might otherwise be, this chapter nevertheless takes a closer look at Macpherson's act of translation in his epic poem *Fingal* and asks whether Macpherson's creativity can be seen as a postcolonial act of rewriting.[3]

In recent years, Translation Studies have increasingly questioned the concept of translation as a linguistic challenge of transmitting authentic meaning, demonstrating that it involves more than just a desire to understand other people and to make their cultural achievements known to a wider public. As Tejaswini Niranjana states, translation is 'tied up with context'.[4] As such it is part of a power structure that can never be impartial or innocent. The attempt to translate meaning into another language necessarily entails a cultural enterprise, as meaning cannot be separated from context. Translators have to take into account the cultural background of a text in a foreign language and seek an equivalent in their own culture. As such, the act of translation is closely related to a feeling of inadequacy, of failure, as translators experience the impossibility of conveying an intended or authentic meaning.[5] Any attempt at 'truthful' translation is doomed to fail; any claim for authenticity is unavoidably lost on the way.

For Niranjana, however, this foregrounding of the subjectivity of the translator opens up a possible space of resistance.[6] Translations no longer exhibit empirical knowledge, but can be questioned in relation to their motivations and aims. In the course of this development, the term 'translation' is increasingly used metaphorically (or perhaps indeed literally) since the focus is not so much on the actual text, but on the cultural features it 'carries across'. Thus 'translation' can be read as a 'transmission of elements from one culture to another'.[7] In addition, the rhetoric of translation has been used for acts of rewriting, a postcolonial strategy of countering the grand narratives of colonialism by adding a different perspective. Postcolonial writers have frequently practised the strategy of rewriting by employing the linguistic structure of a vernacular in English texts and have, thereby, both 'thickened' and defamiliarised the English language and challenged the role of English as a standard.[8] The process of rewriting is of interest if it is interpreted not so much as a 'writing back', as an assertion of one's own perspective against oppression, but as a narrative strategy. One case of rewriting arises when a translation fails to adhere to the 'original', but uses it as a starting point for its own literary creation. Here, the emphasis lies on the shaping influence of the text the translation is based on. This process of what Susan Bassnett and Harish Trivedi call 'transcreation' addresses both contemporary structures of power and questions of tradition and influence.[9]

With regard to James Macpherson, the term 'transcreation' could be seen as summarising the debate on *Ossian*. Macpherson employs the Gaelic folk ballads he finds in the Highlands to create his own oeuvre. His style seems to follow a nationalist aim of resistance to English cultural hegemony. It resembles the rhetorical devices of recent postcolonial writers in that he also utilises a language that draws on the Gaelic language grammatically whereby the English he uses becomes defamiliarised.[10] His mannerisms are usually put down to the fact that they render his poetry more authentic and thus strengthen the process of rewriting.

Another important device for postcolonial 'estrangement' can be seen in the powerful figure of the bard. In *Fingal*, the role of the bards is remarkably prominent. The narrative space given to the songs of the bards by far surpasses the space taken up by battles. As soon as another day has passed and the battles have been fought, the bards are asked to honour the fame of the Scottish ancestors by singing songs handed down from their bardic predecessors. When Ossian, as an old man, laments the fact that he will be the last of the bards to transmit Fingal's fame, Macpherson steps in and authorises himself as one part of what Katie Trumpener calls the 'bardic succession'.[11] Thickening the language and the memories of the bards are instances of rewriting in that they stand in contrast to the prevalent linearity of Enlightenment historiography. Here, cyclical structures vie with teleological ones, when the flow of the narrative is interrupted by recurring epic formulae or the linearity of the bardic succession is evoked just to frustrate a feeling of teleology by singing the old songs over and over again. Macpherson's return to tradition could be seen as a simple return to roots, which anti-colonial texts practise in order to shed the baggage of colonialism. However, as Colin Kidd has shown in his seminal *Subverting Scotland's Past*, Macpherson's political alliances can be found within a Whig tradition championing an Enlightenment infatuation with progress. Thus Macpherson's transcreation propagates a powerful return to an ancient tradition while remaining within the cultural frame of an Enlightenment world picture.[12]

The tradition Macpherson claimed to be purely Scottish Gaelic was also claimed by the Irish as part of their own tradition and led the Irish to accuse him of forgery too, but his transcreation did not stop at the exclusive appropriation of a shared Celtic tradition. He employed the techniques found both in the process of translation itself and in his originals to shape the general picture of Scotland in the eighteenth century. According to the taste of his own generation, he presents a unified picture of an ancient tradition which might be seen as pandering to English tastes. In *Ossian*, the cultural achievements of a Gaelic people are translated into the values of the eighteenth century and mirror both Rousseau's noble savage and the sentimental tradition. In the manner of Rousseau's savages, Macpherson's warriors are hardy; they celebrate bodily strength and live a frugal life close to nature. But the Gaelic warriors also possess the noble features of sentimentalism. They act according to the principles of sensitivity, compassion, and forgiveness.[13] Their wars are led in a similar vein, as Fingal's exhortation of Ossian's son Oscar shows: 'Never seek the battle, nor shun it when it comes' (*Fingal*, 78).[14] Battles are not fought out of aggression, but to defend oneself or a friend. As soon as Fingal is called, he hastens to the aid of the Irish chief Cuchullin.

Dafydd Moore has identified these moral features of sentimentalism as part of the romance tradition, and he argues that Macpherson deployed the romance genre in order to adapt the epic genre to the needs of eighteenth-century notions of subjectivity. Thus Macpherson's transcreation does not simply offer a longed-for national epic to a contemporary audience but troubles it by introducing romance elements that contest the heroic features of his warriors even as they are articulated.[15] This act of troubling the epic heroic tradition leads to what could be termed a 'poetics of defeat'. Macpherson invests his ancient heroes with sentimental values and creates a sublime universe of mist and gloom, defeated heroes and tearful survivors that can only result in despair: 'Ossian misrepresents the Celtic past as one of defeat and despair and inaugurates a self-destructive, retrospective Scottish cult of nostalgia.'[16]

This analysis stands in contrast to the celebratory reading of the Ossianic paratexts by Richard Bauman and Charles Briggs, who proclaim Macpherson's Ossianic poetry as paving the way for a strong Scottish national identity, or Katie Trumpener's more critical assessment that the Ossianic texts act as a safety valve while they nevertheless further nationalist thinking.[17] Murray Pittock holds an even more ambivalent position. He claims that to Scottish readers the poems may have served as an uncomfortable rehearsal of Jacobite glory that is not laid to rest with the defeat of the Jacobites. Thus the Ossianic universe is not just nostalgic but, as Pittock states, suffused with a feeling of injustice.[18] What is clear from this short survey is that most critics propose a prominent nostalgic element in Macpherson's Ossianic poetry, which is incompatible with the surface appearance of the poems or with Macpherson's own (political) agenda in other texts and is thus troubling to any kind of nationalist or postcolonial reading. It is my contention that this troublesome moment in Macpherson's texts is not caused by a clash of diverse ideas but resides in the very structure of nostalgia itself. In the following, I would like to show how the workings of nostalgia lead to ambivalence in Macpherson's *Fingal*.

Fingal's Nostalgic World-Picture

Nostalgia is usually dismissed as escapist: in an effort to mitigate loss, nostalgia provides a mostly fictive image of a supposedly better world in the past. As Svetlana Boym argues, nostalgia is a feeling of longing for the past that results in a utopian and thus creative desire for a past and not a future world. Moreover, it is concerned with a specific period rather than with a desire to be at a different place.[19] Although longing is popularly seen as nurturing fond feelings for a place, nostalgic longing goes further by offering a rose-tinted image of a former lifestyle or memories in general. It has been criticised for deflecting attention from present injustice to a beatified invention of a safe haven in the past. The desire for certainty and safety leads to a projection of positive aspects past and present onto a former period. This conflation of past and present moments in the past ensures that the nostalgic dream is not anchored in a historically sound image of the past. As Boym concludes, 'nostalgia tantalizes us with its fundamental ambivalence; it is about the repetition of the unrepeatable, materialization of the immaterial'.[20]

Nostalgia is a powerful force precisely because of its fictive character. Returning to a supposedly better world in a former period, nostalgics create stories. Yet this creation is fraught with dissonance. Although a nostalgic image is conjured up by recourse to a collective memory, nostalgic yearning is a highly individual process: nostalgics adapt collective images in order to suit their own situation. This new/old world picture is then repeated, and, indeed, performed, so as to take hold and gain authority and authenticity. Any critique will be perceived as treachery. As soon as the translation of collective or personal memory into an account of a former period is identified as a transcreation, nostalgics are deprived of the authenticity of their secret hiding places in the past. They feel betrayed by their fictional creation, which had gained the appearance of a factual reality by the authoritative process of repetition through performance. The nostalgic image is never shared in its entirety. It remains an individual feeling and thus easily questionable even by the nostalgics themselves.

However, Boym is also concerned with the modern condition and its apparently divergent forces of tradition and revolution. While tradition is seen as surrender to acquired norms that might oppose rational thinking, revolution engenders a radical break with tradition. Yet revolution also means 'revolving' and thus 'cyclical repetition'.[21] Only in returning to a former state and its adaptation to a new situation does revolution unfold its radical potential. It could be argued that revolution is in need of the workings of nostalgia in order to achieve a break with the past. The openness of a nostalgic world picture with its merging of the past and the present provides an ideal playground for the creation of new models of explanation as a driving force for revolutionary thought. George Steiner hints at this in his Massey Lectures on 'Nostalgia for the Absolute' where he argues that the common nostalgia for universalising explanations of the state of society, like Marxism or Freud's demotion of the subject, is an effect of the loss of a Christian model.[22] Here, a feeling of nostalgic loss enables thinkers to follow new directions. Or as Boym concludes, 'Nostalgia can be both a social disease and a creative emotion, a poison and a cure'.[23] It can provide an escapist dream or open up new possibilities for different directions of thought. It is my contention that both possibilities figure prominently in Macpherson's Ossianic poetry.

Even though Macpherson's epic poems might be argued to be following Homer's, Virgil's, and Milton's texts' political motivation to become founding myths for a nation, it is noteworthy that *Fingal* does not tell the story of the beginning of the great Scottish nation, but starts *in medias res*. Homer's *Iliad* and Virgil's *Aeneid* recount the beginning of the supremacy of the Greeks or Romans, and John Milton's *Paradise Lost* takes up the biblical creation myth to argue against a Stuart restoration and for Cromwell's Commonwealth. In *Fingal*, however, there is no reference to a beginning of Scotland. The great Scottish warriors are shown travelling to other territories such as Ireland or Scandinavia where they reinstate law and order, but do not reflect those virtues back to a place of origin. There is no recourse to a definite founding myth, and the journeys do not create a palpable picture of Scotland itself. The reader is left instead with an impression of timelessness: the great Scottish nation is always already there; its beginning dates back to a pre-historic state that transcends the grasp of historians.

This eternalising move turns Fingal's Scotland into a form of paradise. It reminds the reader of St Augustine's dictum that the paradisiacal state lies outside time and points towards the biblical creation myth.[24] Here, the Scottish warriors' rootedness in a state of 'always already' provides a background to an ideal *tabula rasa* for nostalgic longing. Fingal and his warriors yearn for their home at the end of the epic, but it is a home that remains a mystery; it is defined neither in time nor in space. One of the few instances where Scotland – or Fingal's home island – is described is in Fingal's statement: 'The desart is enough to me with all its deer and woods' (*Fingal*, 101). The home Fingal yearns for does not seem to have much to offer. It satisfies hardy warriors but does not provide an Edenic resting place for the readers' imagination as does Cuchullin's home island with its lush environment. However, it suggests safety, which is an important factor to the feeling of nostalgia. While Cuchullin's romanticised island might conjure up nostalgic feelings for a paradisiacal environment, Fingal's place grants the safety of a strongly guarded Garden of Eden. And as its depiction remains vague, it is a garden that can be imagined according to the reader's nostalgic needs.

Cuchullin and Fingal can be seen as representatives of the two sides of nostalgia, of escapism and of a starting point. The depiction of the Irish chief Cuchullin and his warriors at the beginning of *Fingal* is reminiscent of Milton's *Paradise Lost*. Cuchullin's epithetical car may remind readers of Milton's God who appears in his 'chariot of paternal deity' (*Paradise Lost*, VI, 750) and by driving the forces of Satan away decides the outcome of the battle. In *Fingal*, however, Cuchullin's car is linked to the satanic forces of final destruction rather than to the paternal duty of correction. As a car 'like the flame of death' (*Fingal*, 59), it is an instrument of fear. However, Cuchullin is portrayed as a broken figure at the beginning of *Fingal*. Although he is introduced as dominating battles with his chariot, the emphasis is on a recollection of past events. When he sees his warriors around him, he finds that his most cherished companions are dead: 'But where are my friends in battle? The companions of my arm in danger?' (*Fingal*, 57). These questions result in a lengthy lament before the epic has even started to unfold properly. From the very beginning the reader is thus introduced to the concept of power as a nostalgic reminiscence, a concept running through the whole epic poem. In the present, Cuchullin has no choice but to depend on the power of the Scottish forces commanded by Fingal. As his messenger Moran reminds him, 'None can meet Swaran in the fight but Fingal, king of stormy hills' (*Fingal*, 55). During the main fight, Cuchullin withdraws to a cave and rejects any offers to join the final feast. He favours a nostalgic return to his former glory which relies on an escapist use of tradition.

Yet the beginning of the epic shows that despite his desolate situation Cuchullin reacts to Swaran's colonial aggression and gathers his warriors:

> Now I behold the chiefs in the pride of their former deeds; their souls are kindled at the battles of old, and the actions of other times. Their eyes are like flames of fire, and roll in search of the foes of the land. – Their mighty hands are on their swords; and lightning pours from their sides of steel. – They came like streams from the mountains; each rushed roaring from his hill. Bright are the chiefs of battle in the armour of their fathers. – Gloomy and dark the heroes followed, like the gathering of the rainy clouds behind the red meteors of heaven. (*Fingal*, 56)

The chiefs are depicted in a transcendental manner. Here, *Fingal* uses similes to endow the warriors with superhuman characteristics. Their eyes shine in an abnormally bright way, their armour sparkles with flashes of lightning, and their force is likened to the sublime power of nature. Like God's battle forces in *Paradise Lost*, they seem beyond wounds and pain, as the text speaks of the natural power they inherit from their surroundings. Yet the image of the chiefs as 'red meteors of heaven' is ambiguously evocative. On the one hand, it portrays their strength, which can only be expressed in terms of a heavenly force, but on the other hand, it also alludes to the Fall.[25] In contrast to the noble direction of God in *Paradise Lost*, who shatters his enemies by driving through them horizontally, Cuchullin's warriors take their powers from a vertical position; they descend on their enemies. Their victory is less predictable in the plains of the battlefield, as they lose force by impact on the ground. As the case of Satan shows, all hope for further damage on the level of the plains is lost with the completion of the Fall. Similarly, Cuchullin's warriors are doomed to failure.

However, the depiction of Cuchullin's warriors goes beyond *Paradise Lost* in that it additionally employs the categories of time and nature to draw up their characteristics. Here, the focus lies on the past. The warriors take pride in their past actions; their former success strengthens their courage. Yet the preoccupation with the past also opens up a less favourable interpretation of the actual strength of these warriors. Dwelling on past events does not necessarily guarantee strength in the present. Rather, strength is evoked by constant repetitions of similes, for example the recurring mention of the 'mountain oak' (*Fragments*, 14 etc.). Cuchullin's chiefs are still compared to forceful entities, but the link is achieved textually via the workings of nostalgia, and not because of their actually depicted strength. Thus, their transcendental force can be read as transcended rather than transcendent; their power is overcome and exists only as a nostalgic memory.

Yet Cuchullin's warriors are not just part of Cuchullin's escapist nostalgia. The description of the warriors avoids allusions to a supernatural heavenly force but takes its similes from the realm of nature. It is in accordance with the statement in the preface to the *Fragments* in which the absence of Christian allusion in the poems vouches their claim to antiquity. Macpherson's transcreation relies on the seemingly scientific preoccupation with nature, which is typical for the eighteenth century. The warriors are no stronger than the metaphors of nature permit. Lightning, fire, streams, mountains, clouds, and meteors strictly belong to a natural and realistic world. Here, nature's characteristics of strength and power are deployed to create the identity of the warriors, an identity which naturalises the force of nature as features of the warriors. The similes transfer their meaning onto the warriors, but, in contrast to a metaphorical use, remind the reader of the realist setting of the epic poem. They allow the warriors to appear as a transcendental force, and still ground them in the world. Thus, the text offers a link to Enlightenment thought. What comes across as transcendence is firmly grounded in rational explanations. The warriors resemble the forces of nature, but they are still human beings without any magical powers.

Nevertheless, the use of similes in the text also unsettles the rational approach. All of these comparisons can be labelled sublime: emotions of horror readers and onlookers perceive in the face of the powers of nature. The warriors in *Fingal* participate in the terrifying force of sublime nature while refraining from contact with the supernatural. Coupled with the gloomy setting of nostalgic reminiscences, the process of enriching the characters of the warriors with rational similes is embedded in memory. The warriors are shrouded in the gloom of their forefathers, which turns the similes into the repetitive structure of epithets and makes them part of the structure of nostalgia. In the end the warriors mainly act on the strength of the epithets of their ancestors. Here, Cuchullin's nostalgic escapism is exchanged for a repetitive invocation of strength, which alludes to the creative side of nostalgia but does not yet unfold all of its creative potential. The less escapist approach shows that nostalgia is even at work when the text situates itself within the frame of Enlightenment thought.

The creative potential of nostalgia is reserved for Fingal. At the outset, Fingal seems to counter Enlightenment thought as he stands for an escapist promise: he is endowed with divine characteristics and thus deeply embedded in a lost culture. Cuchullin is depicted with God's chariot, but it is Fingal who can be compared to Milton's 'paternal deity'. Fingal's appearances are presented in the Old Testament imagery of God: 'But behold the king of Morven; he moves below like a pillar of fire' (*Fingal*, 91). Here, Fingal is likened to the divine fire, which leads the chosen people out of the desert (Exodus 3. 2). Like his warriors, his godlike power rests on similes and seems rationalised, but the comparison goes further. Fingal is called 'first of men' (Fingal, 62). He resembles both biblical characters that are called 'first of man' – Adam, the first of the human race, and Christ, the Messiah, the divine go-between. Fingal acts like Adam in that he follows God's orders to name and procreate; most of Fingal's warriors are in some way related to him, and his patriarchal role within his clan recalls Adam's role as father of mankind.

Fingal's Messianic dimension becomes prominent in his wars – 'he is like the son of heaven that rises in a storm' (*Fingal*, 84) – and the following apocalyptic setting of the battles shows him in a direct line with the Messianic force. He does not fall like a meteor, but rises in his glory. Similar to the apocalyptic scenarios of the Old and New Testament that show the Messiah or Christ ending the regime of original sin, banning Satan, and establishing the kingdom of God, Fingal comes as revenge for injustice. There, he never acts as an aggressor, but reintroduces an order that prevailed previous to the chaos wreaked by unlawful intruders: he beats Swaran and reinstalls Cuchullin before he leaves peacefully. Fingal's behaviour towards Swaran emphasises his Christ-like features. After Swaran's defeat, Fingal spares his life and even invites him to the final feast as a guest of honour. The pity he shows towards Swaran not only mirrors the priorities of eighteenth-century Sensibility, but at the same time points to his similarities with Christ and underlines his exceptional position. But as in the case of the warriors, the text makes sure that Fingal's strength cannot be reduced to magic or other transcendental powers. Fingal shares the messianic features of justice and compassion, yet the depiction of his victory over Swaran shows that Swaran is almost his equal during the fight and Fingal is not endowed with transcendental powers but is a particularly skilled human warrior.

Fingal's strength is closely connected to his ancestors. Like Cuchullin, he carries the memories of dead warriors into battle when he fights with 'the shield of his fathers' (*Fingal*, 99). Yet, unlike the Irish chief, he does not begin his battles with the songs of former heroes, but only asks for them to grant him a moment of peace: 'O Ossian, Carril, and Ullin, you know of heroes that are no more. Give us the song of other years. Let the night pass away on the sound, and morning return with joy' (*Fingal*, 101). For Fingal, the songs of the bards offer an escapist moment of rest before the morning rises and the present takes hold again with its joys. Although he relishes the songs, they do not command his actions, which are of paramount importance to him. Musing on his own demise, Fingal mainly laments that his martial prowess will be gone: 'Our names may be heard in song, but the strength of our arms will cease' (*Fingal*, 101). It is less important to him whether he will be remembered in songs, than that he will have lost his strength. Thus, his nostalgic joy in the bardic songs is depicted as escapist, yet the recollection of heroic songs also serves as a starting point for new, unsung deeds. In contrast to Cuchullin, his actions have triggered and will trigger songs, but they are not defined by songs. They arise from the knowledge of a heroic tradition, without being overdetermined by the structures of this tradition. This creative approach to nostalgia allows him to react in a manner reminiscent of Christ. He is strong where he needs to be and compassionate where his enemies expect revenge.

Towards a Nostalgic Nation

This twofold function of nostalgia can also be seen in the depiction of the bard Ossian himself. The bards are the keepers of the memory of the Scottish nation. They record the great deeds of their clans and secure their eternal value. Thus, they hold important positions. Ossian's decline at the end comes as a surprise:

> By the side of the rock on the hill, beneath the aged trees, old Oscian [*sic*] sat on the moss; the last of the race of Fingal. Sightless are his aged eyes; his beard is waving in the wind. Dull through the leafless trees he heard the voice of the north. Sorrow revived in his soul; he began and lamented the dead. (*Fragments*, 18)

Here, the 'last of the race' motif is introduced. Ossian, the sole survivor of the great clan of Fingal, is blind, old, and lonely. His blindness supports readings which see the 'last of the race' motif as weakening the Scottish cause by a nostalgic grounding of the great warriors in a far distant past. Ossian's old age can be seen as showing the state of decadence and decay the Scottish nation underwent since the time of Fingal's great battles. The grandeur of the ancient nation is irretrievably lost with the extinction of its warriors. Accordingly, Ossian has no longer an audience, but sings to the wind. This has often been seen as a step back in the quest for a Scottish culture and identity and as a politics of rapprochement in the direction of England.[26]

Furthermore, Ossian's blindness troubles in relation to the habits of thought of modernity. Modernity tends to link eyesight both to knowledge and to being. The importance accredited to seeing increased massively with the emergence of the scientific method. As Othello famously demanded, proof had to be 'ocular' since only then did it meet the requirements of the new scientific age and could it be trusted. Although scepticism regarding the truth of empirical proof was widespread, modernity remained preoccupied with the superiority of the eye and eyesight. George Berkeley was celebrated for linking knowing and being by lifting the scientific perspective into the spheres of the divine. As is well known, being depends on being seen, even if it is only by God's eternal eye. Yet in the godless universe of Macpherson's epics, Ossian is deprived of this eternal enveloping vision. Himself blind, he can no longer fill the role of a godlike being who sees everything and who could aid his clan to life and existence.

Yet Ossian's blindness can also be seen as part of a larger tradition of mythological figures such as Homer and the blind seer Tiresias, and poets whose blindness was a matter of record, such as Milton or, closer to home, the Gaelic poet Roderick Morison (?1656–?1714) known as An Clàrsair Dall, The Blind Harper.[27] The mythical allusion strengthens the figure of the bard. Far from being a sign of decadence and decay, the bard gains a new degree of sagacity. His intellectual elevation in his old age translates the physical achievements of a wild tribe into stories of moral importance and ennobles the early Scots. Here, the 'last of the race' motif could be perceived as strengthening the Scottish cause. It could be argued that the possibility of a strong Scottish nation remains, despite the fact that their predecessors died a long time ago. Although Macpherson's transcreation depicts the figure of Ossian as a sentimental old man who laments the lost paradisiacal state of his youth, there is a promise involved, the promise of the 'voice of the north'. But by singing of a past era and the great deeds of a celebrated people, Ossian makes the paradisiacal state accessible. In the figure of the blind bard, tradition is linked to the written word, and the written word to the 'scientific truth' that the Scottish people will rise again, in a messianic manner, to the might of their forefathers. Just as Macpherson unearthed the lost poems of Ossian, the strength of the Scots may simply be buried until it is brought back to light. The dormant strength of the Scots is personified in the figure of the sleeping warrior Fionn and his followers. On the level of narrative technique, this mythical, atemporal argument of the 'sleeping Fianna' is closely linked to the supposedly scientific and progressive approach of historiography.[28] Since this is not the place for mythical effect, the strength of Scotland is made to rise through the addition of the scientific credentials of the Enlightenment. This conflation of myth and Enlightenment thought enables both aspects of nostalgia, escapism and change, to remain in play. Nostalgia functions as a force that preserves the memory of Scottish strength. At the same time, it evokes escapist thoughts of a better past, which can only be accessed as part of the bardic tradition by an always already removed account of the past.

Here, the dilemma of the Ossianic use of nostalgia becomes evident. Due to its ambivalent structure of escapist longing and a possibility for change, the nostalgic pattern frustrates any conclusive reading that favours progress or retreat, postcolonial resistance, or unionist diplomacy. Any argument for change will include at least one instance where an escapist attitude prevails and any escapist reading will bring with it its own promise of progress. Macpherson's transcreation is a nostalgic translation of the notion of Scottish history which does not support a clear political agenda, but which offers a forceful set of possibilities that can be deployed by future generations in new transcreations of Ossianic poetry.

CHAPTER FIVE

Landscape and the Sense of Place in *The Poems of Ossian*

Sebastian Mitchell

In *Improvement and Romance: Constructing the Myth of the Highlands* (1989), Peter Womack took a dim view of the characteristic features of the Ossianic landscape. He thought that Ossian's compositions were 'topographically null', emptily embellished works with meaningless and arbitrary place names, 'all wrapped up in the mystique of tradition'.[1] The distinctive rhythmical prose of Macpherson's translation of the poetry into English was for him a 'negation into style', and the whole concoction had the effect of turning the vacated Highlands into a 'negative sublime', providing calculated justification for the clearance of the region's indigenous population from the middle of the eighteenth century onwards.[2] It is not difficult to see how one might arrive at such a generally disparaging opinion of the aesthetic effect of these works. For it certainly should be conceded that Ossianic poetry draws upon the same limited repertoire of natural and man-made features for the depiction of its landscape, with repeated reference to fire-lit halls, green-headed hills, caves, tombs, memorial stones, rolling oceans, groves, heaths, tall oaks, and distant ruins. Nevertheless, it is still possible to take an opposing position on the artistry and significance of landscape in *Ossian*: to argue that a distinctive aspect of the poetry is the tension it produces between the specific and the general; that it seemingly establishes a distinct sense of location only to dissolve into formless obscurity; and, as we will see in the later stages of this chapter, that it was still possible for continental European readers of *Ossian* to conceive of the poetry as possessing a distinct and an imaginative landscape, capable of being adopted for their own sense of belonging and national purpose.

It has, of course, always been the case that the poetry has been associated with the Highlands of Scotland. The title sheet of the first set of short lyrical pieces (some of which ascribed at that point to the bard Oscian rather than Ossian), the *Fragments of Poetry* (1760), announces that these pieces have been 'Collected in the Highlands of Scotland and translated from the Galic or Erse language'.[3] In the preface to the *Fragments*, Hugh Blair, then acting as mentor and sponsor to the young anonymous translator James Macpherson, declares these short tantalising works to be of an ancient provenance, and 'were certainly composed before the establishment of clanship in the northern part of Scotland' (p. 5). He relates the means of uncorrupted transmission of the poems by the bardic tradition: 'such poems', he says, 'were handed down from race to race; some in manuscript, but more by oral tradition' (p. 5); the reference to their oral nature here suggests a particularly close affinity of the songs of the bards and the lands they inhabited. There is a promissory quality to Blair's further observation that these detached pieces of verse were in all likelihood 'originally episodes of a greater work which related to the wars of Fingal' (p. 5). When Macpherson, now disclosed as the poetry's translator, published the fully reconstructed Celtic epic *Fingal* in London in December 1761 (dated 1762), along with some shorter pieces, the titular poem met with a generally favourable public and critical reception. The initial discussion of *Fingal* in the literary press concentrated on two issues: whether this primitive Celtic epic could really stand comparison with the grandeur, magnificence, and moral purpose of the classical poetry of Virgil and Homer; and whether the proper country of origin for this astonishing discovery of a lengthy complete Gaelic work should not be Ireland rather than Scotland.[4] It was the angry contention of some contemporary Irish antiquarians that Macpherson had appropriated and corrupted cycles of indigenous Irish poems for the cynical and distinctly modern purpose of boosting Scotland's cultural standing within the relatively new nation-state of Great Britain.[5]

Through the 1770s Scottish stadial historiographers, such as Adam Ferguson, William Robertson, and Henry Home, Lord Kames, drew on *Ossian* as evidence of both the necessary state of primitive consciousness and of the kinship networks of hunter-gatherer societies without losing sight of the fact that *Ossian* was intended to be a description of the state of Scotland and its surrounding territories in the third century AD.[6] Even those commentators, who had become uneasy as to the exact provenance and originality of these works when Macpherson published another fully formed ancient Gaelic epic, *Temora*, in 1763, appreciated the indivisibility of a sense of place from the poetry. When the philosopher and historian David Hume recorded his doubts as to the supposed ancientness of the works of Ossian one of his objections was that the state of northern Scotland has always been too barren to support the great armies depicted in *Ossian* by hunting alone, without some rudimentary form of agriculture, and without so much as a passing reference to fishing in the poetry.[7] Even Samuel Johnson, the most condemnatory of English commentators on *Ossian* in the 1770s, mounted his principal assault on the works and Macpherson's role in their supposed fabrication in the midst of a wider discussion on the nature of language and the extent of learning in the Hebridean isles.[8]

Macpherson provides explicit topographical information in *Ossian* in his prefatory materials to the poems and in his extensive annotation of the works from *Fingal* onwards (the light annotation of the *Fragments* is exclusively concerned with elucidating the action of the poems and glossing the names of its principal characters). In all the editions of *Ossian* in which Macpherson had a hand, the notes were located beneath the main text to enable readers to consult them at the same time as they engaged with the poetry. This paratextual material indicated the extensive geography of the works. Given the standard association of *Ossian* with the Highlands of Scotland, one of the surprising aspects of the poetry when one looks at the notes is just how far and wide the action ranges. The main events of both *Fingal* and *Temora* take place in Ulster, the northern region of Ireland, with further references to the more southerly and western kingdom of Connaught, ruled in the Ossianic world by the Fir-Bolg tribe, allies of the Scottish and Irish Celts in *Fingal*, and their foes in *Temora*. Episodes in these epics and in the shorter lyrical and dramatic pieces are also set in the wide archipelagic arc around the northern British coast, in the Hebrides, Orkney and the Shetland isles, and stretching further still across the northern Atlantic Ocean to Scandinavia. The central plot of *Fingal* hinges on an invasion of Ulster by Swaran, a Scandinavian chieftain. As Macpherson makes clear in his book-by-book summary, the poem's action takes place over consecutive days. The task of defending the northern region of Ireland falls to the sympathetic, but ineffectual, chieftain, Cuchullin. His forces are overwhelmed by the invading army, and he spends much of the poem brooding in a mountain cave. The Scottish king, Fingal, father of the warrior bard Ossian, arrives with his troops from across the Irish Sea to aid his fellow Gaels. The action culminates in the set-piece battle between the Gaels and the Scandinavians. Fingal defeats Swaran in single combat, and the Scottish forces prevail. Swaran is bound, but his life is spared (a tragic strand of the sub-plot has already revealed that Fingal was once betrothed in Scandinavia to his departed sister). In the final book, Swaran undertakes not to attack the Celtic lands again and is freed along with his surviving countrymen; the Scottish forces enjoy a victory feast, and the poem concludes on a surprisingly upbeat note with Fingal and his army sailing back to their native Morven on the west coast of Scotland, 'We rose on the waves with songs', Ossian contentedly recalls, 'and rushed, with joy, through the foam of the Ocean' (p. 104).

Macpherson's topographical comments range from speculations on the general areas in which the episodes of *Fingal* are supposed to have taken place to confident identifications of specific features. In the first book, for example, Macpherson glosses a reference to place in an account of the intermingled sounds of martial music, clashing arms, and howling dogs reverberating round the hills, '—Gloomy and dark their heroes followed, like the gathering of the rainy clouds behind the red meteors of heaven.—The sounds of crashing arms ascend. The grey dogs howl between. Unequally bursts the song of battle; and rocking Cromla echoes round' (p. 56). As the translator explains in the accompanying footnote, the name of the principal hill, Cromla, derives from its earlier druidical associations, though its exact location cannot now be stated with any certainty. 'Crom-Leach', Macpherson explains, 'signifies a place of worship among the druids, though here it is the proper name of the hill on the coast of Ullin or Ulster' (p. 421).[9] The conclusion of the fragment 'The Death of Cuchullin: A Poem' describes the eventual demise of the ineffectual chief of the Ulster Gaels, whom Fingal had sailed to defend. In the plangent measured strain of prose poetry, Ossian reports the burial of the young chieftain near the shore of Lake Lego in Ulster: 'By the dark rolling waves of the hero's tomb – Luäth, at a distance, lies, the companion of Cuchullin, at the chace' (p. 138). 'Luäth' is Cuchullin's faithful hound, buried in accordance with ancient warrior custom close to his master. Macpherson's accompanying note states that 'there is a stone shewn still at Dunscaich on the Isle of Skye [from whence he originally came], to which Cuchullin commonly bound his dog Luäth' (p. 451). The observation seems intended to remind the reader that there are supposed to be historical prototypes for the figures described in the poetry, rather than being exclusively the kind of mythical beings that standardly populate Hellenic epics and Norse sagas. Further, while it would not be possible for the overwhelming majority of contemporary readers to visit the remote site of a standing stone in the Inner Hebrides, then the note at least offers the theoretical prospect of a first-hand encounter with the primitive, sowing the seed of an idea that one could conceivably stand and reflect on the very same windswept spot as an ancient king.

Elsewhere Macpherson uses the notes to point out that the Gaelic names often refer to familiar places. 'Lochlin', for example, is the standard term for what is modern Scandinavia, though Macpherson then speculates that the Nordic episodes of *Ossian* are more likely to have been set specifically in the Jutland peninsula of Denmark (p. 421). In the lyric 'Carthon', an elderly warrior Clessámmor relates to Ossian a sad episode from his youth, which begins when he sailed partly by chance into the harbour of a town on the west coast of mainland Scotland. 'I came in my bounding ship to Balclutha's walls of towers', he recalls, 'the winds had roared behind my sails, and Clutha's streams received my dark-bosomed vessel' (p. 128). As Macpherson reveals here, 'Clutha' or 'Cluäth' is the Gaelic name for the Clyde. He then typically suggests that the proper name can be further traced to the distinctive aspect of the object being described, as 'the signification of the word is *bending*', he says, 'in allusion to the winding course of the river' (p. 445). And as part of Macpherson's wider purpose to demonstrate in the accompanying expository material that Gaelic was the original language of Scotland, and exists in a pristine and uncorrupted form in the age of Ossian, the translator avers the Latin name for the Clyde 'Glotta' is a derivation from the Gaelic 'Clutha', rather than the other way round (p. 446).[10] It is also the case that many of the characters are referred to with periphrastic tags that have the purpose of connecting them directly to the landscape. Swaran describes himself at one point as a 'son of Lochlin' [Scandinavia] (p. 92). When Tranar, a young Orcadian warrior, is killed in the opening exchanges between the Irish and Scandinavian armies in *Fingal*, Ossian envisages his grief-stricken fiancé: 'Weep on the rocks of roaring winds, O maid of Inistore' (p. 60), he says. Macpherson then comments at the bottom of the page that 'Inistore' is the Gaelic name for Orkney, which is in turn resolved into a synecdochic feature, as 'Inistore' is said to mean literally an 'island of waves' (p. 423). Ossian refers to himself as the son of Fingal, but he is also associated with the land from whence he comes rather than his noble lineage, poetically describing himself on several occasions as 'the voice of Cona' (Glencoe).

Macpherson's various observations on the geography of the poetry can be understood as an important component in the general ethnographic and anthropological commentary of the textual apparatus; his notes were supposed to convey the cultural vitality of this primitive warrior race. Their manners, expectations, and beliefs needed to be firmly situated in an identifiable region and era for their proper comprehension. Almost all readers of the poems in English have had these topographical markers readily available to them. The references were present in the first edition of *Fingal* and *Temora*, and they were retained in the first complete edition, the *Works of Ossian* (1765). When Macpherson produced his revised edition in 1773 (published 1774), he substantially pruned the annotation and dispensed, in particular, with all the parallel passages from ancient and modern epical works in the notes.[11] However, all the observations on location and the landscape derivations of the place names were kept in the new edition, and the great majority of subsequent editions of *Ossian* in the nineteenth century and twentieth century reprinted these observations.[12] The Scottish poet and critic Robert Crawford approaches the scholarly presentation of a mysterious and allusive primitive verse as a distinctly modern, even modernist, artistic practice, reminiscent of the procedures of an avant-garde poet: 'sublime, yet accompanied by its own handbook, Ossian is *ab initio* both text and paratext', he says, 'simultaneous barbarous and academic [...] being at once "primitive" and book clad'.[13] But as Dafydd Moore observes, such paratextual material in *Fingal* was almost certainly supplied at the instigation of Hugh Blair, Macpherson's mentor, and it seems in some respects Blair acted as collaborator and agent for the publication of the poem.[14] When Macpherson was no longer in daily contact with Blair, having relocated from Edinburgh to London in 1762, there was still no need to change significantly the model for the presentation of *Temora*, given the tremendous success of the launch of *Fingal*. Yet it does seem that Macpherson was always as interested, if not more so, in the historical attributes of the works than their literary qualities. He anticipates his subsequent career as a historian (and in particular as a historian of ancient Britain) by insisting in the preface to *Fingal* 'that the story [of the poem] is so little interlarded with fable, that one cannot help thinking it the genuine history of Fingal's expedition, embellished by poetry. In that case, the compositions of Ossian are not less valuable for the light they throw on the ancient state of Scotland and Ireland than they are for their poetical merit' (p. 37).

Macpherson's insistence on the historical utility of *Ossian* entailed some bold assumptions on the nature of the temporal and spatial relationships as they relate to causation and sense of place in the poems. He evidently believes that it is possible to resolve the often fraught and suggestive episodes of the poetry into a chain of consecutive actions, linked by a standard relationship of cause and effect, and that each of these actions took place in a conventionally understood location, in that events could be seen to follow one another as a series and were computable in terms of a progressive model of linear time. When, say, the Scottish chieftain and his ships are spied sailing toward the coast of Ulster in the third book of *Fingal*, we can reasonably expect them to land shortly afterwards on the coast. In his own influential account of the works, *A Critical Dissertation on the Poetry of Ossian, the Son of Fingal* (1763), Hugh Blair is much more sceptical than his protégé, both as to the degree of temporal and spatial co-ordination one can detect in these works and to their historical reliability. He acknowledges the topographical properties of the works, and the tendency to particularise aspects of the landscape as in the example of 'the storm of the sea of Malmor, or the reeds of the lake of Lego'.[15] However, he rejects outright the notion that just because there may be the occasional decipherable geographical feature this should lead us to believe the texts can be relied upon as robust evidence for an actual series of events. In Blair's interpretation of the poetry, *Ossian* is the expression of an era in which modern notions of absolute time, space, and place have no bearing. The poetry, he believes, is the product of an age of 'fabulous confusion', in which its rich figuration is a consequence of the intrinsic volatility of primitive language. Such expression is indicative of a period in which signs have not settled into having fixed relationships with concrete objects. While this lack of stability in language prevents the construction of a credible historical narrative, it does allow for a suffusion of overwhelming passion into all speech, giving rise to those remarkable Ossianic traits of the solemn, the grave, and the sublime.

We can certainly see some of these dislocative qualities when we turn to the poetry itself. In the following passage the Irish chieftains Calmar and Cuchullin, and the invading Scandinavian king, Swaran, watch the approach of the Scottish flotilla toward the coast of Ulster in Book III of *Fingal*:

> Morning is gray on Cromla; the sons of the sea ascend. Calmar stood forth to meet them in the pride of his kindling soul. But pale was the face of the warrior; he leaned on his father's spear. That spear which he brought from Lara's Hall where the soul of his mother was sad.——But slowly now the hero falls like a tree on the plains of Cona. Dark Cuchullin stands alone like a rock in a sandy vale. The sea comes with its waves and roars on its hardened sides. Its head is covered with foam and the hills are echoing around.——Now from the gray mist of the ocean, the white-sailed ships of Fingal appear. High is the grove of their masts as they nod, by turns, on the rolling wave.
>
> Swaran saw them from the hill, and returned from the sons of Erin. (p. 75)

The location is Cromla, the mountain overlooking the coast of Ulster. We can infer that the majority of actions described in successive clauses are supposed to take place one after another. The passage begins with the warrior Calmar, a chieftain of the Fir-Bolg tribe and a key ally of Cuchullin, looking out to sea. Calmar falls to the ground. At the same time, or perhaps slightly afterwards, Cuchullin is described standing alone, and, although the passage is not explicit on this point, the implication is that he too is looking out to sea. The second double-em dash seems to indicate a moment of contemplative silence, which is then followed by the 'now', introducing the appearance of Fingal's ships emerging from the bank of mist. The paragraph break suggests the Scandinavian Swaran sees Fingal's boats shortly after their sighting by Calmar and Cuchullin. The distinctive style of this piece is due to its parataxis, that is, the extensive use of propositional clauses with few connecting and co-ordinating prepositions between the adjacent statements. Walter Ong has argued that parataxis is a common feature of oral cultures, with such expression essentially operating by an additive rather than a subordinate principle, and that the oral work accumulates ideas in order to impress a notion or an image on the mind of the listener.[16] However, when such oral formulations are then written down, they can take on a paradoxical and ambivalent quality. On the one hand, the even-paced level sequence of the writing can lend the work a semblance of disinterested historicity, where one documented action follows on from another. But, on the other hand, the absence of any grammatical hierarchy and any evident means of co-ordinating temporal relations in a given passage can have exactly the opposite effect: producing a sense of confusion between successive terms, with orderly development now lapsing into uncertainty and elusiveness.

In this apparently straightforward episode of the Irish and Scandinavian warriors spotting Fingal's ships as they emerge from the sea mist, there are some intriguing moments of local temporal and spatial disturbance. The mention of Calmar's spear, for instance, initiates an associative analepsis (a sudden leaping backwards in time) as the weapon reminds the warrior of his mother grieving in the hall in Connaught over the death of his father. The conjunctive 'But' after the dash appears ungrammatical, not being adversative; its purpose in the passage would seem to be to haul both reader and character back into the present moment of the action, an action which is then intensified by the use of the adverbial 'now' in the phrase as 'slowly *now* the hero falls like a tree on the plains of Cona' (emphasis added), when the Irish warrior is momentarily associated with Glencoe (Cona), the native soil of the bard Ossian rather than that of Calmar. The landscape feature, even when it is modified or qualified with an identifiable place name, is still often used figuratively, and, as such, operates as a means of momentary displacement from the main narrative frame. The specificity of the reference intensifies rather than diminishes the sense of displacement in the simile, transporting the reader in that instant from the shores of Ulster to the forests of Glencoe. The vividness of the image, moreover, is indicative of the ways in which figuration tends to operate in the poem as a whole, such that a given simile or metaphor is ostensibly employed as a telling example of an event or incident in the main story, but this supplementary image then possesses more force than the object or action it was intended to illustrate in the first place; it draws the reader's attention away from the immediate event to some distant contemplative prospect. The cumulative effect of this style of displaced composition, as both Fiona Stafford and Howard Gaskill have concluded, is to produce a poetic idiom in which landscape, and an abstracted version of landscape at that, becomes more significant and memorable than the actions performed by the characters.[17]

Perhaps, then, there is less of a sense of dialectic in the paratextual materials of *Ossian* and the poetry itself, and rather more of the sense that the annotation was supposed to encourage two discrete approaches to the works and then to keep both these modes of reading in play at the same time. One was supposed to respond to this world of heightened sensibility with its unmoored relationship of time and space and with its topography always about to vanish into a beguiling formlessness, and to do so while also keeping in mind the supposed reality of the events described in these poems, set as they are in the ancient lands of Scotland, Ireland, and Scandinavia. In such circumstances, it is not surprising that the many tourists who began to visit the Highland region of Scotland from the late eighteenth century onwards were often in search of the distinctively Ossianic in this mountainous northern landscape. As Nigel Leask has argued, the approaches of late Georgian and early Victorian travellers to the poetry ranged from searching for those features associated with specific scenes in the works to the more general attempt to configure what they saw through the prism of received Ossianic aesthetic expectations – that is, to conceive of the landscape before them in terms of the sublime scenery of the star-filled firmament, the red disc of the setting sun, heather, gauze, barren hills, the rock-lined shore, and stormy weather.[18] One can detect a similar dynamic in the work of landscape artists of the period. Murdo Macdonald has recently identified a realistic impression of the region of Loch Lomond by the most prominent British painter of the nineteenth century, J. M. W. Turner, as being, in fact, an illustration of an episode from Ossian's lyrical fragment, 'The War of Caros'.[19] However, other painters working in England at that time made no attempt to represent the actual appearance of either Scotland or the northern region of Ireland in their pictures, as though to undertake such straightforward mimesis would be to miss the point of the poetry's emotionally charged scenery. Thomas Girtin, John Sell Cotman, and François Louis Thomas Francia, for example, all produced impressive Ossian watercolours as distillations of poetical mood with their depictions of vaporous trails, ghostly warriors, and moonlit mountains.[20]

Yet there is also a sense in which *Ossian* could come to stand not just for a purely imaginative terrain, but also for a vision of a vanished world, which could then be dramatically relocated with both a personal and collective sense of time and place; that its distinctive amalgam of precision and vagueness meant that it could seemingly evoke the distant Highlands of Scotland as well as serving as an imaginative account of one's own country. Ossian was translated throughout Europe, until there was a version of the poems in all of the major languages on the continent by the middle of the nineteenth century. Sometimes mapping the poetry's landscape on to domestic scenery was a relatively straightforward process, such as in the case of its Swiss reception where the Alps were viewed through the lens of Ossian's sublime mountains and lakes, and Swedish readers could be persuaded to set aside the unfavourable portrayal of Scandinavian warriors in the poetry to see the resemblance of their own land in the bard's descriptions of seas and shores.[21] However, the sense that the poetry described a similar set of geographical features was of lesser significance than the symbolism it was capable of investing in the idea of a homeland. Ossian acted as a spur to burgeoning Romantic movements across Europe.

Within its European context, the poetry can be understood to be closely associated with the development of ideas of independent nationhood. The most influential example of eighteenth-century Ossian translation was the inclusion of passages from the lyrics 'Berrathon' and 'The Songs of Selma' by Goethe in his seminal early *Die Leiden des jungen Werthers* (*The Sorrows of Young Werther*, 1774).[22] The novel represented a startlingly original use of *Ossian* in a work of contemporary fiction, and *Werther*'s European success meant that it would become a principal means by which many continental readers became aware of this distinctive, primitive Caledonian poetry.[23] However, *Ossian* was also being used in *Werther* as a significant element in the furnishing of a form of modern literary expressiveness. That invigorated idiom could, in itself, link to the desire for a unified Germany beyond its current politically and culturally fragmented circumstances, constituted as a patchwork of autonomous principalities. And as Gabriella Hartvig has demonstrated, the nationalistic associations of *Ossian* were especially pronounced in its reception in Hungary, where artists, writers, and intellectuals encountered the poetry via German editions in the late eighteenth century. A significant purpose of the Hungarian translations and Ossian-inspired original verse of the 1850s, she says, was to express through its fraught landscape a yearning for independence and to signal resistance to the governance of the Hapsburg Empire.[24] The works of Ossian had evidently travelled a long way from the Highlands of Scotland in their Hungarian incarnation, to become the means of articulating the aspirations for a cherished homeland in central Europe in the middle of the nineteenth century.

CHAPTER SIX

Ossian's Impact on the Discovery of Ancient Scandinavian Literature

Robert W. Rix

In the late eighteenth century, classical literary models of Greece and Rome were challenged as benchmarks of cultural prestige. It was no longer sufficient only to regurgitate the fruits of timeless and transcultural classicism. Instead, cultural prestige was now increasingly to be won through reconstructing one's own ethnic history. James Macpherson's *The Poems of Ossian* was central to this change. Indeed the enormous popularity these poems enjoyed has made it appear as if they were the cause of this reorientation, but *Ossian* should rather be seen as the flagship riding the swell of interest in ancient vernacular poetry that had been growing for some time. The sensational 'discovery' of *Ossian* came at an opportune moment and accelerated developments. Macpherson's poems were a significant catalyst for the renewed awareness of ancient Germanic or (in the parlance of the day) 'Gothic' tradition. This chapter will examine some of the dynamics that *Ossian* helped set in motion in respect to antiquarian and literary interest in the 'Gothic' tradition.

The Germanic past was often recovered through Scandinavian sources, in particular Icelandic texts, which represented the most significant fount of knowledge about beliefs, manners, and poetic practice of the 'Gothic' peoples. But it was generally believed that what could be gleaned from this Norse material had once been widely shared by peoples living around the North Sea littoral. This chapter will concentrate on two case studies. The first will focus on Britain, where the recovery of 'Gothic' tradition was a reaction to *Ossian*, partly carried out in the spirit of admiration and partly in the spirit of competition, and partly in the spirit of both. The second focus will be on Denmark, where Copenhagen became a hub for both German and Danish writers exploring a new repertoire of vernacular antiquity with more or less direct reference to an appreciation of *Ossian*.

Celtic and Germanic

In much eighteenth-century scholarship, no distinct fault lines were drawn between Celtic and Germanic cultures. So much is clear from Paul-Henri Mallet's *Introduction à l'histoire de Dannemarc, où l'on traite de la religion, des loix, des moeurs, et des usages des anciens Danois* [Introduction to the History of Denmark, or Discussion of the Religion, Laws and Manners of the Ancient Danes] (1755) and *Monuments de la mythologie et de la poésie des Celtes, et particulièrement des anciens Scandinaves* [Monuments of the Mythology and the Poetry of the Celts, in Particular the Ancient Scandinavians] (1756). Mallet was a Genevan professor at Copenhagen, and his *Introduction* was sponsored by the Danish government in order to improve the reputation of Denmark. It proved a successful gambit, as both publications became popular books of reference throughout Europe. Much work had already been done by seventeenth-century Scandinavian scholars, such as Ole Worm, Thomas Bartholin and Johan Peringskiöld, but these Latin treatises were mostly appreciated by a cadre of dedicated antiquarians. Mallet's studies in French kick-started a renewed interest in Nordic antiquity. This was in turn helped by the success of *Ossian*, which undoubtedly reinforced the popularity of Mallet's works, resulting in new editions of his books in 1760, 1763, 1787 and 1790 – as well as translations into German (1764–1766) and English (1770). *Ossian* far from invented the interest in vernacular literary tradition, but its added measure of eighteenth-century sentimentalism was instrumental in relocating vernacular antiquities at the centre of fashionable culture. For example, in the collected 1765 edition of Ossian's poetry, Mallet's *Introduction* is mentioned in a footnote to *Temora*, annotating the remarks the bard makes about the religion of their Scandinavian enemies. This is one of the annotations that falls under the 'historical-cum-cultural context and speculation' category of notes.[1] Through reference to Mallet, Ossian's reference to the 'stone of Loda' is related to the worship of Loda or Loden, purportedly cognate names of the Norse god Odin.[2] This was in fact nonsense, as the Ossian detractor Malcolm Laing pointed out.[3] Either Macpherson or Hugh Blair had misread Mallet in their eagerness to provide a historical paratext that would seem to authenticate Ossian's poetry.

Regardless of escalating misgivings about Macpherson's scholarship and credentials, antiquarians in Scandinavia often turned to Ossian as an important testimonial of the old Norsemen and their religion. Because Fingal had fought Scandinavians, the bard Ossian was believed to have provided a first-hand account of their religion and manners. The eighteenth-century Danish scholar Peter Frederik Suhm, for example, mined *Ossian* for information in both his history of Denmark and his study of the ancient religion of Odin.[4] The important, albeit often credulous, nineteenth-century Icelandic–Danish philologer and archaeologist Finnur Magnússon similarly had recourse to *Ossian*.[5]

The transition between the two adjacent traditions in the north seemed natural enough, not only because they were assimilated in critical studies, but also because the traditions were believed to have interacted. Macpherson himself printed a 'fragment' of an originally Norse poem (on the Norwegian King Harald Fairhair, who annexed the Orkneys and Shetlands in the ninth century) in the preface to the collected poems of Ossian (1773). This Macpherson translated from 'the Norse to the Gaëlic language', in which form it had allegedly survived.[6]

The somewhat surprising revelation that high and elevated poetry had been produced in the north was a spur for broader examinations of northern antiquity. In Germany, Johann Gottfried Herder's project of collecting folk poetry, including ancient Scandinavian poetry, was closely connected with his reading of *Ossian*, as is evident from his *Auszug aus einem Briefwechsel über Ossian und die Lieder alter Völker* [Extract from a Correspondence about Ossian and the Songs of Ancient Peoples] (1773). In Sweden, Erik Skjöldebrand, a member of the Stockholm Royal Academy of Letters, History, and Antiquities, published an 1802 paper on how the Ossian poetry acted as an impetus for collecting the songs of the old Scandinavian bards.[7] Clearly, recourse to Ossian did not only aid Norse scholarship, it also helped to popularise it.

Thomas Percy and Gothic Tradition in Britain

In Britain, the antiquarian Thomas Percy was inspired by Macpherson's short collection *Fragments of Ancient Poetry, Collected in the Highlands of Scotland* (1760) to publish five poems taken from the skaldic tradition of Norse poetry. These appeared in 1763 under the title *Five Pieces of Runic Poetry Translated from the Islandic Language*. Originally, it seems likely that Percy had wanted to translate the Norse poetry as an extension of the northern tradition Macpherson was discovering in Scotland. But his attention to ethnographic categories – the divide between Celtic and Anglo-Saxon cultures – was sharpened by the debate that ensued after the Ossian poems were published. Thus in the years 1760 and 1761, when Percy was preparing the Norse poems for publication, he several times referred to them as 'Celtic' in his correspondence.⁸ But, when he wrote the foreword to the printed book, there was no wavering that the material is decidedly 'Gothic' and 'Teutonic'.⁹

The disseverance was underlined in Percy's translation of Mallet's books into English, *Northern Antiquities* (1770). In 'The Translator's Preface', Percy explains Mallet's mix-up of Celtic and Germanic as an unfortunate error that had existed since classical times. Percy further clarifies that the 'Goths' (or Germanic peoples) and the Celts were 'two races of men *ab origine* distinct'.¹⁰ Percy's faithfully translated text appears as a palimpsest, in which Mallet's inaccurate usage of 'Celtic' is assiduously corrected throughout by means of footnotes and bracketed interpolations in the text. When I. A. Blackwell edited Percy's translation of *Northern Antiquities* for republication in 1847 he added several of his own chapters, presenting a taxonomy of the human races with a strong pro-Germanic bias, and going so far as separating the Teutonic from the Celtic race in terms of physiological characteristics, including references to craniology, and their psychological constitution.¹¹

Although Mallet's references to the Anglo-Saxons are scant, the title page of Percy's English edition boldly advertises it as a history of 'Northern nations; including [...] our own Saxon ancestors'. The purpose was clearly to appropriate the Norse tradition to the pre-Christian Anglo-Saxons. The idea that otherwise scant information on the manners of the pagan Anglo-Saxons could be enhanced through recourse to Norse poetry had already been suggested by seventeenth-century scholars Robert Sheringham, Aylett Sammes, and William Temple. But, in the wake of Macpherson's remarkable success with ancient poetry from the Celtic fringe, there was an increased push to find something that could promote the vernacular antiquities of Britain's Germanic ancestors.

Macpherson's literary patron, Hugh Blair, had made a comparison between the Norse and Gaelic traditions in 'A Critical Dissertation on the Poems of Ossian' (1763). While he suggests similarities between them he also distinguishes them in terms of their aesthetic appeal. Using the Norse poem 'The Death Song of Regnar Lodbrog' as an example, Blair notes that Norse skaldic poetry breathes 'a most ferocious spirit [...] animated and strong', but fails in the 'tenderness, and even delicacy of sentiment'. In contrast, Ossian melts the listeners' hearts 'with the softest feelings' yet without giving up 'the spirit of true heroism'.¹²

Percy, who published his *Five Pieces* almost simultaneously with Blair's essay, had made similar observations and clearly attempts to 'Ossianise' the Germanic tradition. In the preface, he accuses the antiquaries of Norse literature of attending only to poems of death and warfare, leaving the public with the impression that the skalds never 'addressed themselves to the softer passions, or that they did not leave behind them many pieces on the gentler subjects of love or friendship'.[13] To drive home this point, Percy selected 'The Complaint of Harold', a skaldic composition from the thirteenth-century *Knýtlinga saga*, in which the Viking King Harald III speaks a refrain of unrequited love. Nonetheless, the repetition of the recurring line 'And yet a Russian maid disdains me' is hardly enough to justify the Oxford Professor Thomas Warton's description of the ode in the first volume of his *The History of English Poetry* (1774–1781) as having the 'romantic air of a set of stanzas, composed by a Provencial troubadour'.[14] In the same place, Warton describes the Ossianic tradition as essentially secondary and derivative, claiming that the Celtic poets had learned from the Norse skalds.[15]

Evidently, opinion was divided on what constituted the merits of Celtic and Norse poetry. To the Scottish antiquarian and anti-Celtic racial theorist John Pinkerton, Ossian's poetry was so 'wholly melancholic in a supreme degree' that it exposed a weakness of the Celtic race. Pinkerton points to 'The Death Song of Regnar Lodbrog' as an example of the undaunted Germanic warrior welcoming death in song as a salutary counterpoint to Celtic whimpering.[16] Regnar's exit line, 'I die laughing', was regularly seen to represent the epitome of Scandinavian death-defiance, not least in the oft-quoted work of the Danish antiquarian Thomas Bartholin, *Antiquitatum Danicarum de causis contemptæ a Danis adhuc gentilibus mortis* [Danish Antiquities about the Pagan Danes' Disdain of Death] (1689). In Pinkerton's ethnographic work, the two northern traditions were taken hostage in the development of pro-Anglo-Saxon racialist discourse that would gather force in the course of the nineteenth century, culminating with the Scottish author Robert Knox's fiercely prejudiced *Races of Men* (1850).

Ossian's gloomy sentimentalism was also seen as an obstacle for the reception of the Germanic tradition. In J. G. Herder's philosophical dialogue *Iduna, oder Apfel der Verjüngung* [Iduna, or the Apple of Rejuvenation] (1796), Norse mythology is recommended as a suitable subject that could help artists work for societal renewal. Here, the speaker named Alfred, who has read deeply in the Norse *Edda*, complains that the soft and sentimental poetics of Ossian is regularly transposed onto the Norse tradition, thereby distorting its reception.[17]

The publication of Norse specimens was not, however, solely conceived as an ethno-cultural standoff. Whether it was believed to be historical or not, *Ossian* was recognised for opening up a popular market for ancient poetry. Although Percy casts doubts on the authenticity of Ossian in the preface to *Five Pieces*, he does not try to hide that his own publication was an attempt to capitalise on the rapturous reception that Macpherson's *Fragments* had received: '[i]t would be as vain to deny, as it is perhaps impolitic to mention' he writes, 'that this attempt is owing to the success of the ERSE fragments'.[18] In a letter of 4 December 1761, William Shenstone reproached Percy for delaying the publication of *Five Pieces* so much that Macpherson had time to publish his *Fingal*. In Shenstone's opinion, Percy had failed to take advantage of a book market characterised by conspicuous consumption of ancient vernacular poetry: 'Why will you suffer the Publick to be quite *cloyed* with this kind of writing [Macpherson's Ossian], ere you avail yourself of their *Appetite*.'[19]

Percy's selection of Norse verse was intended to emulate the poems in the *Fragments*, both in its scope and format. This is evident when comparing the design of the two title pages. Percy even quoted a passage from the same text by the Roman poet Lucan. The translated poems inside are cast in a similar style of rhythmical prose translation as that which Macpherson had utilised, and the layout in the dialogue of 'The Incantations of Hervor' was an imitation of Macpherson's *Fragments*.[20] However, Percy does try to gain an edge over Macpherson. In the preface to *Five Pieces*, Percy maintains that the public's suspicion of *Ossian* as a forgery 'will not be eradicated until the Translator of those poems thinks it proper to produce his originals'.[21] This demand was somewhat unreasonable, as Macpherson had always claimed the majority of the Ossian material was collected from oral sources. Percy decided to print transcripts of his five Icelandic original texts as 'vouchers for the authenticity' of the poems. In his correspondence, Percy had previously stated that printing the originals served little purpose, since it was in a language 'nobody will understand'.[22] But, he eventually realised that printing the transcripts was both a legitimising measure and a sensible marketing ploy.

The use of the designation *runic* in the title of Percy's anthology had also been painstakingly considered. Percy explains the term in the preface immediately before the passage questioning the authenticity of Macpherson's translations: 'The Characters, in which this language was originally written, were called Runic [...] at first applied to the letters only: tho' later writers have extended it to the verses written in them.'[23]

This appears to be a riposte to the dominant perception of the Celtic tradition in the eighteenth century as essentially scriptless. Percy clearly associates the Norse poems that he translates with the supposed existence of early runic manuscripts. The theory that the Germanic poetry of the north had regularly been committed to manuscript through the use of runes was propounded by Ole Worm in his authoritative *Runir: seu Danica literatura antiquissima, vulgo Gothica dicta luci reddita* [Runes: or the Most Ancient Danish Letters, Popularly Called Gothic, Brought to Light] (1636, rev. 1651).

To substantiate this claim, Percy adorned the title page with runic writing, quoting from two of the poems, 'The Ransome of Egil the Scald' and 'The Dying Ode of Regner Lodbrog', translated in the anthology. The runes were copied from Worm's transcription of the two texts into the younger *futhark* rune script – the medium in which the Danish antiquarian presumed they would originally have appeared. These runic 'back-translations' were purely hypothetical. Worm's runic version had most probably never existed. It is ironic, of course, that in his zeal to give his publication the stamp of both ancientness and authenticity, Percy unwittingly perpetuated the text-without-an-original counterfeit which he had set out to discredit.

Norse-Inspired Poetry in Britain

Percy's publication was the first gambit for the popular market with Norse poetry. Ossian had shown that there was literary value to be found in vernacular tradition, which had otherwise been unceremoniously jettisoned in favour of classical models. Percy later published the more successful *Reliques of Ancient English Poetry* (1765), a seminal collection of historical ballads that came to define the canon of popular, vernacular poetry.

On a European scale, the popularity of *Ossian* was pivotal in bringing attention to medieval Nordic poetry as a marketable commodity, either through translation or as a commercially viable subject for new compositions. To borrow a term from the culture researcher Itamar Even-Zohar, Macpherson's work was a 'primary' text, that is, a productive principle to which the economy of literary texts reacts. The success of *Ossian* precipitated a new *dynamic canonicity*, the introduction not just of a single text but of a new literary model that entered the repertoire of possible models in a literary system.[24] In other words, Ossian served as a canon-forming model, which made possible the construction of more texts of the ancient-vernacular variety. It is the production of Norse-inspired poetry in Britain that will be examined below.

The most successful exponent of the new formalistic and thematic experiment was Thomas Gray. Before the Ossian poems appeared in print, Gray had in fact perused two specimens of Macpherson's 'translations'. In a letter of 1760, Gray professes that he was 'charmed', 'gone mad about them' and in 'extasie with their infinite beauty'.[25] The year after, he composed two Norse odes, 'The Fatal Sisters' and 'The Descent of Odin'. Both these texts can be seen to take up the themes of doom and fate in battle that can also be found in the Ossianic poems. Gray's odes were not published until 1768, at which time they were accompanied with a note explaining that they had originally been intended for a 'History of English Poetry', in which they would represent the style of those nations 'who had subdued the greater part of this Island, and were our Progenitors'.[26] Both poems were taken from the scholarly studies of Thomas Bartholin and the Orkney historian Thormod Torfæus, but Gray's English versions altered the source texts considerably, which shows that he saw them more as material for experimentation within a new aesthetic paradigm rather than a straightforward translation.

A number of writers in Britain took up the lead that Gray had provided and tried their hand at pseudo-Norse poetry with Ossian in the baggage. The scholar and poet Thomas James Mathias, for example, included in his *Runic Odes: Imitated from the Norse Tongue in the Manner of Mr. Gray* (1781) two poems which (notwithstanding the title of the volume) focused on Celtic themes. One of these was inspired by 'Images selected from the Works attributed to Ossian'.[27] Edward Jerningham, who had made his fame as an imitator of Thomas Gray, published the long poem *The Rise and Progress of the Scandinavian Poetry* in 1784. The first part of this poem tracks the power of the Norse muse in awakening the old Northmen to courageous battle, a theme that has clear affinities with Ossian's poetry. Frank Sayers's much-revered *Dramatic Sketches of the Ancient Northern Mythology* (1790) contains the pseudo-Norse poem 'The Descent of Frea'. Sayer's aim was to provide a full map of British literary past, and this poem is placed alongside the respective dramas on *Moina* and *Starno* (names to be found in Ossian), with their several scenes of Celtic bards and druids in action.[28] Richard Polwhele edited a collection of *Poems Chiefly by Gentlemen of Devonshire and Cornwall* (1792), which contains several translations and imitations of both Norse and Ossianic poetry. Polwhele's own 'Ossian Departing to His Fathers: Imitated from Macpherson's Ossian' is printed alongside other Norse-themed imitations:

'Gram and Gro', 'Hother', 'The Incantation of Hervor', and 'The Tomb of Gunnar'. Richard Hole, who contributed the last poem on this list (based on *Njal's Saga*) had previously published a *Poetical Translation of Fingal* (1772). He would later write the poetical romance *Arthur; or, The Northern Enchantment* (1789) about the clash between native Celts in Britain and invading Germanic armies. Finally, Thomas Love Peacock's Norse-inspired juvenilia *Fiolfar* (1806) uses Macpherson's Ossianic terminology for Scandinavia.

For Walter Scott, *Ossian* acted as a spur for his interest in Norse antiquity. In the years 1792 and 1793, he delivered both the (sceptical) essay 'On the authenticity of Ossian's Poems' and 'On the Origin of the Scandinavian Mythology' to the Speculative Society in Edinburgh.[29] If the title of the latter appears to have followed a customary eighteenth-century investigation of mythology as part of the development of the human mind and society, Scott soon realised the national importance of Norse tradition for Scotland. Around 1800, Scott made contact with the antiquary Robert Jamieson, whom Scott admired for his discovery of the kinship between Scandinavian and Scottish folklore ('a circumstance, which no antiquary had hitherto so much as suspected').[30] Scott learned that Scotland had preserved a rival Norse/Germanic tradition. In the medieval tale *The Lay of the Last Minstrel* (1805), Scott incorporates the 'customs and manners which anciently prevailed on the Borders of England and Scotland'. Among these were purportedly the belief in Valkyries, fleshy ghosts and reverence of magic swords, for which parallels could be found in Icelandic manuscripts.[31]

What was seen at the time as Macpherson's 'discredited' forgery appears to have also encouraged Scott to write a *faux* tale: the poem *Harold the Dauntless*, which was published anonymously in 1817. The poem focuses on the Viking past of northern Britain and flags up its status as a counterfeit by adopting a voice 'supposed to be that of a rude minstrel, or Scald'.[32] A central scene of the plot concerns the eponymous hero confronting Odin, the Norse deity who rules over Viking-dominated Britain and is modelled on Fingal's battle with the spirit of Loda in *Carric-Thura*. Harold defeats the pagan deity, which serves Scott as an allegory of Britain's final acceptance of Christianity. However, the 'champion of the north' also brings a strain of 'light, to liberty, and life' to the shores of Britain (Canto VI, 319–22). In the last lines of this mock-medieval tale, Scott launches what may be construed as an ironic gibe at Macpherson's scholarship based on scriptless sources. After listing examples of the many scholarly studies on ancient Scandinavian courage produced since the thirteenth century, he asks the reader's pardon for having committed to writing a 'tale six cantos long' and 'yet scorn'd to add a note'.[33]

The legacy of the Scandinavian tradition was taken up again in the novel *The Pirate* (1822). Here, Scott creates a melodramatic tale based on the survival of Norse culture, traditions, and language in the Shetland Islands into the late seventeenth century. In fact, Scott helped to raise awareness that one could discover remnants of Scandinavian lore in the Northern Isles. In his *Life of Scott,* John Lockhart mentions that a visitor to North Ronaldsay had recited Thomas Gray's Norse imitation 'The Fatal Sisters' (recorded in Thormod Torfæus's Orkney-history *Orcades* [1697]) to the inhabitants there, after which an old person among them supposedly recognised the poem as one known on the island.[34] In the same manner that Macpherson had undertaken field trips in the Highlands, travellers sought out the archipelago of the Northern Isles. In the year 1774, for example, the Scottish theologian George Low visited Shetland in order to collect material for a description of the country and was able to take down thirty-five stanzas of the Norn ballad 'The Earl of Orkney and the King of Norway's Daughter' from an elderly farmer of Foula. The ballad was first printed in George Barry's *History of the Orkney Islands* (1808).[35] This was part of a flurry of books on North Britain, which was increasingly seen as a repository of ancient vernacular traditions. Barry's book was published by Scott's Edinburgh publisher Archibald Constable (in collaboration with the London firm Longman & co.) and was advertised alongside Laing's critical edition of Ossian and other books on the Highlands and Islands.[36]

Composition of Norse-Inspired Works in Scandinavia

We now turn to Scandinavia, where the popularity of Ossian helped project a new awareness of Nordic antiquity.[37] Through translations into German, Italian, and Danish (first full translation 1790–1791), Ossian helped activate a new repertoire of national antiquities. One place where this had a significant impact was in the visual arts. The Danish painter Nicolai Abildgaard was one of the pioneers who took up subjects from Nordic mythology. During the late 1770s and early 1780s, he pursued this interest alongside his painting and sketching scenes from Ossian, such as *Fingal Sees the Ghosts of his Forefathers by Moonlight* (1782) and his often reprinted *Ossian Sings His Swan Song* (1782). In the work of one of Abildgaard's students, Asmus Jacob Carstens, we also find an overlap of interests. Carstens painted scenes from Nordic mythology, but he is also known for his 1796 painting *Fingal Battling Loda*, depicting the scene of the battle with the spirit of Odin.[38]

The use of Norse mythology as a subject for the arts was a highly controversial issue, since it was seen to lack the beauty of classical mythology and the edification inherent in biblical subjects. The heated debate is recorded in a collection of pamphlets published between 1812 and 1821, filed as 'The Mythology Dispute' in the Danish National Library of Art. The debate illustrates how the introduction of a new repertoire causes instability in the established canon and can meet with resistance.[39] However, in 1819, Crown Prince Christian VIII employed the antiquarian Finnur Magnússon to teach Nordic mythology and literature at the Royal Academy of Arts in Copenhagen. Royal backing signified a change in the economy of genres that were permissible. The Crown Prince's motives are clear: Danish patriotism was running high at this time, after a series of spectacular national misfortunes including the British bombardment of Copenhagen in 1807, the state bankruptcy in 1813, and the cession of Norway to Sweden in 1814.

In terms of the influence of *Ossian* on literary developments, the earliest traces lead back to the German-speaking poet Heinrich Wilhelm von Gerstenberg. This seminal, albeit somewhat forgotten, figure came to Copenhagen in 1765. Gerstenberg read Ossian through the partial German translations of 1762 and 1764, although he shows sound scepticism of their authenticity.[40] He composed *Gedicht eines Skalden* [Poem of a Skald] (1766): a sentimental poem stages the Ossian-like awakening of an ancestral ghost, the Norse skald Thorlaug. In the fifth and final song, Thorlaug muses on the death of the Norse gods and how much more enlightened religion has become with the introduction of Christianity. But there seems to be a parallel with Ossian, who describes a Golden Age that is wasting away. In any case, this and other of Gersternberg's poems show unequivocal Ossianic inflections, especially in their animated descriptions of the Scandinavian landscape.[41] If Macpherson straddled a bi-cultural divide in Scotland, the interest in the pan-Germanic mythology of Odin and the Aesir had unifying significance for Gersternberg, who hailed from the German-speaking minority in the southernmost parts of Denmark.[42]

Gerstenberg became a close friend of the German expatriate poet Friedrich Gottlieb Klopstock, who had resided in Copenhagen since 1751. Klopstock had probably read Ossian early and certainly knew parts of Michael Denis's translation before it appeared in print (during 1768 and

1769). Klopstock wrote to Denis on 8 September 1767: 'Ossian's works are truly masterpieces. If we could only find such a bard!'.[43] In Klopstock's poem 'Unsere Sprache' [Our Language] (1767), references to 'Gothic' tradition abound, but it is Ossian who is held up as a model of a bard whose poetry creates an unbroken continuity with the past. The first four verses, in which the Celtic bard is eulogised, were occasionally prefixed to German translations of Ossian. In the conclusion of the poem, Bragi, the skaldic god of poetry in Norse mythology, is resting on a harp, but he may in future pick it up and strike its strings.[44]

A significant moment is reached in Klopstock's 'Der Hügel und der Hain' [The Hill and the Grove] (1767), in which he expresses the intention to leave behind classical literary ideals (symbolised by Mount Parnassus) for the German bard, who sings in the ancient grove of Odin. After this, he abandons interest in classical figures. Klopstock finds a parallel to Fingal in the Germanic hero Arminius, who had successfully fought the Roman Empire (as recounted in Tacitus's *Germania*). This hero appears most prominently in the historical drama *Hermanns Schlacht* [Hermann's Battle] (1769), which was written at the height of Klopstock's fascination with Ossian.[45] Klopstock's work was instrumental in kindling what classically inclined poets would refer to as the *Bardengebrüll*, a 'bardic roar', pursued among his followers and imitators in Germany.

Klopstock's Copenhagen circle included a young Dane, Johannes Ewald. Klopstock, who had a keen interest in verse metrics, was disappointed that Macpherson had not supplied the public with the melodies that purportedly accompanied the Gaelic verses and therefore came up with a plan by which Ewald should travel around the Highlands, the Orkneys, and Iceland accompanied by a composer to record 'the old songs that Macpherson had missed or not even sought'. Nothing came of this due to Ewald's failing health.[46]

Nonetheless, Norse texts were readily available in print to furnish writers with material for composition. In a retrospective collection of his works, Ewald recounts that Ossian (together with Shakespeare) gave 'my taste a new turn'.[47] A product of this turn was the drama *Rolf Krake* (1770), based on the story of this legendary king in Saxo Grammaticus's thirteenth-century chronicle *Gesta Danorum* [The Deeds of the Danes], a work pre-Romantic and Romantic writers mined time and again for its heroic tales of ancient Danish kings and warriors. In 1773, Ewald wrote the musical drama *Balders Død* [The Death of Balder], based on the mythic narrative recounted in Saxo's history. In this play, the god Balder is the passionate lover who will not bow to social conventions but insists on pursuing his love without restraint – thereby, unwittingly, opening up a gateway for evil forces, which eventually lead to Ragnarök. The invocation of strong passions and the sentimentalised scenario of an era coming to its end would have found a ready audience amongst those familiar with Ossian. Ewald's play deepens and darkens the story of love between gods compared to Anna Catharina von Passow's one-act play *Den uventede Forlibelse, eller Cupido Philosoph* [Unexpected Love, or Cupid the Philosopher] (1757). This trifle, in which the playful Cupid shoots his arrows at the goddess Freya, was inspired by Mallet's publications and was the first Danish play to refer to Norse gods. Ewald's later play is tragic in the manner of the love story between Fingal and Agandecca – to which is added a dash of Goethe's obsessive Werther. Following Ewald's lead, the Dano-Norwegian author Christen Pram wrote the tragedy *Frode and Fingal* (1790). This much-maligned play stages a meeting between two legendary kings – Danish and Scottish. The play was written for the Danish Crown Prince's wedding, and the tribulations of the ancient kings were intended as an allegorical 'mirror for princes'. This shows how vernacular narratives were now used in place of classical models as vehicles for moral and political philosophy.

Success for Nordic-themed writing came with the Danish national poet Adam Oehlenschläger. He produced a number of poems and dramas based on both mythology and legend, including *Balder the Good: A Mythological Tragedy* (1807), *Palnatoke* (1809), *Starkad* (1812), *Hroar's Saga* (1817), *The Gods of the North: An Epic Poem* (1819), *Ørvarodd's Saga: An Old Norse Story* (1841), and *Regnar Lodbrok: A Heroic Poem* (1849). Oehlenschläger had Ewald as his admired model, but also complained that the older poet dressed the Norse gods in 'southern apparel'.[48] Oehlenschläger's antidote to Ewald's French rococo inspiration was his various experiments with adaptation and his reformulation of Norse metric patterns, such as *fornyrðislag*, *rimur*, and *dróttkvætt*.[49]

In the manner of Macpherson's field trips to the Highlands, Oehlenschläger set out from Copenhagen to travel rural Denmark in pursuit of its legendary and ancestral past. An account of the trip is given in the poetic suite *Langelands-Reise* [Journey to Langeland] (1805). At the outset, Oehlenschläger declares that his purpose was to visit ancient national monuments and listen to legends taken from 'the peasant's simple mouth'. However, against a backdrop of the *Ossian* authenticity debate that had raged for almost four decades at the time, Oehlenschläger discarded any attempt at collecting empirical evidence. Instead, he decided to use Saxo's medieval collection of fabulous national legends as a guide to the places visited – employing the 'poet's view' by using what is inwards and 'radiate it outwards'.⁵⁰

Evidently, Oehlenschläger approached the new fount of Nordic material through his reading of Ossian, having acquired Edmund von Harold's German prose translation *Die Gedichte Ossian* [The Poems of Ossian] (1775).⁵¹ In 1800, before Oehlenschläger had made his poetic debut, he wrote an article on Nordic literature, in which he comments on a Danish translation of the Icelandic skald Eyvindr Skáldaspillir's poem *Hakonarmaal*. This poem, he declares, was so close to Ossian in respect to 'poetic spirit and strength' that it could be called 'a holler of Northern Scotland's great singer'.⁵² In the same year, Oehlenschläger submitted an entry for an essay competition at the University of Copenhagen, answering the prize question: 'Is it useful for the *belles lettres* of the North to use and commonly accept Norse mythology in place of Grecian myths?' In his affirmative response, Oehlenschläger points to the works of Gersternberg and Klopstock as pointing the way, but, above them stands Ossian, who intermingles 'masculine spirit' with a 'sweet temper'.⁵³

Both these qualities can be found in Oehlenschläger's masterpiece 'Guldhornene' [The Golden Horns], a poem which concerns the chance discoveries of two ancient ceremonial horns in a field of rural Jutland.⁵⁴ In Oehlenschläger's narrative, the first of the ornamented artifacts is found by a rosy-cheeked maiden with lilywhite hands, the second by a sturdy farmer, who is 'strong-armed and tall, / Like his forefathers all'. These peasants intuitively understand the glory of the divine imagination which envelops the 'eternal works'. The horns are 'given' to them by 'war stained' ancients who reside 'in the sky' – recalling Ossian's 'forms of the dead […] blended with the clouds' (*Temora* VI, 113) – here, translated into the gods and men in Valhalla. In contrast, erudite antiquarians who later examine the horns are left 'with thoughts perplexed / In darkness they grope / Vainly they hope', but find only an impenetrable 'mist'.

That Oehlenschläger saw Ossian's martial, yet sentimentalised, poetry as a template for a new national art is clear from his speech given at a celebration for the famous sculptor Bertel Thorvaldsen in 1819. Here, Oehlenschläger expresses the hope that Thorvaldsen would 'give thought at times to the North's ancient race of gods, to the first noble ideas of a people from whom you descend! Like the spirits of Fingal and Ossian, they waft in the sky, waiting only for you in order – to put it Homerically – to dwell again on earth, and be granted form and life'.⁵⁵

If Macpherson's work gave the first impetus to the discovery and editing of national heritage, the nation was not always the only unit of collective identity. Ossian also inspired regional dissociations, challenging the 'nation' as the only or most important yardstick on which heritage could be measured. *Ossian* awoke in the Danish cleric and author Steen Steensen Blicher a focus on the regional. Blicher translated the *Ossian* into Danish in two volumes (1807, 1809). In the debut collection *Digte* [Poems] (1814) he includes a number of 'Ossianic Elegies', which draw directly on Macpherson's material. Blicher focused his literary works on the peninsula of Jutland, much of which was still uncultivated heathland with a primarily rural population. It seems that the vast and desolate heathland, its legends, nonstandard dialect, and its remoteness inspired in Blicher a comparison with Ossian's Highland vistas. In the poetic suite *Jyllandsrejse i sex Døgn* [Travels in Jutland over Six Days] (1817), the sixth day is a lament over the loss of heroism in the fatherland, where the name of Odin had once made men fearlessly embrace death. The sixth day concludes with a series of references to Selma having lost its Bard, Morven its king, Fingal his son, and Oscar his father, etc. Evidently, these images are meant to epitomise the feeling of loss for Blicher, but also the hope that his national harp may be as loud and long-lasting as that of Ossian.[56] The image of Ossian singing on the ruins of his collapsing nation impressed itself with much symbolic significance at a time of Danish national losses and misfortunes. For the patriotic Blicher, Ossian was a nostalgic poet of departed glory, who expressed the sentiments of a once-proud nation.

However, Ossian also served as a stimulus for regional discourses. In his autobiography, Blicher refers to 'Morven's royal bard, whose mighty sounds of the harp have certainly assisted in giving a direction to the poetry of Jutland'.[57] Thus Blicher constructs an image of Jutland as the place where the most archaic vestiges of culture and tradition have lingered and can still be heard and includes it as part of his Ossian reception. In the comments to his translation of the poems, he writes that it may be difficult to determine exactly what Ossian means by the oft-used term 'Lochlin', but that it may either refer to all of Scandinavia or to Jutland alone.[58] Blicher's Jutland-based works often document a rich tradition of folklore and ballads. His work *E Bindstouw* (1842) is a masterpiece of local patriotism. Here, Blicher sets up a *Decameron*-like framing story of a provincial knitting room, where Jutlanders exchange ballads and folklore (in dialect). Blicher's works can be said to parallel the structural position Ossian took up in Britain, insofar as Blicher was attracted to the idea that the vitality and robustness of a nation came from the fringe rather than the centre. Like Macpherson and his Scottish supporters,

Blicher was a unionist. He believed in a federal system of government, which – at the same time – needed a culturally strengthened Jutland. In this way, Blicher transposes Macpherson's antiquarian brand of regional (but unionist) patriotism to a new culture-political arena.

Conclusion

This chapter has documented how Macpherson's work formed the groundswell of a new intellectual and artistic paradigm. Macpherson's work was by no means the 'Big Bang' of antiquarian interest in northern antiquities, but it reactivated the long-standing interest in Norse/Germanic antiquity as a vehicle for cultural, ethnic, and political consciousness. In England, the new canon of vernacular past could be ecumenical, but 'Gothic' tradition was sometimes recovered in cultural competition with the Celtic bardism whose contours it found conducive even as it sought to resist its ethnic and even moral implications. As part of an assessment of the larger cultural trends *Ossian* set in motion, we can see that the selection of 'Gothic' tradition was to a degree determined by a set of Ossianic themes with which contemporary audiences were familiar. In Denmark, *Ossian* ignited a renewed interest in Nordic-related antiquarianism, as well as made available a new aesthetic paradigm for composition. That *Ossian* symbolised a stylistic departure from previously dominant French-classical strictures was acknowledged when the bookseller C. F. W. Lahde gave the title *Ossian* to his weekly magazine (published from 1826 to 1836), the aim of which was to publish literary experiments focused on national and non-classical themes.

The influence *Ossian* exerted on the Norse/Germanic register presented itself as a mixed picture of intentions and ambitions. But it is clear that *Ossian* was important and shows the extent to which the negotiation of identities could take place on the basis of ancient tradition rediscovered. What it invited was a frequently inseparable synthesis of deeply felt ethno-cultural patriotism, Romantic Nationalism, literary fashion, and commercial sense.

CHAPTER SEVEN

The Significance of James Macpherson's *Ossian* for Visual Artists

Murdo Macdonald

The response of visual artists to James Macpherson's *Ossian* is an astonishing aspect of Macpherson's influence. Artists began making work based on *Ossian* with the publication of *Fingal* in 1762 and are still making such work today. Many images – for example, the earliest, those of Samuel Wale (1721?–1786) and Isaac Taylor (1730–1807), published in 1762 and 1763 respectively – were intended to be engraved, and appear as illustrations of Macpherson's text. But many were independent works of art, and it is important to emphasise that *Ossian* was, from its earliest appearance, giving impetus to the thinking of artists rather than simply providing a source of imagery for illustration. This is underlined by the variety of approaches taken to Macpherson's text. For example, in 1802 one finds the English painter J. M. W. Turner (1775–1851) using the inspiration of *Ossian* to develop his poetical vision of landscape. In complete contrast but at around the same time the French artist Anne-Louis Girodet (1767–1824) was developing a new form of dream-like figurative painting on the cusp of neoclassicism and romanticism, again with the inspiration of *Ossian* at its heart. The fact that Turner's 1802 work *Ben Lomond Mountains, Scotland: The Traveller – Vide Ossian's War of Caros* was presumed lost, only to be discovered in plain view but wrongly titled in 2013, echoes the cultural-political 'losing' of Macpherson's text itself within academia.[1] In contrast, Girodet's *Ossian Receiving the Ghosts of French Heroes*, commissioned by Napoleon in 1801, has always been well known. It was part of a remarkable series of works commissioned by Napoleon from leading French artists, among them Ingres (1780–1867) and Gérard (1770–1837).[2]

This chapter introduces some of the extensive body of visual art to which Macpherson's *Ossian* gave birth, and some of the more significant discussions of this body of work within scholarship.[3] It is in four parts. First of all it considers at greater length a key feature of *Ossian* art touched on above: the way it is closely and often self-consciously engaged in cultural and artistic questions of the day. This discussion necessarily broaches some of the key interpretations of this artistic response, and the second section completes this review of the key literature on the field. The third section offers something of a chronological survey of work made in response to *Ossian*, though it is one as alive to questions of thematic preoccupation and the influence of schools of thinking and the dynamics of the coterie as it is to those of date. Finally, and by way of conclusion, I suggest some ways in which the field might yet evolve and develop, in particular in its understanding of the transnational importance of *Ossian* as an inspiration for art.

Image, Text, and Context

Girodet's work already noted was given proper context with respect to his other works in 2005, when it gave rise to one of the core themes of the major reassessment of his achievement mounted by the Louvre in Paris.[4] As chance would have it, in Paris at the same time, at the UNESCO building, was an exhibition of *Ossian* work by an artist of our own day, Calum Colvin. The French capital thus brought together works inspired by *Ossian* spanning two centuries, and that conjunction is emblematic of the international and historical durability of *Ossian* as a starting point for visual artists. Colvin's exhibition *Ossian: Fragments of Ancient Poetry / Oisein: Bloighean de Sheann Bhàrdachd* was first shown in 2002 at the Scottish National Portrait Gallery in Edinburgh.[5] It is not merely a response to *Ossian*, but as thorough a meditation on Macpherson's place within Scottish culture as many of those published in written form. Its wider impact has been such that it was cited on the timeline of research in Howard Gaskill's introduction to *The Reception of Ossian in Europe*.[6]

This linkage between visual artists and scholarly consideration of *Ossian* is characteristic. One can find that interdisciplinary effort certainly as far back as Alexander Runciman, who was associated with the Society of Antiquaries of Scotland in the late eighteenth century, and it can also be seen in Turner, who shared his interest in *Ossian* with his patron, the antiquarian and archaeologist Richard Colt Hoare (1758–1838). Like Turner, Richard Colt Hoare was deeply interested in the Latin poet Virgil, and this complementarity of the Celtic and classical is typical of many of the artists who have explored *Ossian*.[7] In most cases the classical complement to *Ossian* is Homer, but with respect to Turner, Virgil is more prominent. Indeed, Turner's early *Ossian*-inspired art can be thought of as complementing his illustration of Virgil, *Aeneas and the Sibyl, Lake Avernus*, which was painted in about 1798. That painting by Turner was based on a sketch by Richard Colt Hoare. As well as being a distinguished antiquarian, Richard Colt Hoare was the owner of Stourhead in Wiltshire, the most perfectly 'Claudian' of all English manipulated landscapes, complete with perfectly proportioned classical architecture by Henry Flitcroft (1697–1769). That landscape transformation had been the project of Richard Colt Hoare's grandfather Henry Hoare (1705–1785). The point here is that Virgil was a key source for the paintings of Claude Lorrain (1604/5?–1682), after whom the 'Claudian' landscape was named, and both Turner and his patron were keenly aware of the fact. Thus the landscape at Stourhead is implicitly Virgilian as well as explicitly Claudian. And *Ossian*, as a northern European legendary text, provided the perfect complement to that thinking driven by Italy and Greece. Indeed, it was in the course of reflections on Stourhead and classicism that John Gage suggested the correct identity of Turner's 1802 *Ossian* painting.[8] Turner's later *Ossian* picture *Staffa, Fingal's Cave*, from 1832, can thus be seen as a northern complement to a number of Virgil-based works, not least *The Golden Bough* painted in 1834.[9]

The close links between visual artists and those researching other aspects of *Ossian* has remained a key feature of the artistic response to the poems.[10] For example, the cultural context of Colvin's work was considered in detail by Tom Normand in the catalogue accompanying the original exhibition. Further, Colvin's UNESCO exhibition in 2005 was accompanied by a conference, *Ossian Then and Now*, which led to a special issue of the journal *Interfaces – Image, Texte, Language* published in 2008.[11] More recently Colvin's work has been explored by Sebastian Mitchell in his 'Celtic Postmodernism: Ossian and Contemporary Art' (2013).[12] In that article Mitchell also explored work derived from *Ossian* of other contemporary artists: the photographer Gayle Chong Kwan,[13] the painter and printmaker Geoff MacEwan,[14] and the sculptor Alexander Stoddart.[15] Also of note is Norman Shaw, whose work has an added dimension in that it links back into issues of emigration and language, via a print contributed to *An Leabhar Mòr / The Great Book of Gaelic*, published in 2002.[16] *Ossian*-related work by both Colvin and Shaw formed part of an exhibition at the City Art Centre in Edinburgh in 2010, which had the purpose of rethinking the idea of art and the Scottish Highlands, both from historical and present-day perspectives. In that exhibition their work was given context by a wood-block print of Ossian dating from about 1910 by the Celtic Revival artist John Duncan (1866-1945) and etchings from the 1770s by one of the earliest of all artists who responded to Macpherson's work, Alexander Runciman (1736-1785).[17]

The Artistic Response to Ossian in Scholarship

The intervention of artistic responses to *Ossian* within wider scholarly and cultural debates described above has already brought forward a number of the key critical works on *Ossian* art. It is worth, however, considering explicitly some others. Other key contributions to the literature include a number from Duncan Macmillan, in particular in relationship to the pioneering work derived from *Ossian* of Runciman. This begins with Macmillan's papers in *The Burlington Magazine* in 1970 and in *Art History* in 1978. Runciman's *Ossian* painting plays an important part in Macmillan's books, *Painting in Scotland: The Golden Age* (1986) and *Scottish Art* (1990, 2000). An account of how Runciman fits in with the wider Scottish print culture of the time has been given by Macmillan in 2012.[18] In 2006 Martin Myrone devoted a chapter to Runciman in his rethinking of eighteenth-century figurative iconography, *Bodybuilding: Reforming Masculinities in British Art 1750-1810*,[19] and in 2008 Sebastian Mitchell made an invaluable exploration of the image of Ossian made by Runciman's friend, the Irish painter James Barry (1741-1806).[20] Another recent contribution to the visual debate is Joep Leerssen's chapter 'The Bard's Garb: Ossian's Dress Sense' for the volume *Ossian and the National Epic* published in 2012, edited by Gerald Bar and Howard Gaskill.[21] That book also includes a reflection by Calum Colvin upon his own work on Ossianic material.[22]

The foundation of much current research into *Ossian* and visual art is Henry Okun's paper 'Ossian in Painting' from 1967 published in *Journal of the Warburg and Courtauld Institutes*.[23] A crucial complement to that paper are the two catalogues produced in 1974 for the major *Ossian* exhibitions held at the Grand Palais in Paris and the Kunsthalle in Hamburg.[24] The exhibitions received a review by Werner Spies, which can be considered part of the literature.[25] The Paris and Hamburg exhibition catalogues provide good visual guides to Ossian and art, focusing on northern European art around the year 1800. They identify a grouping of the most innovative artists operating at the time. Building on such material was my above-mentioned 'Ossian and Art: Scotland into Europe via Rome', which formed a chapter in Howard Gaskill's *Reception of Ossian in Europe*, published in 2004.

Both catalogues can be recommended, but the Hamburg catalogue is preferable because it contains more material including a timeline. This timeline is an important research tool because it includes reference to and images from editions, rather than simply independent works of art. There is important material illustrated here, for example the title page designed by Goethe (1749–1832) for his 1777 edition and the little-remarked wood engravings of Paolo Priolo (1820–1890), published in 1873. Priolo's images have a further significance because they accompany text by the Gaelic-speaking Highland land-rights activist John Murdoch, and that association firmly reinserts Macpherson's *Ossian* into the Highland political context from which it originated. On the Hamburg timeline the point is also made that *Ossian*'s influence can be found in twentieth-century art. A single image by Max Ernst, dating from 1972, is included. Werner Spies notes Ernst's work in his review, and that prefigures the continuing interest one finds in *Ossian* among artists of our own day.

Despite its availability since the 1960s and 1970s, no British gallery has built on this body of art-historical scholarship. That failure is a further indication of the ignorance of *Ossian* that still characterises the view of so many otherwise adequately informed commentators. It has been another casualty of a cultural political issue that has not resolved itself after two hundred and fifty years. To show how profound that slippage with respect to the significance of *Ossian* can be, one has only to look at William St Clair's *The Reading Nation in the Romantic Period*.[26] This magisterial work is a recognised standard, and rightly so. That the author ignores Macpherson's work while simultaneously drawing attention to the importance of that of Hugh Blair, Macpherson's most important advocate, is thus all the more puzzling. In a wider context Dafydd Moore has commented: 'The story of the present-day reception of *Ossian* is, then, an intriguing one.'[27] Indeed so.

Ossianic Art: Forms and Themes

I now turn to an account of some of the key works that respond to *Ossian*. This survey is broadly chronological in organisation, but equally seeks to outline some of the more important thematic preoccupations of the work, and keeps a close eye on questions of medium. It will also draw out some important dynamics of group and school within the ways in which Ossianic matter has been represented in art. It is appropriate to start with the two earliest images illustrating *Ossian*, by Samuel Wale and Isaac Taylor. Wale's image appears, engraved by Isaac Taylor, on the title page of the first edition of *Fingal* dated 1762 and published by Becket and de Hondt in London. The scene that it shows is from *Berrathon*: Ossian awaits his death and imagines the ghost of Malvina plucking at the strings of his harp. Samuel Wale was a distinguished and prolific book illustrator. He was a founder member of the Royal Academy in London, in 1768, and became its first professor of perspective. The second image made in response to *Ossian* dates from 1763 and is both drawn and engraved by Taylor. It is for the title page of *Temora*, again published by Becket and de Hondt in London in the same format as *Fingal*. It shows an incident in *Cath-Loda*, when Fingal finds Conban-Carglas held prisoner in a cave. This passage would be revisited in due course by a number of other artists, including Runciman in his murals and etchings of 1772. Indeed, Runciman etched three different versions of the scene.

Both the earliest images, by Wale engraved by Taylor and Taylor engraved by himself, are constrained by their limits as title page illustrations. Whatever their quality, they were designed to fit in with the typography rather than to exist as artworks in their own right. The first full-page illustration of *Ossian* is in fact by an Italian artist in an Italian book. It is the frontispiece of the translation by Melchiorre Cesarotti (1730–1808) of a substantial portion of *Fingal*, published in Padua as *Poesie di Ossian* and dated 1763. This image further emphasises the internationalism of *Ossian* both from the point of view of translation and with respect to visual art. The frontispiece is the work of the distinguished Venetian engraver Antonio Baratti (1724–1787), and it is based on the title-page engraving made by the Samuel Wale for *Fingal*. It is, however, a much more substantial response than that of Wale because Baratti had a full page available to him: he did not have to fit his image into the typographical constraints of a title page. Paradoxically, the passage from *Berrathon* to which the frontispiece refers was not translated into Italian until a later edition. That indicates, if further indication were needed, that Baratti is using Wale's image rather than Cesarotti's text as his immediate inspiration. Although this frontispiece can be considered as the first fully realised illustration of *Ossian*, it should be noted that in 1763 another important image was made, which was engraved and printed the same year. That was the drawing of Cathmor's shield by William Stukeley (1687–1765), contained in his letter sent to James Macpherson after the publication of *Temora*, and duly published.[28] This interaction of Macpherson and Stukeley is an important part of the visual/intellectual context of *Ossian*, not least because of the subsequent influence of the work of both men on William Blake (1757-1827). It is also worth pointing out that Stukeley's astrological approach to *Ossian* echoes earlier alchemical imagery and prefigures the assignation of particularly heavenly bodies to particular characters in *Ossian* by Goethe's friend, the painter Philipp Otto Runge (1777-1810), early in the nineteenth century.

If Baratti provides the first full-page illustration for an edition of *Ossian*, then distinction for making the first major independent art work taking its inspiration from *Ossian*, with respect to painting at least, seems to be shared in the early 1770s between the Swiss artist Angelica Kauffmann (1741-1807) and the Scot Alexander Runciman. Both had been part of the circle of the painter Henry Fuseli (1741-1825) in Rome. With respect to sculpture, the earliest work seems to be a lost *Head of Ossian* in Coade Stone by John Bacon (1740-1799), which dates from after 1769. It was made while he was employed at Coade's workshop in London, around the same time as he entered the Royal Academy as a student.[29] Bacon may also have been the sculptor of the medallion of Macpherson based on the Joshua Reynolds portrait, which can be seen on Macpherson's monument on his estate of Balavil near Aviemore.[30] Bacon's *Head of Ossian* attracted some interest at the time:

> One of the first works from his hand which attracted public attention, was a colossal head of Ossian. The poems of Macpherson were then exciting public attention, and the head of the blind bard, conceived and executed with uncommon skill, made the learned and the illiterate gaze with wonder, when they saw it placed over the gateway of Coade's establishment.[31]

It is possible that this head, now lost, inspired the sculpted head of Ossian that appears in an undated print entitled *Calliope* by Robert Edge Pine (1730-1788).[32]

It is also worth noting here an etching made by Alexander Nasmyth (1758-1840), who is best known today as the artist who was to become Robert Burns's close friend and portraitist. It is marked with the remarkably early date of 1771.[33] At the time, Nasmyth would have been only thirteen years old, probably studying at the Trustees' Academy in Edinburgh under Runciman and inspired by his teacher's interests. The etching attests to his early skill as an artist. Three years later Nasmyth was to be employed by Allan Ramsay to assist him in London. By the end of the 1770s another of Fuseli's circle, Runciman's friend, the Irish painter James Barry, had made a notable image of Ossian as part of his mural cycle, *The Progress of Human Culture*, made for the main hall of the Society of Arts in London.[34]

Because of their residence in Rome one can speculate that Runciman, Kauffmann, and Barry would have known *Ossian* both through Macpherson's work directly and through Cesarotti's Italian translation. By extension they would have known both Wale's title page image and Baratti's frontispiece. This speculation with respect to Baratti would also apply to another member of Fuseli's circle, the Dane Nicolai Abildgaard (1743–1809), who made a series of major paintings relating to Ossian beginning in about 1780. Indeed, Okun (1967) suggested that Wale's image may have been an influence on Abildgaard's *Blind Ossian Singing*. That has, however, been disputed.[35] If, however, one suggests that the influence comes from Barrati rather than Wale, the suggestion, while not necessarily right, has more force. The vertical orientation of Abildgaard's composition has far more in common with the format of Baratti's frontispiece for Cesarotti's *Poesie di Ossian*, than it does with Wale's landscape-format title page image for the first edition of *Fingal*.

Another work from 1780 is Charles Cordiner's (1746?–1794) remarkable image *Cascade near Carril*, which shows Ossian in the foreground of a landscape of trees and waterfalls lit by moonlight.[36] Cordiner was minister at Banff, but he was also an accomplished artist, having trained at one of Scotland's earliest art schools, the Foulis Academy in Glasgow. This is an important work as it pioneers an emphasis upon the Ossianic landscape as a subject for the visual artist in which the landscape is the primary subject, and, while it is informed by figures, it is not dominated by them. That is to say, the figures serve the landscape rather than the other way around, and they become a way of getting at the poetry of the place being represented. J. M. W. Turner, Thomas Girtin (1775–1802), John Sell Cotman (1782–1842), Joseph Anton Koch (1768–1839), and George Augustus Wallis (1770–1847), among others, were to take this further with respect to subjects from *Ossian*, while William Blake in particular was to develop it with reference to the notion of the bard-in-landscape in general. It is interesting to note that Blake may have seen this image by Cordiner at the time it was engraved, for he was around that time finishing his apprenticeship with James Basire (1730–1802), whose workshop engraved the work. It was published in 1780 in Cordiner's book *Antiquities and Scenery in the North of Scotland*. The book includes a number of other images by Cordiner that can be read from an Ossianic cultural and political point of view: for example, *Monument at Sandwick*, which shows a Pictish stone with a tartan-clad Highlander leaning on it[37] – innocuous enough, except for the fact that in the wake of Culloden tartan was still an illegal form of dress in 1780. The Act of 1747 was not repealed until 1782. Perhaps that is why, in *Cascade near Carril*, Cordiner makes a point of giving Ossian tartan socks.

With such a wealth of visual art activity around *Ossian* after its first publication, it seems strange that the editions of 1765 and 1773 are without any illustration, not even on the title pages. However, there is a letter from John Pinkerton to Malcolm Laing of 6 September 1799 in which he refers to a person being present 'when M'Pherson brought to Mortimer the painter, an Ossian for him to draw designs'.[38] This refers to John Hamilton Mortimer (1740-1779), who would certainly have been an appropriate choice to illustrate an edition. It is not clear whether the 1765 or the 1773 edition was under discussion. However, another frontispiece from this decade should be mentioned: it is the work of William Walker (dates unknown) for Ewen Cameron's versification of Macpherson's prose poetry, published in 1776.[39] Like Samuel Wale's image from 1762, this again shows Ossian and Malvina, but where Wale's image refers to Malvina's ghostly presence in *Berrathon*, Walker's image shows her in human form listening to Ossian singing about the heroic deeds of Oscar, her dead lover and his dead son. Ossian and Malvina scenes occur frequently in Macpherson's text, for Malvina was the fellow bard to whom Ossian transmits much of his work. Scenes involving Malvina were explored by artists over a period of at least one hundred and fifty years, a relatively recent example being a treatment of the subject by Stewart Carmichael (1867-1950), which dates from 1928.[40] It is worth dwelling a little on this as a key preoccupation of the artistic response.

A particularly interesting French version is by Elizabeth Harvey (dates unknown) *Malvina lamenting the Death of Oscar*.[41] It was exhibited at the Paris salon in 1806, and in his pioneering book published in 1967, *Transformations in Late Eighteenth Century Art*, Robert Rosenblum comments extensively on it, noting, for example, the presence of Fingal's Cave in the background.[42] One can also note here an image of Ossian and Malvina by Luigi Zandomeneghi (1778-1850), which specifies the crucial scene in *Cathlin of Clutha* just before Ossian begins to sing to Malvina to sooth her in her sadness at the loss of Oscar.[43] Thanks to the research of Fernando Mazzocca, and to the work of the Cesarotti Project at the University of Padua, Zandomeneghi's *Ossian* material is now beginning to get some of the attention it merits.[44] Zandomeneghi was best known as a sculptor: a student of Antonio Canova (1757-1822), he was a major figure in the artistic life of Venice in the first half of the nineteenth century. Among his works is the tomb of Titian in the Frari in Venice. In his *Ossian* illustrations he was inspired by the designs made to illustrate Homer and Dante by his fellow sculptor, the Englishman John Flaxman (1755–1826). Ossian and Malvina scenes are the subject of a number of other Italian artists to whom Mazzocca draws attention. They include in 1825 Camillo Guerra (1797–1874),[45] in 1846 Giacomo Trécourt (1812–1882),[46] and in 1859 Guiseppe De Nigris (1832–1903).[47] In addition to the work of these Italian artists, a little-known work by the English artist and engineer William Brockedon (1787–1854) is of interest. Brockedon spent a considerable amount of time in Italy, and he became a member of the academies of art in both Florence and Rome. One might therefore consider Brockedon's *Ossian Relating the Fate of Oscar to Malvina*, which was probably painted in the 1820s, to be as much a response to Cesarotti as it is to Macpherson.[48]

The subject of Ossian and Malvina had a resurgence in the art of the Scottish Celtic Revival. In addition to the version by Stewart Carmichael already noted, the subject was also an important part of the background of John Duncan's visual manifesto for the Celtic Revival, *Anima Celtica*, published in Patrick Geddes's magazine *The Evergreen* in 1895. Another Ossian and Malvina image was made in the context of a work reflecting on the authenticity of Macpherson's work. By Robert Traill Rose (1860–1930), it appears as the frontispiece of Keith Norman MacDonald's *In Defence of Macpherson's Ossian*, a collection of pieces that first appeared in the *Oban Times* and were published together in Glasgow by Alexander Maclaren in 1906. It is interesting to see the simplified linearity of the Scottish Celtic Revival work of John Duncan and Robert Traill Rose in the context of Luigi Zandomeneghi, who adopts a similarly radically linear approach to *Ossian* the best part of a century earlier. His *Ossian invita al canto la mesta Malvina* is particularly analogous to later Celtic Revival work.

Elsewhere, I have begun to explore the significance of female bard, warrior, and hunter figures, for there are many besides Malvina that appear in visual art responding to *Ossian*.[49] James Macpherson routinely represents women in active physical and creative roles, in distinct contrast to many of the nineteenth-century writers who followed him. In passing one can note that the first person to edit a selection from *Ossian* – under the title *Poetry of Nature* – was a woman: Mary Potter (dates unknown). It was published in 1789. It is an under-researched book, significant not least for its visual presence, for it makes its 'natural' point by using an experimental Caslon typeface to emulate handwriting.[50] As in so many other aspects of *Ossian*, in his approach to female characters Macpherson can be seen as a precursor of Tolkien. But, in contrast to Tolkien, Macpherson would have had models for such women available to him in the culture of the Scottish Gàidhealtachd of his childhood. They would have included bards such as Sìleas na Ceapaich (1660?–1729)[51] and Màiri Nighean Alasdair Ruaidh (1615?–1707?),[52] and Jacobite heroines such as Anne Macintosh (1723-1787) and Flora Macdonald (1722–1790), each of the latter only a decade or so older than Macpherson himself. John Duncan's *Anima Celtica* is of interest from this perspective also, for, as well as making its *Ossian* point, it alludes to Jacobite iconography (notably a white cockade) and uses for the features of its main figure those of the distinguished Celtic scholar Ella Carmichael (1870–1928).[53]

Another Ossian and Malvina work from the time of Zandomeneghi can be mentioned here. It dates from 1810 and is by the Austrian artist Johann Peter Krafft (1780–1856). Artists like Krafft and the Tyrolese born Joseph Anton Koch made a significant geographical link between the northern Europe of Runciman and Abildgaard (however mediated by Rome) and the north of Italy, and that helps to situate the Veneto of Cesarotti with reference to *Ossian*. At this time the north of Italy was becoming the driving cultural and political force that resulted in the Risorgimento. Cesarotti's *Poesie di Ossian* can be thought of as an early indication of that trend for it is a pioneer work in the establishment of a modern Italian literature. And, crucially, it looked north to the Alps and beyond for its inspiration. Thus, artists like Krafft and Koch must be seen not only in the context of Goethe but also of Cesarotti. Krafft had a distinguished career, which included a period as director of the Belvedere Gallery in Vienna. Where Zandomeneghi looks back to the classicism of Flaxman and forward to the art of the Celtic Revival, Krafft inhabits an equally interesting place between the Ossianic vision of Abildgaard in the 1780s and the development of Symbolism later in the later nineteenth century. *Ossian*-related visual art can thus be seen as a key link in the history of art of this period whether seen through the Venetian lens of Zandomeneghi or the Viennese lens of Krafft.

Conclusion

There is much else to be said on the topic of *Ossian* and art beyond the scope of the current chapter.[54] For example, in the 1780s, Abildgaard had shifted the image of Ossian in a Scandinavian and Germanic direction, helping to give strength to the idea of Ossian as a Nordic rather than

Celtic Homer, an idea which has had currency ever since. Abildgaard's commitment to subjects from *Ossian* provided an example for other northern European artists, among them the German/Danish painter Asmus Jacob Carstens (1754–1798) who studied briefly with him in Copenhagen. Like William Blake, Carstens thought of himself as 'a kind of universal artist and thinker, working in some supranational realm of idea and spirit'.[55] The best known of his works on Ossianic subjects is *Fingal and the Spirit of Loda*[56] painted in Rome in 1796. It is a highly individual work in which the armoured Fingal is dominated by the titanic and threatening figure of Loda emanating from a cloud. In it Carstens, on the one hand, looked back to Michelangelo and, on the other, pointed the way to the development of popular fantasy illustration one hundred and fifty years later. As Colin Bailey has pointed out, Carstens had a strong influence on the *Ossian* work of the English artist George Augustus Wallis. Wallis was much better known in Europe than in his homeland, impressing, among others, Madame de Staël, who refers to an *Ossian* piece by Wallis in her novel *Corinne*.[57] Wallis's *Ossian* paintings have disappeared, but, if Turner's early *Ossian* artwork can be identified in 2013, it seems worth suggesting that these works may be hiding in plain sight also. As I have noted, Carstens' friend Koch contributed to the idea of Ossianic landscape, which had been pioneered by Cordiner and was later taken up by Turner, Girtin, and Cotman. An example of such a work by Koch from about 1800 can be found in the National Gallery of Canada. It is reproduced in the catalogue of *Central European Drawings* alongside Cordiner's *Cascade near Carril* for comparison.[58] The suggestion that this is an Ossianic subject was made by Mitchell Frank, who also quotes the following illuminating passage from Koch's writings: 'No landscape painting can achieve an ideal character without a human figure.'[59] Complementing his landscape aspect, Koch made a significant contribution to the development of *Ossian* as a fully articulated figurative narrative through two extensive series of drawings, now held in Copenhagen and Vienna.[60] These sorts of influences and friendships among artists indicate the power of Macpherson's text to inspire complex and sustained visual response across national boundaries.

In the context of this transnational perspective, it is perhaps fitting to end with reference to another neglected axis of influence and response: the American dimension needs to be considered much more than it has been to date. Three artists are of particular importance. One is John Trumbull (1756–1843), very well known for *The Declaration of Independence*, painted in 1817–1819 and since 1826 on permanent view in Washington. His *Ossian*-influenced *Lamderg and Gelchossa* was painted in 1792.[61] Trumbull's teacher, the Anglo-American painter Benjamin West (1738–1820), is also important here because of the substantial Ossianic references in his design for the Certificate of the Highland Society of London. West's commission dates from 1805.[62] Another American artist who should be mentioned is Alexander Anderson (1775–1870). Anderson was of Scottish parentage, and he is widely acknowledged as the key figure in the development of American wood engraving. In 1810 six of his wood engravings were published to illustrate a New York edition of *Ossian*.[63] This transatlantic dimension of visual art as it relates to *Ossian* is well worth further scrutiny and re-emphasises the enduring interest of Macpherson's text as an international phenomenon.

CHAPTER EIGHT

Macpherson's *Iliad* and the Logic of Literary Primitivism

Dafydd Moore

Macpherson's *The Iliad of Homer* (1773) rendered all twenty-four books of *The Iliad* in the measured prose that was so striking a feature of *Ossian*. For friends and allies, presenting Homer in the manner of *The Poems of Ossian* was a logical progression in the primitivist project of remediating epic poetry for the late eighteenth century. As Hugh Blair, Macpherson's one-time mentor and the man who not only provided much of the critical underpinning to *Ossian* but also then testified to the value of the poems in his *Critical Dissertation on the Poems of Ossian*, put it to Macpherson:

> I am exceedingly glad to hear that you have undertaken Homer. [Adam] Ferguson's idea that you were the proper person for such a work is not new. Ever since your translation of Ossian, we have often been saying the same in this country; and, if I mistake not, I have more than once told you so.[1]

Ossian – or rather the Ossianic prose-poem style – represented a distillation of eighteenth-century linguistic and literary critical notions of primitive poetic form as they emerged from the work in different fields of, amongst others, Robert Lowth, Thomas Blackwell, Adam Smith, Hugh Blair, and Edmund Burke. As such, the reconfiguration of Homer in this light was but a natural and necessary next step. Not all, however, were convinced. One-time supporter David Hume was not sure whether the 'attempt or the execution be worse'; William Mason affected outrage at the idea that 'Homer a la Erse' would 'Fingalize'; while Horace Walpole was merely content to think that Macpherson's attempt to 'make a Fingal out of Homer' was yet more evidence that he lived in an age of contraries.[2]

Posterity has tended to follow the latter camp when it has come to its view of Macpherson's *Iliad*. It is widely considered a failure, evidence of the moment when the pretensions of the Ossianic mode were revealed as such: if there had been something of the tragic in *Ossian*'s misguided brilliance, then there was something merely ludicrous in the *Iliad*'s misguided inanity. Generally, critics have been content to write it off as an oddity or as a sign of Macpherson's cynical manipulation of the literary marketplace, with Homer sacrificed in the cause of making money off the back of the *Ossian* craze. Else it has been considered a curio, its attempts to produce a version of Homer in line with the northern bard Ossian as a somewhat embarrassing document of the ways in which an emergent British national literary identity was competed over in the last third of the eighteenth century. Alternative views are thin on the ground. George Steiner anthologised a sample from it in his *Homer in English* (1996), while in 2012 David Hopkins took it seriously enough to include it as one of four translations (alongside those of John Dryden, Alexander Pope, and William Cowper) discussed at significant length in his essay on Homer in the *Oxford History of Classical Reception in English Literature*.[3] However, the seriousness with which Sebastian Mitchell treats the translation when he considers it 'the culmination of a sustained attempt by [Macpherson] to consider the appropriate modern form for the effective transmission of ancient artefacts' is rare.[4]

Along with a predominant attitude of disdain, the other inheritance from the eighteenth-century verdict on Macpherson's *Iliad* is the unproblematic sense (shared by supporters and critics alike) in which it is understood as an attempt to 'Fingalize' Homer; in other words, that the text aims to render Homer as Ossian and fails miserably in the attempt. This chapter will argue that while it might be hard to maintain that Macpherson's *Iliad* is anything other than an artistic and aesthetic failure, the reasons for that failure are more interesting and sophisticated than have been assumed. In particular, it will suggest that the relationship between *Ossian* and Macpherson's *Iliad* is more enlightening than the received wisdom that, with the Homer, Macpherson tried and failed to do as he had with *Ossian*. It will take as its starting point Mitchell's conclusion, in the face of the assumptions made manifest in that label 'Homer a la Erse', that one of the problems with Macpherson's *Iliad* is 'not that Macpherson had introduced too many of the distinctive elements of *Fingal*, but too few' (67–68). Mitchell suggests that, at bottom, this was because Macpherson's heart was not really in it and that he did not have the appetite to produce the fully worked-through version of a meaningfully Ossianic Homer at a time when his attentions were increasingly being drawn elsewhere. The result was *Ossian*-lite, little more than a gesture in the direction of a rhetorical treatment of Homer in the Ossianic manner. Mitchell's conclusion is based upon his sophisticated understanding both of the Ossianic effect as it can be observed through close attention to the poems, and of Macpherson's career in the early 1770s as he sought to move away from his previous reputation as a translator and reinvent himself as a historian. This chapter will suggest another reason for the hesitancy on Macpherson's part, a reason grounded within the logic of Macpherson's earlier position and the primitivist theories upon which it is in turn based. It will argue that the ultimate point of the original comparison with Homer in *Ossian* was difference, not similarity, and that therefore to render Homer in Ossianics was fundamentally oxymoronic. As such, it argues that the aesthetic failure of Macpherson's *Iliad* can in part be understood in terms of a tension between two contradictory impulses within literary primitivism: on the one hand, its desire to offer a universal model of literary expression (which suggests that Homer literally rendered can be like Ossian) and, on the other, its desire to root literary sensibility in the material and local (which suggests that he can never be). As such the *Iliad* and its failure reveal much about the assumptions upon which *Ossian* itself is predicated, and can provide another angle on the questions of translation and mediation widely seen as key to the poems themselves.

Never one overly burdened with self-doubt, Macpherson set out his stall in a forthright preface that acts as a manifesto for the translation to come. In it he made no reference to *The Poems of Ossian* and instead offered an ambitious aim:

> To do all the justice, in his power, to his Author, as well as to render his version useful to such, as may wish to study the original, through an English medium, he has translated the Greek VERBATIM: Even to the minute attention to the very arrangement of the words, where the different strengths and idioms of the two languages required not a freedom of expression, to preserve the strength and elegance of the thought.[5]

The Critical Review had great fun with this in its notice of March 1773. It counted fifty occasions where the single English (and indeed rather Ossianic) noun 'hall' was used instead of a variety of other nouns in the Greek, and the reviewer noted with disdain repeated examples of the opposite tendency whereby Macpherson rendered the same Greek word in different ways in English. Of course Macpherson had in fact immediately qualified the claim to verbatim translation with a caveat so all-encompassing as to render the initial assertion as good as worthless: his translation will be extremely literal, he says, as long as the 'different strengths and idioms' of the languages do not require 'a freedom of expression'. This is in effect a restatement of the dilemma central to all translation and explains why many translations are not 'verbatim'. More generously, it might be said that Macpherson's point is a comparative one as he seeks to distance his effort from the manner of translation most closely associated in the eighteenth century with Dryden and Pope and their efforts to make Homer speak as a recognisably modern Englishman – what he terms 'the antithetical quaintness of modern fine writing', the 'modernized turns of language, which, however pleasing in themselves, are utterly inconsistent with the solemn gravity of an ancient epic poem':

> The simplicity, the gravity, the characteristical diction, and, perhaps, a great part of the dignity of Homer, are left untouched. They have rendered the father of poetry, in great measure, their own: and, in stripping him of his ancient weeds, they have made him too much of the modern beau.
> (1, p. xv–xvi)

Whatever the over-simplification (and indeed derivativeness) of this post-Popean position, it does not in itself preclude Macpherson from presenting 'a literal prose translation' in which 'simplicity is studied' while still using 'hall' as the translation of a number of Greek words. Macpherson's aim in his translation is a measure prose that approximates Greek hexameter (aided with the use of a long dash to mark pauses not otherwise apparent through what passed for standard punctuation in the 1770s) and which allows him the flexibility to convey the 'fire and vigour' and the 'simplicity of expression and smoothness of language' of Homer (xviii, xix).[6] Macpherson's ultimate desire to ensure that Homer 'speak[s] English, with his own dignified simplicity and energy' is a pointed revision of Dryden's famous dictum that he had desired to render the *Iliad* 'such as would have been composed by the original author were he alive now and speaking English' (xx). Thus, opening Macpherson's translation, the reader is confronted with:

> The wrath of the son of Peleus,—O goddess of song, unfold! The deadly wrath of Achilles: To Greece the source of many woes! Which peopled the regions of death,—with shades of heroes untimely slain: While pale

they lay along the shore: Torn by beasts and birds of prey: But such was the will of Jove! Begin the verse, from the source of rage,—between Achilles and the sovereign of men. (1, p. 1)

Alexander Pope, in the best known translation of the age, has these lines as such:

> The Wrath of Peleus' son, the direful spring
> Of all the Grecian woes, O Goddess, sing!
> That wrath which hurl'd to Pluto's gloomy reign
> The souls of mighty chiefs untimely slain,
> Whose limbs, unburied on the naked shore,
> Devouring dogs and hungry vultures tore:
> Since great Achilles and Atrides strove,
> Such was the sovereign doom, and such the will of Jove. (I, ll. 1–8)[7]

Space does not allow for a full comparison of these lines, but, in the immediate context, it is worth observing the treatment of what is the fourth line of Pope's translation. Those looking for the Celtification of Homer via an Ossianic vocabulary would surely be disappointed by Macpherson swapping Pope's 'chiefs' for the less ethnically loaded 'heroes'. Dryden had used 'hero' (amongst others) at this point, but he had also been keener on what might otherwise be considered an Ossianic interest in premature death than either Pope or Macpherson with his 'many a Heroe, King and Hardy Knight | Were sent, in early youth, to Shades of night'.[8] It seems then that Macpherson's opening is somewhat less Ossianic than that of either Pope or Dryden, *avant la lettre*. This suggests that it is worth putting the question of Macpherson's Ossianic Homer under some more significant scrutiny. For argument's sake, the chapter will continue a comparison with Pope's on the grounds that it offered the best-known version of Homer at the time, the version Macpherson himself treats virtually co-extensively with Homer himself in *Ossian*, as we shall see.

Mitchell notes that Macpherson 'was clearly most comfortable and rhythmically confident in those passages where he felt it was appropriate to employ Ossianic diction and imagery, such as in the descriptions of mourning warriors' (67), and it would be foolish to deny that his *Iliad* does not bear the trace of its Ossianic predecessor. The rendition of key moments could only have been by the author of *Ossian* as surely as Pope's translation bears a recognisably Popean hallmark (albeit a Popean diction attuned to the needs of rendering Greek epic). A clear example is afforded by book fifteen's description of the battle for the ship of Protosilaus. Pope offers:

> No room to poise the lance or bend the bow;
> But hand to hand, and man to man, they grow;
> Wounded, they wound; and seek each other's hearts
> With falchions, axes, swords, and shorten'd darts.
> The falchions ring, shields rattle, axes sound,
> Swords flash in air, or glitter on the ground;
> With streaming blood the slippery shores are dyed,
> And slaughter'd heroes swell the dreadful tide. (XV, ll. 860–67)

Bearing in mind Macpherson's strictures about 'antithetical quaintness' it comes as no surprise that the same passage in his own translation replaces Pope's balanced emphasis on the reciprocal cut and thrust of battle with an elaboration of something that detains Pope but half a line:

> Hand to hand, and face to face; with one mind, they mingled war. With axes, with halberds, they fought; with mighty swords, with steel-pointed spears. Many bright swords fell on earth: With dark handles, with large polished hilts. Many fell, from the shoulders of heroes; and glittered, as they lay in the dust. Confusion spread, with tumult, around. The dark earth floated with blood. (2: p. 114)

This emphasis on the accoutrements of battle and an attendant shyness about explicit descriptions of scenes of wounding has been consistently identified as a key part of what Adam Potkay has termed 'the literal and figurative mystification of violence' at the heart of *Ossian*, a text in which 'primeval force is advertised but concealed; paraded but veiled behind a polite aesthetic'.[9] That Macpherson should focus attention on the abandoned swords as a metonym for the carnage of battle (so that 'many fell' refers literally to swords rather than men) is of a piece with his earlier Ossianic 'poetry of aftermath', what Paul deGategno has identified as a tendency to move 'away from military engagement in order to linger amongst the various half-lights produced by the battle'.[10]

Similarly, a comparison of Pope and Macpherson's rendering of the oath of Achilles at the climax of his argument with Agamemnon reveals Macpherson emphasising an Ossianic diction. Macpherson has:

By this sceptre, I say, I swear and great and binding is the oath! That when the loss of Achilles shall be felt by all: When thy feeble arm shall fail: When grief shall overwhelm thy soul—when dreadful Hector shall riot in blood and death: Then THOU, with bitter anguish torn, –shalt, when too late, lament—that thus thou hast presumed to dishonour—the bravest of the Argive powers. (1, pp. 12–13)

Pope's eye had again been caught by a different dimension of this passage:

> By this I swear:—when bleeding Greece again
> Shall call Achilles, she shall call in vain.
> When, flush'd with slaughter, Hector comes to spread
> The purpl'd shore with mountains of the dead,
> Then shalt thou mourn the afront thy madness gave,
> Forced to deplore when impotent to save:
> The rage in bitterness of soul to know
> This act had made the bravest Greek thy foe. (I, ll. 317–24)

If Pope's 'forced to deplore when impotent to save' could only have been written by him, then 'thy feeble arm shall fail' could hardly have been written by anyone other than Macpherson. More broadly, Macpherson has little to say about slaughter – no bleeding Greece, blood-stained shore or mountains of dead – but instead focuses attention on the regret of Agamemnon.

Following for a moment the stated nature of Macpherson's translation – that it is much more literal than any previous – such goings-on would reveal the ways in which Homer and Ossian, when translated literally by Macpherson, share much more in common than would be assumed by those who knew Homer via Pope's translation. This is the 'Homer a la Erse' anticipated by Blair and Ferguson and lamented by Mason, Walpole, and Hume, the proof that the epic idiom of the Scottish Gael Ossian was in fact the epic idiom of Europe. So it is a little curious to discover that in the final analysis not only are such Ossianic moments relatively few and far between in Macpherson's *Iliad*, but also, what is more, plenty of opportunities go begging; significant moments a reader might assume would be ripe for a newly discovered Ossianic emphasis are in the event curiously muted in execution. So, for example, episodes such as Andromache's description of herself as the last of her family, Hector's prayer for his son, and his sense of the allotted portion of human life are all moments where we might expect an amplification of Ossianic philosophising – if only because readers of *Ossian* would have been forgiven for thinking that such moments in *Ossian* were originally inspired by such moments in Homer. Yet at these crucial episodes, Macpherson's Homer fluffs his Ossianic lines and, if anything, Pope 'out-*Ossians*' Macpherson as here in book six:

> Andromache! My soul's far better part,
> Why with untimely sorrows heaves thy heart?
> No hostile hand can antedate my doom,
> Till fate condemns me to the silent tomb.
> Fix'd is the term to all the race of earth;
> And such the hard condition of our birth:
> No force can then resist, no flight can save,
> All sink alike, the fearful and the brave. (VI, ll. 614–21)

Macpherson on the other hand has:

> 'Cease, my beloved,' he said. 'Let not sorrow shade wholly thy soul. Me no warrior, before mine hour, shall send, untimely to the shades. None ever could his fate avoid;– of mortal men, I deem, that none! Whether feeble or brave in arms, none could shun the fate assigned, at his birth.' (1, p. 191)

Hopkins notes the irony of the fact that, while Macpherson's style, 'clearly designed for vocal rendering, can sometimes achieve an impressive grandeur' in narration, when it comes to speeches it is 'often stiff and stilted'.[11] At such moments, it is as if Macpherson is elevating Dryden's notion of metaphrase to the level of self-conscious literary style, as if the literalness of the translation is vouched by the fact that it is virtually unreadable.

A consciously cultivated awkwardness of style which provides a break on Ossianic poignancy might be one of the reasons why Macpherson's *Iliad* is in the final analysis tentative about turning up the Ossianic volume on Homer. There are, however, others. Mitchell suggests that a second is Macpherson's lack of appetite for the task of 'develop[ing] the Ossianic idiom into a more pliant diction capable of making an effective equivalence between the language of the *Iliad* and modern notions of the primitive' (p. 68). It is possible to suggest a third, which is that the internal logic of those modern notions of the primitive militated against Macpherson offering a full-throatedly Ossianic Homer. His *Iliad* does not offer a solution to this, but it does outline the dilemma with some force. Some sense of the logical difficulties of Macpherson's position can be gained from considering a moment where it is possible to align *Ossian* with Homer as represented by Pope and then Macpherson.

In *Fingal*, Macpherson invites the reader to compare the visitation of the ghost of Crugal to the sleeping Connal to those of Hector to Aeneas in the *Aeneid*, and Patroclus to Achilles in book twenty-three of the *Iliad*. To aid comparison, Macpherson provides the relevant passages in Latin and Greek, along with the translations of Dryden and Pope respectively.[12] At such moments he is making three interconnected points. Firstly, he is demonstrating how Ossian qualifies as an epic poet by pointing attention to the ways in which he covers the same material as Homer and Virgil. In 1735, Thomas Blackwell the Younger had in his *Enquiry into the Life and Writings of Homer* suggested that there was 'no greater proof of the power that *Manners* and the *Publick* character have over poetry, than the surprising resemblance of the oldest writings', something, he noted, could be observed on the level of the 'very same expressions and phrases.'[13] As we shall see this takes rather a lot for granted about the similarity of primitive 'manners and the public character', but nevertheless it was key to the equation that vouched for Ossian via a similarity with Homer. Secondly, Macpherson is asserting his academic and intellectual credentials as the translator/editor of Ossian, not least for knowing (it is implied) Homer and Virgil in the Greek and Latin, via what Kathryn Temple calls 'the authenticity effect' and Margaret Russet seeks to uncover as part of the 'archaeology of the spurious' in relation to eighteenth-century texts of problematic provenance.[14] Thirdly, and perhaps most importantly (and this is what would come back to haunt Macpherson when it came to his own *Iliad*), such moments are part of a strategy through which the reader is invited to discern difference within the overall similarity. Ossian and Homer share an artistic sensibility that is drawn to such an episode, but they do so in ways that are quite different from each other, and it is those differences to which the reader is asked to attend most closely. As Macpherson puts it in the first note to book eight of *Temora*:

> The [Greeks] were lively and loquacious; and manly conciseness of expression distinguished the [Celtae]. We find, accordingly, that the compositions of Homer and Ossian are marked with the general and opposite characters of their respective nations, and consequently, it is improper to compare the minutiae of their poems together. There

are however, general rules, in the conduct of an epic poem, which, as they are natural, are likewise, universal. In these the two poets exactly correspond. (*Temora*, p. 137)

This comment comes in the second of the *Ossian* volumes and is itself part of the critical debate prompted by the first. In effect, Macpherson is himself engaging with the critical arguments to do with the similarities and differences between Homer and Ossian. Some of those were about authenticity – as the 1763 pamphlet *Fingal Regained* had rather dryly put it, 'Mr Pope is at times less like Homer than is Ossian himself', further observing that 'if Ossian had *not* read Homer, his translator had' – and some were about the grounds upon which comparisons could be drawn.[15] This latter dispute was most notably played out across four lengthy reviews in the *Critical* and *Monthly Reviews* through 1762.[16] This point about similarity-and-yet-difference is straightforwardly applicable to the Crugal example. Homer and Ossian both use the visit of a fallen comrade to the hero to warn of imminent disaster because it is a universal component of epic. However, the handling of the moment will be different because the 'genius of the Greeks and the Celtae were extremely dissimilar'. So this is Ossian's Crugal as rendered by Macpherson:

> Crugal sat upon the beam, a chief that lately fell. [...] His face is like the beam of the setting moon; his robes are of the clouds of the hill: his eyes are like two decaying flames. Dark is the wound of his breast [...].
>
> Dim, and in tears, he stood and stretched his pale hand over the hero—Faintly he raised his feeble voice, like the gale of the reedy Lego. (*Fingal*, p. 22)

Macpherson compares this with the same moment in Homer as rendered by Pope (given that Macpherson provides Pope's translation after the Greek, the reader is presumably supposed to think it capable of standing as a serviceable version of it in order to get his point across):

> When lo! The shade, before his closing eyes,
> Of sad Patroclus rose or seem'd to rise,
> In the same robe he living wore, he came
> In stature, voice, and pleasing look the same.
> The form familiar hover'd o'er his head,
> And sleeps Achilles thus? The phantom said. (XXIII, ll. 78–83)

The point of the comparison is clear (and reinforced by the Virgil/Dryden example). Where the Classical is concrete, the Ossianic is diffuse; where Patroclus is a 'form familiar', looking exactly as he did in life even down to his dress, Crugal is melting into (or perhaps out of) the environment given that his robe is of the cloud of the hill; where Patroclus sounds exactly like he did in life, Crugal's voice is a murmur of the wind across a lake. Indeed, so enervated is Crugal that he can only summon the wherewithal to be as the beam of the setting moon: he hasn't even got the strength to be like the beam of the setting sun.

So far, things are consistent, if a little fraught. As universal primitive geniuses, Homer and Ossian are, as Blackwell says, drawn to similar ideas, but, as representatives of different primitive peoples, they articulate the moment differently. So, when Macpherson comes to render this moment in the *Iliad* in his own 'verbatim' translation, there should be a palpable and significant difference between Homer and Ossian by dint of Macpherson's own previous observations on the subject and his distinction between the similarity of episode and the handling of episode. But Macpherson forgets himself:

> Pale-bending, o'er the mighty chief—came the ghost of the hapless Patrolcus: In shape, in manly stature the same,—in voice, in bright-rolling eyes. The same flowed his airy robe,—round the empty shade of the chief. he stood, by the hero's head,—and thus, with feeble voice, began: 'Sleeps the son of mighty Peleus?' (2, p. 359)

Patroclus might not be exactly the same as Crugal, but he is more the same than he is different. 'Pale-bending' sets the tone, and, while the passage asserts the similarity to life (which, unlike in Pope, notably avoids any explicit mention of 'living'), the reader would be forgiven for thinking that Homer did not really mean it. After all, he has an 'airy robe', is called an 'empty shade', and is described as having a 'feeble voice' (the last of course being a feature directly shared with Crugal). It may be life, but not as it is usually described, and this hints perhaps at the unreconciled tensions within Macpherson's handling of the passage. Freed from the shadow of Pope's modern quaintness, Macpherson reveals that Homer is in fact quite close to rendering a moment such as this, just as Ossian had done. In effect, Macpherson demonstrates that Homer's Patroclus is much more like Ossian's Crugal than the reader of Pope could have ever imagined, despite the fact that Homer and Ossian have supposedly very different poetic sensibilities, according to Macpherson. They may not be identical, but they are an awfully long way from being 'extremely dissimilar'.

Homer could be revealed to be like Ossian, or he could be rendered literally, but, by the logic of Macpherson's own previous position, he could not be both at the same time. A literal Homer might be more similar to a literal Ossian than a Homer filtered through Pope, but could not in any meaningful way be the same. Macpherson does not solve this impasse, and the half-heartedly uneven Ossianics of his Homer is the result. It is going too far to say that Macpherson was consciously aware of and trying to mitigate this issue, but it is possible that the imperative of attending to the logic of his previous position does lurk somewhere within the creative process. If a part of Macpherson, along with Blair and Ferguson, had forgotten that Homer could not in any real way be like Ossian, a part had remembered. The curiously underdone Ossianics of Macpherson's version of the *Iliad* is the result.

Commenting on later eighteenth-century engagements with Homer, Hopkins suggests that 'the post Popean dream of direct, unmediated access to the "real" Homer was more difficult to attain – and perhaps, anyway, less desirable – than its advocates realised'.[17] The immediate context for this observation is Cowper's notorious swapping of the Popean for the Miltonic in his rendering of Homer, but it is equally applicable in the case of Macpherson's attenuated mediation of the *Iliad* via *Ossian*. Furthermore, the reluctant nature of an engagement in the face of the previously established relationship between Homer and Ossian only underlines the importance of the insight that literary translation is rarely, if ever, autochthonic but is always and ever a 'dialogic, conversational, encounter[s] between the classical past and the English present', a dialogue undertaken by translators 'with Homer, with their predecessors, with their own culture'.[18] Seeing Macpherson's Homer in this light is one way of understanding his efforts within the wider context of the dilemmas and challenges of eighteenth-century (or indeed any) translation, even if he is unusual in being in large measure in conversation with himself in the shape of Ossian. There are other and connected points to offer by way of a conclusion.

The question of how Ossianic Macpherson's Homer is necessarily leads to questions of where the essence of the Ossianic itself might be, as a literary style, a vocabulary, a set of images, a particular sensibility. Macpherson's *Iliad* suggests that these elements can be uncoupled, and that there is some case to think about the prose-poem style and the claims to literalness they underwrite as separate phenomena. After all, by 1773 there had been two complete versifications of Ossian/Macpherson's *Fingal* (as well as significant numbers of other poems). It seems that, never mind the Ossianic Homer, even some of Macpherson's most sympathetic readers were not in fact quite ready for an Ossianic Ossian. Mitchell has gone so far as to suggest that many of the changes introduced in the revised text of *Ossian* in 1774 – he notes for example that Macpherson was removing long dashes from *Ossian* just as he was adding them to Homer – were a response to the implicit (and indeed explicit) calls represented most vividly by the versifications for 'polish and standardised expression'.[19] Whatever we make of this, it suggests that the issue was a matter of live debate and 'the Ossianic' was a more complex and layered aesthetic formulation than the use of the commonplace label suggests.

Equally, the logical difficulties Macpherson's Homer ties itself up in offer more than just testimony to Macpherson's shallowness. They can be seen as being generated out of potential fault lines within eighteenth-century primitivist aesthetics, and indeed the wider sociological enquiries of conjectural and cosmopolitan history into whose service literary texts could be recruited.[20] Donald Foerster, commenting on the rival models of significance for Homer that emerged with the rise of Enlightenment historicism in the eighteenth century, stated that 'the true value of the *Iliad* was found, therefore, in its universal presentations of human nature or in its specific pictures of Greek life – not in both', yet in practice primitivist perspectives did attempt to have it both ways.[21] These aesthetics tended to be at the same time both universalising (to the extent that it was possible to read across a common frame of experience) and specific (to the extent that they came to emphasise the unique nature of individual manifestations of culture); that is to say, they are committed both to a natural history of man and to an awareness of the differences derived from climate, geography, and social organisation. Similarly, they are built out of a belief in both the difference and similarity between primitive and modern people. The stadial historiography refined in Scotland by Macpherson's friends and collaborators such as Smith and Ferguson emphasises both the sharp separations that characterise the stages of development through which human societies pass and the common values held via different means in the earliest and most advanced stages, a balance which leaves such models poised between being entirely assimilative and alive to the possibility of resistance and difference.[22] As Macpherson himself puts it:

> As the first [stage] is formed on nature, it is the most disinterested and noble. Men in the last have leisure to cultivate the mind, and restore it, with reflection, to a primaeval dignity of sentiment. (*Temora*, p. xii)

In purely literary terms, primitivist aesthetics are by their nature committed both to a determinist, materialist view of literary production – early societies make for particular types of literary expression – and to the particular encouragement for original genius within the earliest stages of society, genius which is usually expressed in terms of its ability to transcend its own narrow circumstances. Accordingly, poetry is both historical document and document of the imagination, the universal expression of universal feelings through universal forms and the intensely unique productions of any given people. *Ossian* is born from the conviction that the works of primitive cultures the world over are comparable and goes in to be itself key to the growth of ideas about the specific and unique value of an individual nation's indigenous culture, for example through the sway it holds in Germany in the case of the likes of J. G. Herder. These questions are part of a debate about the meaning of the natural and of the cultural, about the nature of cultural perception and enquiry, which animates much eighteenth-century sociological and historical enquiry. Equally, the tensions and apparent contradictions within these positions remain active to this day, for example between the historicist, or cultural relativist attitude to the past, and the aesthetic, reader-response-led engagement with literary history, between 'what it meant to them' and 'what it means to me' approaches to the literature of the past.[23] The problem of Macpherson's Ossianic *Iliad* then, its half-hearted Ossianism, is the problem of sameness-and-difference and difference-and-sameness that haunts all attempts to render the foreign meaningful both in its own terms and ours. That Blair and Macpherson imagined it possible at all marks the potentialities of the cosmopolitan enlightenment venture; that it failed offers striking evidence of the necessary contradictions upon which it was founded.

CHAPTER NINE

Principles, Prejudices, and the Politics of James Macpherson's Historical Writing

Robert W. Jones

This chapter explores James Macpherson's historical writing, an extensive and demanding body of work. Macpherson's histories have received little scholarly attention, but their time might at last have come. The last two decades have witnessed a resurgence of interest in eighteenth-century historiography, its aims, methods, and published forms. Scholars have charted the key developments in the enlightened and sentimental historical writing of, among others, David Hume, Edward Gibbon, and William Robertson.[1] Macpherson's work has not featured in this reappraisal either because its author is still (erroneously) associated with 'forged' histories or, more interestingly, because Macpherson is a rather awkward presence, neither fully committed to new developments in historiographic writing nor truly against them. He is furthermore ardently polemical, a trait reflecting both conviction and habit.[2] This essay will begin a process of re-reading Macpherson's histories in the light of these concerns and underline the most distinctive aspects of his work.

Macpherson's most significant interventions almost always involve an anxious musing on the nature of opposition, legitimate or otherwise. This is most clearly expressed in his *Short History of the Opposition during the Last Session of Parliament*, published in support of Lord North's beleaguered Ministry in 1779, and, in the same year, *The History and Management of the East-India Company, from its Origin in 1600 to the Present Times*.[3] The focus here will, however, fall on Macpherson's engaging and often scrupulous *The History of Great Britain, from the Restoration, to the Accession of the House of Hannover*, published by William Strahan and Thomas Cadell in two handsome volumes in 1775.[4] At one level Macpherson sought to continue Hume's celebrated *History of Great Britain* (1754–62), hoping presumably for comparable success and remuneration, but he seems also to have been keen, as this essay will explore, to challenge Hume's reorientation of historiography away from 'the rhetoric of disclosure'.[5] To this end, the *History* was supplemented by the publication of what amounted to Macpherson's sources: *Original Papers: Containing the Secret History of Great Britain, from the Restoration, to the Accession of the House of Hannover*. *Original Papers*, with its alluring promise of a 'Secret History', is suggestive of Macpherson's deep interest in exploring and, crucially, revealing otherwise hidden motives, returning historical writing, in the process, to the exploration of illustrative anecdote.[6]

The densely compiled *Original Papers* is indicative equally of Macpherson's canny awareness of the expanding horizons and increasingly professionalised methods of modern historians. Perhaps scarred by the controversy provoked by *Ossian*, Macpherson provides what is a very modern response to the past, one that invites further investigation, offering readers the opportunity via his sources to become active students of the past.[7] Macpherson was a confident user of footnotes, a practice which, like the publication of source documents, enabled the reader to enquire further, even if the notes are, by modern standards, rather elliptic.[8] Macpherson would have been conscious of the already illustrious range of Scottish historical writing. By the 1770s this impressive canon included not only Hume's *History*, but also Tobias Smollett's *The Complete History of England* (1758–60), Robertson's *History of Scotland* (1759), and later his *History of America* (1777). Hume thought he was working in 'a historical age' and that Scotland was a superlatively 'historical nation'.[9] If Hume, along with Robertson, represents a high-water mark in historical writing in these isles, then it is equally the case that the writing of multi-volume histories, especially of Britain, was a lucrative and not always conspicuously meritorious genre, as Oliver Goldsmith's career as a hack writer of popular histories, natural and otherwise, demonstrates. Macpherson's historical writing ought to be seen in relation to this market, as much as to the conceptual ambitions of historicism on the one hand and the pleasures of controversy on the other.

Controversy was certainly never far from Macpherson's mind in the 1770s. He was working, and he was deeply conscious of this, at a critical moment in British history as the American colonies declared their independence, with rebellion very much in the air and the authority of the Crown contested. Macpherson was no friend to the Americans and served as one of the North government's best propagandists.[10] He was not alone in his endeavour, even if the path he took was uniquely explicit. Nor was the writing of what claimed to be history removed from present political concerns. It is impossible to know, as Pocock has observed, just how this precarious political scene shaped Edward Gibbon's *Decline and Fall of the Roman Empire* (1775–1788), but it is hard to imagine no point of contact at all.[11] Writing with clearer polemical intentions were Catherine Macaulay and Edmund Burke, whose view of politics, especially opposition politics, Macpherson would have despised.[12] It will be necessary to take cognisance of all these modes; this will require analysis of the methods and textual strategies that Macpherson deploys. The accuracy of his writing, judged as an account of the past, will consequently be less immediately a concern.

Macpherson's historical writing soon reveals that he is a historian in the august classical tradition inaugurated by the Roman historian Tacitus. This adherence is crucial as it determines Macpherson's style of historical writing and his subject matter. Like his great predecessor, Macpherson's focus is politics, statecraft, and war. His object is what he terms 'the great line of history', but he complicates it with tantalising references to the 'secret' springs behind historical action (*History*, I: iv-v). The conduct of kings, the fall of princes, and the motions of parliament are his business. There is little discussion of events, people, or developments beyond these parameters; the reader discovers nothing of the achievements of Henry Purcell, Sir Christopher Wren, or Edmund Waller. The Great Fire of London receives little attention, while the plague is noted only in passing. Astonishingly both events receive fuller treatment in the *Short History* (*History*, I, 88–89, 80; *Short History*, 54). Without art, culture, or indeed much that can be described convincingly as non-partisan, Macpherson's work necessarily confronts the twin problem of the royal prerogative and its opponents. Royal power seemed to grow markedly under Charles II and his successors, making its presence felt most powerfully in relation to matters of religion. Opposition grew proportionately and with equal daring. Attempting to capture the details of these clashes, the workings of power and faction, Macpherson's work becomes, to all intents and purposes, a history of civil war. The scope of the *History* is consequently challenging: nothing less than a narrative of one of the most controversial and convoluted passages of British, indeed, Scottish, Irish, and English history. The cast of historical actors is proportionately long. The events of this troubled era, of which there are a large number, are intricate, controversial, and frequently arcane. Yet throughout, the abiding concern, one that unites the *History* with Macpherson's more avowedly political writing, is the question of opposition to the Crown and later to government. Macpherson would have known Burke's reflections on parliamentary opposition, especially in *Thoughts on the Cause of the Present Discontents* (1770) where the formation of an opposition party is presented as an honourable undertaking incumbent upon all right-thinking and rightly-connected individuals.[13] Macpherson was never persuaded by the honour of opposition, and often represents it, contrary to Burke's high-mindedness, as a species of factiousness bordering on fanaticism (*Short History*, 4, 6).

Questions of Character: Understanding Kings in *A History of Great Britain*

Questions of power, policy, and opposition are central to the *History*. But these concerns aside, Macpherson does not look for general causes, for patterns, or developments. Instead he essays explanations based almost entirely on the actions, motives, and, fundamentally, characters of his chosen historical actors. In this respect he was joining a much wider trend in historicist and novelistic narration. As Deidre Shauna Lynch has argued, 'character' was pursued in eighteenth-century writing as a means of negotiating an increasingly complex world, one in which actions and intentions required greater elaboration. Character could become a progressively subtle point of literary and philosophical inquiry, notably in the work of Hume and Samuel Richardson, but for many historians character retained its ancient sense of denoting a fixed entity, which the pressures of events would inevitably reveal. Personality did not change or evolve, rather it was discovered.[14] Macpherson's use of character is mostly, but not exclusively, in this older mode. Character is central to the account of the 'secret' causes of historical events. His first description of the newly restored Charles II is a fine case in point:

> The disposition and character of Charles, as far as they were then known, were well suited to the times. Attached to no system of religion, he seemed favourable to all. In appearance destitute of political ambition, his sudden elevation was more an object of admiration, than of jealousy. Accommodating in his possession and easy in his manner, he pleased even those he could not gratify. Men, from principle, enemies to monarchy, were prejudiced in favour of the person of the Prince. Those in whom fear might excite aversion, lost their hated, in his apparent forgetfulness of past injuries [...]. The carelessness of his measures raised him many opponents; but the easiness of his temper prevented him from having personal enemies. (*History*, I: 3)

This portrait of a man offensively inoffensive recurs time and again: 'He conveyed agreeable things, in a pleasing manner. He promised good husbandry; but he was by nature profuse.' It is not long before the consequences, personal and political, of such easiness manifest themselves. The king, according to Macpherson, was repeatedly 'disturbed by domestic distractions' not least of which was his 'immoderate love of women'. Increasingly under the influence of the Countess of Castlemaine, his 'virtue, for he had some, came seldom into view' (*History*, I: 44, 53). This judgement of the lolling and priapic king is hardly unique, but the careful use of the clause 'for he had some' requires notice. The refinement implies some calibration, a grading of character that encourages finer judgement, even as it alludes to a fixed identity. Yet Macpherson is soon obliged to deplore the mounting 'debauchery' and 'scenes of riot and pleasure' that define the Court (*History*, I: 114).

Unwilling and unable to restrain himself, yet always eager to act the part of a king, Charles was increasingly opposed by a Parliament equally keen to assert its privileges and responsibilities (*History*, I: 142–4). The consequences of this mutual distrust, exacerbated by the affront to Parliament represented by the Duke of York's Catholicism, became apparent when Charles introduced a measure of toleration for both English dissenters and Catholics on the eve of the second Dutch war (*History*, I: 146, 152). The policy, Macpherson explains, was not ill-timed or ill-judged; yet it proved vexatious, precisely because Charles's reputation, and suspicions of his character, provoked unease and opposition:

> By virtue of the inherent power to which he laid claim, in ecclesiastical matters, he suspended the penal laws against all non-conformists and recusants. He indulged Protestant Dissenters with places of public worship. He restricted the Catholics to the exercise of their religion, in private houses. To mollify the Church of England, he declared his own adherence to its tenets; and that no person should be capable of holding any benefice or ecclesiastical dignity, who would not conform to the faith. The manner only of this indulgence was blameable. The King did by proclamation, what the parliament should have done by law. Though Ashley was the advisor of the measure, it was ascribed to the bigotry of the Duke of York; and the nation entertaining that opinion, had some ground for their fears. (*History*, I: 155)

A careless personality rather than poor policy is signified by the deliberately doubled meaning granted to the term 'indulgence', which comprehends here not only a description of religious allowance and permission, but also Charles II's effete lack of self-control. Macpherson is equally alive to the pressures generated by the contest between the king and his subjects, especially those in parliament. Strikingly, the fears of the people seem both to be accepted – there are some grounds for them – and to be regarded merely as unwarranted doubts. Causation therefore appears both predictable and yet capricious, not least when it stems from inaccurate or prejudicial information.

Macpherson's account of the fall of James VII and II and the gaining of the English, Scottish, and finally Irish crowns by William of Orange exhibits this uncertain emphasis repeatedly. During the eighteenth century any narrative of James II's fall required the historian to describe a complex political and religious contest, marshalling their evidence accordingly, but also to declare or disguise their allegiance. The extent of Macpherson's Jacobitism or otherwise remains subject to dispute.[15] The evidence, for want of a better word, offered by Macpherson's *History* is mixed. The politics of the volumes are not easily determined, as the list of errata included with the first volume reveals. There the reader is advised that, on page 571 and at line 22, they should 'for prejudices' read 'principles' (*History*, I, endpaper). The sentence to which the reader is asked to return forms part of a damning summation of James II's failings; as printed it reads: 'His whole reign, in short, was full of imprudencies in his own conduct, and with attacks on the favourite prejudices of his people' (*History*, I, 571). A printer's mistake perhaps, but the confusion hints at a greater equivocation. Although the error, if that it was, was corrected for the Dublin edition of the same year, it would be unwise to underestimate the hiatus it implies. The amended sentence is even more damning, though the implications of the term 'favourite' are equally problematic, appearing to disqualify principles far more than it might elaborate prejudices.[16] The hesitation between principles and prejudices marks both the ways in which the events of 1688–89 continued to press on Macpherson's historical imagination, and also his difficulty of finding a place outside the factionalism he seeks to present. Throughout the *History* there is little sense of civil society; political events are not mediated, nor are the effects of faction dispelled by a history of manners, as Hume would have done. Opinions, when they are adduced, are robust, masculine, and suspicious to the point of prejudice (or principle). Writing of the tense domestic atmosphere in Britain after William III's accession, he observes: 'Men in general believed, that some secret machinations existed in favour of the late King' (*History*, II: 20). This explicitly gendered formulation says much about how Macpherson represented the past: not for his *History* the appeal to women readers that distinguishes Hume's work; he insists instead on a robust and manly presentation of civil and religious conflict.[17]

As befits his Tacitean mode of historical narration, Macpherson employs character portraits repeatedly, along with reported speech (invented speech, common in Roman histories, is eschewed) as his central heuristic and literary modes. Much of Macpherson's account of the events of the 1680s, including the machinations of the Popish, Rye House and Meal Tub plots, the factionalism of the Exclusion Crisis, Monmouth Rebellion, and finally the Glorious Revolution, is concerned with the arcana of intrigues and the clash of personalities. The narrative is necessarily involved, but the verbal portraits and direct speech with which Macpherson inlays his account give direction and animation. Contrast and comparison are repeatedly sought, and never more so than when he contrasts James II with his rival the Prince of Orange. Macpherson has two words which he bestows frequently on James II. The first term to really make itself prominent (largely through repetition) is 'obstinate'. The term is most frequently used to describe the tenacity of religious faith exhibited by James, first as Duke of York and later as king. Obstinacy might, on certain occasions, be viewed as something akin to a virtue, denoting a credible persistence of character. Burke uses the term in this sense in his *History of American Taxation* (1775), seeing it as part of 'the whole line of the great and masculine virtues'.[18] Macpherson hints at this sense of the term when he writes: 'Charles was ever willing to purchase ease by concession. But the obstinate temper of James was known. None expected he would yield' (*History*, I: 433). However, Macpherson generally uses the term, and this recurs as his account of James II's troubled reign gathers pace, in a way that is entirely synonymous with 'bigot', a term he deploys increasingly. Some examples make the point: 'his bigotry for the Romish faith sullied his good qualities'; 'This bigotted prince embraced with gladness a proposal so favourable to his own superstitious views'; 'courage degenerated into a vice, in a mind disgraced with weakness and bigotry' (*History*, I: 430, 465, 498). To use the word 'bigot' and its cognates is to abolish, at the level of language, any possibility of 'historical distance' and the forms of dispassionate analysis that go with it.[19] The term indicates a present concern, specifically a sectarian factionalism that continues to exert pressure. Macpherson's use of the word, and the tone it sets, is not only partisan but deliberately impolite. The *History* is not a reconciliatory account of the past, nor does it aspire to be.

It is not the case, however, that Macpherson's *History* is unsympathetic to James II, not least because this ill-fated monarch seems, as a consequence of his own personality, to have precipitated his own fall. The king's character and the issue of his conduct on the throne are presented both as the cause and symptom of national crisis in a striking passage in which Macpherson reviews his position during the brutal aftermath of the Monmouth Rebellion in 1685, an excess of judicial violence from which James is neither exempted nor excused (*History*, I: 453–55). It is the mental and constitutional effects of these barbarities, however, that is crucial:

> The severities which attended the suppression of the Duke of Monmouth's rebellion, by intimidating his enemies, seemed to confirm the authority of the King. Had he confined his ambitions to power alone, he might have reigned in tranquillity and died in peace on the throne of his ancestors [...] His excessive good fortune was the source of his ruin. He became powerful with such facility, that he seemed to be resolved to be absolute. His own free exercise of the Romish religion was seen with so little disgust, that he formed the vain, though perhaps distant hope of converting the nation. He descended from the character of a King to that of an apostle; and an excess of folly deprived his very misfortunes of pity.

Although Macpherson gives further grounds for supposing the king to have been advantageously placed, the point is that this foundation is really a quagmire, based, as it is, on an excessive and treacherous tranquillity abroad and 'an obsequious parliament at home' (*History*, I: 456). The king's security is conditional, everything 'seems' secure, but nothing endures. It does not last, moreover, because the king presumes to act on the supine nature of his parliament, first with a bid to form a standing army, alarming ancient anxieties, and most scandalously by adopting the doctrine that 'the King as supreme law giver' meant that he had the power to dispense with the law, principally concerning the appointment of bishops (*History*, I: 458, 468). This last move was fatal: 'Men might perceive from that instant, that he was destined to fall by a religious zeal similar to his own', Macpherson reflects. The slim distinction between a prejudice and a principle in the minds of the people is once again apparent. James's opponents act from the principles of their religion and their political convictions, but they are as bigoted and presumptuous in this respect as the king whom they seek to bring down (*History*, I: 471). There is equally a problem with opposition: it is too little, then too much.

Once exiled, however, James II is different, translated unwillingly but irresistibly into 'this unfortunate Prince'. He becomes no longer an obstinate king but a mournful spectacle. As Macpherson puts it: 'Deserted, avoided, despised, feeling much and fearing more, his mind became unequal to the difficulties of his situation; and though naturally possessed of some perseverance, which had obtained the name of firmness, he became wavering and distracted in all his counsels' (*History*, I: 535). In the end he resolves to flee, slipping out of the palace at Whitehall and making for the Kent coast.

> When the King was brought to [an] inn, a seaman, who had served under him, knew him, and melted before him, in silence, into tears. James himself was so much moved at this instance of affection, that he wept. The other fishermen, who had treated him with such indignity before, when they saw his tears, fell upon their knees. The lower inhabitants of the whole village gathered around him, with every mark of respect. The better sort fled from his presence. Their prudence overcame their affection; or the memory of his past misconduct was not to be obliterated by his present misfortunes. The seaman formed themselves into a guard round his person, and declared aloud, 'that a hair of his head should not be touched' (*History*, I: 539)

Macpherson has a source for this lachrymose encounter, mostly from the king's own account (on which he often relies), but, even if this story is not unique, and even indeed if it is an accurate report of what occurred, it is still a striking moment in the context of the wider development of the *History*. An anecdote or 'secret history' has been suffused with sentiment. The kind of response which this passage elicits is not one that requires much judgement, but rather a felt apprehension, one enabled in no small part by the absence of any kind of opposition or even much in the way of speech. Certainly James does not speak. The point of the scene, surely, is that pity and sentiment are placed alongside culpability.

Macpherson maintains his dual response to James II, alternately portraying him as an enthusiast and a bigot (a fault that is more matched by his most fiery former subjects) and pitying him as a man excluded by largely foul means. His death, in 1701, as events in Europe turn favourably for William III, is the most vivid example, but also one in which the deployment of literary devices associated with sensibility overpower the rhetorical and political organisation of the *History* and produce, perhaps, a fusion of sentimentalism and putative Jacobitism. The exiled king was certainly in a desperate position. After the Treaty of Ryswick (1697) ended his hopes of Restoration, James II became a depressed and introverted figure. At the time of his death he had, Macpherson claims, 'resigned himself to all the austerities of religious enthusiasm', adding, in a significant act of framing, that Louis XIV 'with great humanity [...] exhibited every symptom of compassion, affection, and even of respect' during his final days (*History*, II, 214). It is the French king's decision to recognise the Prince of Wales as king of Great Britain that enables one of Macpherson's greatest sentimental passages:

> When [Louis] arrived at St. Germains, he acquainted first the Queen, and then her son of his design. He then approached the bed in which James lay, almost insensible with his disorder. When James, rouzing himself, began to thank his most Christian Majesty for all his favours, the latter interrupted him, and said: 'Sir, what I have done is but a small matter. But what I have to say is of the utmost importance.' The people present began to retire. 'Let no person withdraw,' he said, 'I come to acquaint you, Sir, that when God shall please to call your Majesty from this world, I shall take your family into my protection, and acknowledge your son, as then he will certainly be, King of Great Britain and Ireland'.

Tears and applause break out immediately; indeed, the 'voice of divinity could not have made a greater impression on the unfortunate servants of James', who were immediately rapturous. In response, James 'in a kind of extacy, half-raised himself on the bed, and endeavoured to speak', but could not be heard above the clamour the French king had raised. Macpherson describes how, having provoked these effusions, Louis was 'unable longer to bear this melancholy scene' and so 'retired' (*History*, II, 215). His withdrawal prefigures that of the historian and his readers, who must similarly turn away. Read in isolation, Macpherson's phrasings hint at a kind of irony, an amused eyebrow raised to Catholic infatuation. However, the scene, which borrows from the sentimental literature of Richardson and Sterne, is much more complex. The genre codes of sensibility, which were primarily concerned with the legibility of emotions and the body, enable a narrative of legitimation (if not fully legitimacy) to emerge.[20] The kindness of foreign kings and the agonies of a dying exile combine in an affective tableau that claims something more than pity. Religious feelings are consequently channelled in a new direction, and an enthusiasm that might have provoked action (whether prompted by principle or prejudice) is replaced by a more contemplative literary mode that presupposes emotional reflection. The transition is such that if irony is part of Macpherson's intention, then it is a modulated and moderating gesture, reflecting upon the potential absurdity of the individual in fractious times.

In these passages sentimental imitation rather than the public lessons of Roman didacticism is the dominant feature.[21] James II's character, fall, and subsequent estrangement from his kingdom become a narrative of suffering that effects a great enrichment of his character. He becomes not really obstinate at all, but withdrawn and pliable; however, above all he seems more complex (*History*, I, 535–36, 542, 546; II, 94, 110). James II, Macpherson reveals often enough, is actually rather pleasant company in private. The possibility of this transition has in fact been foreshadowed: unlike his nemesis, and indeed his brother, James has more obvious domestic virtues – they are simply obscured when he is acting as king, and especially by his religion (*History*, I, 146). This complication means that his character becomes readable in different ways. Readers of Macpherson's *History* are shown James being read, at least in part, by the sailor in Kent and Louis XIV, but they are given much more scope to make their own judgements, indeed are encouraged to do so. Crucial is the imagined integrity of private feelings. James II is revealed suffering and to possess, consequently, that richness of character that by the later eighteenth century was associated with the experience of distress. He seems to have an inner life, one that does not always manifest itself in his public actions, but is inferred through affect. William III is presented very differently and appears throughout merely as a function of his public actions. He has no character beyond these achievements, which Macpherson even tends to play down – he is not such a great general, for example. He is certainly not a complex or attractive personality. The new king has no inner life, no ability to be private beyond the comfort of his favourites. His character is merely Tacitean, a limited, shallow schemer, happy only in the 'mad bigotry of his opponent' (*History*, I, 163–64; 310, 552). More precisely, where James II seems to acquire new layers, William III remains always the same, not unlike one of Fielding's characters, a matter of visible external effects. In essence, William III is Blifil: although not to James II's Tom Jones, but rather to a personality much more akin to Richardson's doomed Clarissa or Lovelace (*History*, II, 26, 51).

Parliamentary Politics: Characterising the Opposition in *A Short History*

In common with many other larger-scale historical studies (Hume would be a clear example), Macpherson's *History* changed as its focus changed.[22] Methods suited to one period can lack explanatory power when applied to another, later epoch. It is the nature of politics, Macpherson's preferred field, in which the change is most readily seen and which causes the shift in method and address it is now necessary to consider. Under William III and later Queen Anne, politics become endlessly complex but also technocratic. Taxation and representation, opposition and governance are centrally the concern. Characters, at least the kind of great and commanding characters found in the Stuart brothers, are notably absent. Big personalities, if they exist at all, lie with scheming opposition politicians, such as Marlborough and Russell. James II even begins to resume a kingly personality (*History*, II, 52, 61–63). There is, perhaps, a Jacobite edge to this distinction. If so, it is an allegiance of the heart and the literary affect, but not of the head. This is an important development, and it becomes an emerging feature of the *History*. The language of sensibility plays an increasingly active role in Macpherson's dynamically realised characters, whose clashing ambitions are the impetus for history. These features are important, and perhaps are the most dynamic aspects of his project; however, it ought to be conceded that Macpherson's historiographic interests change as he turns to the later phases of William III's reign.

During the 1690s, when issues such as the need for reliable coinage, credit, and all other forms of finance emerge more fully as the basis not only of the state and its security but also of modernity itself, Macpherson must step beyond the confines of his earlier discussions. Character and secret motivations are less apparent and have less explanatory value. Parliament, and distinctly the House of Commons, becomes a central focus, and not solely as an opposition to the operations of the royal prerogative (*History*, II, 778–79, 100–02, 119–20, 145–46). Macpherson is disgusted by the excesses of opposition, even as he is upset by the presumption of the prerogative (*History*, I, 196, 202, 207). These tensions are most marked during Queen Anne's reign, and the *History* reflects these developments. It is a story of greater subtlety and much modification, if also of the enlargement of the sphere of government, most notably in relation to the Act of Union in 1707. If politics becomes more clearly negotiated by the beginning of the eighteenth century, and consequently less immediately threatened by the possibility of civil war, then it is equally the case, and often palpably so, that these new political forms and pressures rest upon, and are the consequences of, the violent struggles of the recent past. It is a legacy that will always require attention and effort in order to keep it in the past. In this context, the oscillation between principles and prejudices would be critical.

If the *History* essays, however dubiously, a truce between principles and prejudices and a wider and more complex sense of government, then it was not one which Macpherson was minded to honour throughout his career as a historian. The *Short History of the Opposition* was published at the end of the 1778–79 parliamentary session, a significantly abysmal period during Britain's quest to keep her American colonies. At this grim moment, Macpherson writes, it is incumbent on those unable to draw their swords in the nation's defence that they 'expose to just indignation, those, who have proved themselves her internal, and consequently, her unnatural enemies' (*Short History*, v). In this spirit the *Short History* is not short on execration. After an initial flurry of quotation from speeches by Charles James Fox and other members of the largely Rockinghamite opposition, Macpherson settles down to attack those MPs (Fox, Thomas Townshend, and others) and the Admirals and Generals (notably Augustus Keppel and John Burgoyne) who had assailed their own parliament or who had, in his eyes, given succour or support to the rebels. Macpherson is particularly exercised by what he sees as the unmanly nature of this activity. He complains that although the 'dignity and honour of the nation' were once the proper concern of the Opposition, 'melancholy, meanness, and despair, now fill the whole circle of patriotic oratory'. Macpherson is particularly keen to attack the 'mortifying pictures of age, misfortune and disease' that rose from the 'feeling bosom of Mr. E____d B__ke'. Burke appears correspondingly as dubious and unmanly (*Short History*, 11–12, 4, 24, 17). Macpherson's insinuations underscore the ferocity of his attack on the Ministry's opponents, who he consistently represents as degenerate, fractious, and wholly incapable of restraint. From this committed perspective it is hard to imagine how any form of opposition could be legitimate. This is especially so in times of war when Macpherson expects loyalty and application, come what may. It was this aspect of the text perhaps more than any other that drew criticism (*Short History*, 52–53).[23]

Although it is focussed on a single session, *Short History* offers a wider and more reflective history of opposition and its origins, while also seeking to proscribe limits to protest. Macpherson claims that parliamentary opposition was initially a valuable and acceptable part of public life, not least as a way of balancing royal favours and powers. He has in mind when he makes this claim, though he is not explicit about it, the period immediately following the Restoration. In his account of that initial impetus some familiar paired terms are prominent in the analysis:

> As a degree of the public confidence was necessary to direct the Sovereign in his choice of servants, men who wished to be employed, took care to support, in their public appearance, the principles and perhaps the prejudices of the people. A habitual jealousy of the power of the Crown, kept open the ears of the public to every alarm (*Short History*, 2)

Macpherson's language is striking. As in the discussion of James II and his troubles, it is equivocal, undermining the very point it appears to make. Opposition is, on this account, less a check to executive power (though it retains that function) than a sop to 'jealousy' and 'prejudice'. It stirs up trouble more than it achieves balance. Later at the accession of George III a remedy appeared possible:

> The present reign began, with advantages, calculated to put an end to foolish distinctions, which ought to have expired, with the prejudices, on which they had been founded [...] The door of preferment was laid open to all his subjects; but though this liberal conduct might have pleased the unprejudiced, it was incapable of extinguishing party among the interested. These, though of different principles and characters, by imposing on the weak and the credulous, formed new factions, on the shadows of departed political tenets (*Short History*, 3)

Prejudice is not only injurious, but persistent. Even peace and good governance cannot dispel its effects. Macpherson is writing these words as an implacable and unwavering loyalist, keen to do down his enemies: Fox, Burke, and their cronies. By entering the contemporary political fray Macpherson has removed the burden and obstacle of James II's obstinate Catholicism (a bigotry that could justify even prejudice) that so clouded and confused his account of opposition in the 1680s. Modern politics and the calamities of war confirm the dangers of unrestricted opposition, danger glimpsed during the Exclusion Crisis, but felt just as strongly in the present moment (*History*, I, 323–25, 333–38). This is strident and unyielding; opposition to the Crown appears dangerous and, moreover, inimical to the fabric of the nation. The lesson, however, is equivocal. Macpherson has some rousing as well as dejected sentiments to convey at the close of his tirade:

> We may suffer some losses, at the beginning; for what people was ever uniformly successful in war? The Romans themselves were not always invincible. They frequently lost provinces and armies; yet they rose superior to all nations. The profits and losses of war can only be estimated, on the day, which concludes a peace. Let us be unanimous among ourselves, and that day cannot be distant, disadvantageous, or dishonourable [...].
> (*Short History*, 58)

This is an odd sort of consolation. Perhaps for Macpherson defeat had its own particular and salutary merits.[24]

Endnotes

Introduction

1. The most comprehensive and still unsurpassed analysis is that of Derick Thomson in his *The Gaelic Sources of Macpherson's Ossian* (Aberdeen: Aberdeen University Press, 1952). See also Derick Thomson, 'James Macpherson – the Gaelic Dimension' in Fiona Stafford and Howard Gaskill (eds), *From Gaelic to Romantic: Ossianic Translations* (Amsterdam: Rodopi, 1998), pp. 17–26.
2. Hume to Blair, 19 September 1763, reproduced in Thomas Bailey Saunders, *The Life and Letters of James Macpherson* (London and New York: S. Sonnenschein & Co., 1894), p. 206; 'Preface' in Howard Gaskill (ed.), *The Poems of Ossian and Related Works* (Edinburgh: Edinburgh University Press, 1995), p. 412.
3. Fiona Stafford, *The Sublime Savage: James Macpherson and the Poems of Ossian* (Edinburgh: Edinburgh University Press, 1988), p. 165.
4. Saunders, *Life*, p. 217.
5. Ibid., p. 232.
6. This was published anonymously and is attributed to James, though Saunders believes John responsible for some of it. The Carnatic is a coastal region of South East India.
7. Balavil is rendered in a number of ways: sometimes Belleville, Belville, or Bellville.
8. See Saunders, pp. 281–84.
9. Jerome McGann, *The Poetics of Sensibility: A Revolution in Literary Style* (Oxford: Oxford University Press, 1996), p. 33; Robert Crawford, *The Modern Poet* (Oxford: Oxford University Press, 2001), p. 41.
10. See Dafydd Moore (ed.), *Ossian and Ossianism* vol. 3 (London: Routledge, 2004) for a collection of the range of critical responses evoked by the poems during the first thirty years after their publication.

11 Saunders, *Life*, J. S. Smart, *James Macpherson: An Episode in Literature* (London: D. Nutt, 1905).
12 See for example, Leith Davis, *Acts of Union* (Cambridge: Cambridge University Press, 1999).
13 For Macpherson and the Gaelic world, see Lesa Ní Mhunghaile's contribution to this collection. For Macpherson and folklore studies, see the special issue of the *Journal of American Folklore* 114.454 (2001), in particular the contributions of Thomas McKean and James Porter. For interpretations of the forgery row see, as a selection, Kevin Hart, *Samuel Johnson and the Culture of Property* (Cambridge, 1999), pp. 136–50; Andrew Hook, '"Ossian" Macpherson as Image Maker', *Scottish Review* 36 (1984), pp. 39–44; Jack Lynch, 'Samuel Johnson's "Love of Truth" and Literary Fraud', *Studies in English Literature* 42.3 (2002), pp. 601–18; Katie Trumpener, *Bardic Nationalism: The Romantic Novel and the British Empire* (Princeton: Princeton University Press, 1997), chapter 2; Ian Haywood, *The Making of History: A Study of the Literary Forgeries of James Macpherson and Thomas Chatterton in Relation to Eighteenth-Century Ideas of History and Fiction* (Rutherford NJ: Fairleigh Dickenson University Press, 1986); Susan Manning, 'Henry Mackenzie's Report on Ossian: Cultural Authority in Transition', *Modern Language Quarterly* 68.4 (2007), pp. 517–39; Matthew Wickman, 'The Allure of the Improbable: Fingal, Evidence, and the Testimony of the 'Echoing Heath'', *PMLA* 115.2 (2000), pp. 181–94.
14 See Howard Gaskill (ed.), *The Reception of Ossian in Europe* (London: Continuum, 2004) for an unrivalled survey of Macpherson's influence across thirteen European languages. On the question of *Ossian*'s impact on art, see Murdo Macdonald's contribution to the current volume for a continuation of and updating to his contribution to Gaskill's collection.
15 The single exception would be John Dunn's unpublished PhD thesis 'The Role of Macpherson's *Ossian* in the Development of British Romanticism' (University of Michigan, 1965). For a sample of the work that has been carried out, see Fiona Stafford, '"Dangerous Success": Ossian, Wordsworth and English Romantic Literature', in Howard Gaskill (ed.), *Ossian Revisited*, (Edinburgh: Edinburgh University Press, 1991), pp. 49–72 and 'Romantic Macpherson' in Murray Pittock (ed.), *The Edinburgh Companion to Scottish Romanticism*, (Edinburgh: Edinburgh University Press, 2011), pp. 27–38; 'Macpherson's Ossian: A Special Issue', *Scotlands* 4.1 (1997);

Dafydd Moore, 'Tennyson, Malory and the Ossianic Mode: The Poems of Ossian and the Death of Arthur', *Review of English Studies* 57.230 (2006), pp. 374–91.

16 See Murray Pittock, *Irish and Scottish Romanticism* (Oxford: Oxford University Press, 2008) for a full discussion of the methodological dilemmas of Romantic revisionism in these terms (and also pp. 71–80 for specific discussion of Macpherson).

17 John Kerrigan, *Archipelagic English: Literature, History and Politics 1603–1707* (Oxford: Oxford University Press, 2009).

18 Gerard Carruthers and Alan Rawes, 'Introduction', *English Romanticism and the Celtic World* (Cambridge: Cambridge University Press, 2003), p. 19. For a clear account of the approach and the way it changes our perception of the field, see also Ian Duncan, Leith Davis and Janet Sorensen's introduction to their edited collection *Scotland and the Borders of Romanticism* (Cambridge: Cambridge University Press, 2004), pp. 1–9; Pittock, *Irish and Scottish Romanticism* and also his earlier work *Inventing and Resisting Britain: Cultural Identities in Britain and Ireland 1685–1789* (London: Palgrave, 1997).

19 Fiona Stafford, 'Primitivism and the Primitive Poet: A Cultural Context for Macpherson's *Ossian*' in Terence Brown (ed.), *Celticism*, (Amsterdam: Rodopi, 1996), pp. 273–92. See also, Howard Weinbrot, *Britannia's Issue: The Rise of British Literature from Dryden to Ossian* (Cambridge: Cambridge University Press, 1994), p. 529; Peter Womack, *Improvement and Romance: Constructing the Myth of the Highlands* (London: Macmillan, 1989).

20 Pittock, *The Myth of the Jacobite Clans* (Edinburgh: Edinburgh University Press, 1995), p. 39.

21 See for example, Mary Margaret Rubel, *Savage and Barbarian: Historical Attitudes in the Criticism of Homer and Ossian in Britain, 1760–1800* (Amsterdam: North Holland Publishing, 1978).

22 Luke Gibbons, 'The Sympathetic Bond: Ossian, Celticism and Colonialism', in Terence Brown (ed.), *Celticism*, (Amsterdam: Rodopi, 1996), pp. 273–92. For the more general view, see Richard Sher, *Church and University in the Scottish Enlightenment* (Edinburgh: Edinburgh University Press, 1985); John Dwyer, 'The Melancholy Savage: Text and Context in the Poems of Ossian' in *Ossian Revisited*, pp. 164–206.

23 See for example, Adam Potkay, *The Fate of Eloquence in the Age of Hume* (Ithaca: Cornell University Press, 1992); Dafydd Moore, *Enlightenment and Romance in the Poems of Ossian* (Aldershot: Ashgate, 2003).

1: The Correspondence of James Macpherson

1. T. Bailey Saunders, *The Life and Letters of James Macpherson* (1894; New York: Haskell House, 1968); Fiona Stafford, *The Sublime Savage: A Study of James Macpherson and the Poems of Ossian* (Edinburgh: Edinburgh University Press, 1988); and Henry Mackenzie (ed.), *Report of the Committee of the Highland Society of Scotland* (Edinburgh, 1805). See Fiona Stafford, 'Dr. Johnson and the Ruffian: New Evidence in the Dispute between Samuel Johnson and James Macpherson', *Notes and Queries* (1989), pp. 70–77, offering a full analysis of their quarrel, including the pertinent Macpherson correspondence (three letters), along with Johnson's famous reply.
2. James Macpherson, 'To George Lawrie'. 27 February 1760; 18 March 1760; 22 March 1760; 11 April 1760. MS. Boswell Collection. GEN MSS. 89/27/f. 650. Yale University Lib., New Haven. See Robert Crawford, *Scotland's Books: The Penguin History of Scottish Literature* (London: Penguin, 2007).
3. See Paul deGategno, 'The Sublime Savage in America: James "Ossian" Macpherson's Tour of Duty in West Florida', *Scotia: Interdisciplinary Journal of Scottish Studies* 16 (1992), pp. 1–20. West Florida, and its capital Pensacola, containing an excellent harbour, was secured from the Spanish in August 1763.
4. James Macpherson, 'To Allan Macpherson', 21 January 1783 and 24 January 1783. National Register of Archives for Scotland (NRAS), 2614. 158.
5. See deGategno, 'Sublime Savage in America', p. 20. For information on James Macpherson's role in supervising a favourable press for the government, see Robert Rea. *The English Press in Politics: 1760–1774* (Lincoln: University of Nebraska Press, 1963), pp. 133, 167.
6. For example, James Macpherson, 'To Charles Jenkinson', 16 February 1764. BM, MS, 38,202, f. 101. See J. N. M. Maclean, who states clearly the two men have already developed a valued relationship, in *The Early Political Careers of James 'Fingal' Macpherson and Sir John Macpherson* (Diss. Edinburgh University, 1967) pp. 65–121.
7. George McElroy, 'Ossianic Imagination and the History of India: James and John Macpherson as Propagandists and Intriguers', in Jennifer J. Carter and Joan H. Pittock (eds), *Aberdeen and the Enlightenment* (Aberdeen: Aberdeen University Press, 1987), pp. 363–74.
8. See Saunders, p. 215; Maclean, pp. 112, 131; and McElroy, p. 364. Also, for the once conventional view, see Hugh Trevor-Roper, *The Invention*

of Scotland: Myth and History (New Haven: Yale University Press, 2009), p. 127.
9   See Paul J. deGategno, *James Macpherson* (Boston: Twayne, 1989), pp. 139, 157. See original citation in Sir John Fortescue, ed., *The Correspondence of King George III: 1760–83*. 6 vols. (London: Macmillan, 1927–28, 5:414). Maclean also mentions this point (p. 179).
10 See BM. MS. ADD. 38729. 'James Macpherson. Resolution of Partners of the *London Packet*', 6 January 1770. Stanley Morison, *The English Newspaper, 1622–1932: An Account of the Physical Development of Journals Printed in London* (Cambridge: Cambridge University Press, 2009), p. 145 notes this joint stock arrangement. The *London Packet* began publication in May 1769 and changed its title to the *London Packet, or, New Evening Post* in early 1771. Strahan relinquished to William Woodfall in 1772. See the *17th–18th Century Burney Collection Newspapers*.
11 Strahan did not print anti-government letters in the *London Chronicle*, certainly not Junius's 'Letter to the King'. But Strahan was an astute businessman and saw an opportunity for improving his financial condition, even with a paper which would print opposition news. See Lance Bertelsen, 'The Education of Henry Sampson Woodfall, Newspaperman', in Anthony W. Lee (ed.), *Mentoring in Eighteenth-Century British Literature and Culture* (Burlington: Ashgate, 2010), p. 166. I appreciate his help on eighteenth-century newspaper reports.
12 Caleb Whitefoord was a Scot who had moved to London as a wine merchant and sometime diplomat, but he knew men of letters and journalists including Benjamin Franklin. With the end of the American Revolution, Lord Shelburne chose Whitefoord as secretary to the commission that would conclude the peace with the US. See D. G. C. Allan, 'Caleb Whitefoord', in the online *Oxford Dictionary of National Biography* (cited as DNB). David Garrick by 1770 was a successful and respected actor and co-manager of Drury Lane Theatre known for his business acumen, while always seeking opportunities for improving his finances. Though he was not at this meeting, his friend William Strahan paid the subscription price for him. In 1769, Alexander Carlyle reports on a dinner where both James and John Macpherson were present, as well as Garrick, John Home, and David Hume, in John Hill Burton (ed.), *The Autobiography of Dr. Alexander Carlyle* (London: Foulis, 1910), p. 530. Garrick and James Boswell would later correspond about Macpherson and the Ossian poems, as well as the dispute between Samuel Johnson and James Macpherson.

Boswell writes to Garrick about Ossian on 4 February 1775 in George Kahrl, et al. (eds), *The Correspondence of James Boswell with David Garrick, Edmund Burke, and Edmund Malone* (New York: McGraw-Hill, 1987), 4:61–64. Garrick became one of the proprietors of *The Public Advertiser* in 1771: see Robert Rea, *The English Press in Politics, 1760–1774*, p. 214.

13 James Macpherson, 'To H. S. Woodfall', 13 June N.d. BM ADD. 27,780. f. 54. Colonel Allan Macpherson and James Macpherson were childhood friends, and in 1758 he enlisted in the Black Watch serving in North America and the Caribbean; after his discharge, he joined the army of the East India Company in 1763, becoming Quartermaster-General to Warren Hastings and later Sir John Macpherson, to whom he was also Private Secretary. See William C. Macpherson, *Soldiering in India, 1764–1787* (Edinburgh, 1928).

14 Saunders, pp. 275–76. Also 'To H. S. Woodfall'. 21 July N.d. BM, ADD., 27,780. Keith Feiling, *Warren Hastings* (Hamden, CT: Archon., 1967), pp. 71, 240, 297. As Feiling notes, a well-known connection existed between Benfield and John Macpherson, 'at the heart of the Carnatic politics [...] were two first-class scoundrels [...] Benfield and John Macpherson' (p. 71). See P. J. Marshall, 'Paul Benfield', DNB.

15 James Macpherson, 'To John Macpherson', 3 February 1770 (correct date: 3 March 1770). BM, MSS, EUR. F291/122: 1770. The letter is referenced in Maclean, pp. 181–83. See Bruce Redford (ed.), *The Letters of Samuel Johnson*, 5 vols (Princeton: Princeton UP, 1992), 1: x.

16 P. J. Marshall, 'The British in Asia', pp. 501–02.

17 James Macpherson, 'To Lord Macartney', 11 April 1782. MS. Department of Western Manuscripts, Bodleian Lib., University of Oxford. Macartney would soon prove an unreliable ally of Hastings and become suspicious about the Macphersons' motives.

18 James Macpherson, 'To His Highness the Nabob of Arcot and the Carnatic', 15 April 1782. MS. Department of Western Manuscripts, Bodleian Lib., University of Oxford.

19 James Macpherson, 'To Allan Macpherson', 21 February 1781, NRAS 2614. 157; 'To John MacIntyre', 10 March 1781, NRAS 2614. 147; 'To Allan Macpherson', 23 April 1781, NRAS 2614. 157. Macpherson had first written to Hastings in August 1778 (BM, ADD, 29141, ff. 311,342). Keith Feiling reports Hastings had read *Fingal* in 1769 on his return to India (*Warren Hastings*, p. 61). John MacIntyre was James's nephew, a son of James's sister, Janet, born at Knappach in the Parish of Kingussie. James Macpherson secured him a posting in the East India

Company army. I appreciate this information from Professor Alan G. Macpherson, Memorial University of Newfoundland. Message to author, 6 June 2000 (email).
20 James Macpherson, 'My dear friend (Unnamed)', 18 June 1782, SRO GD80/907/7.
21 James Macpherson, 'To Allan Macpherson', 24 July 1782, NRAS 2614, 157 and 8 September 1783, NRAS 2614, 158.
22 James Macpherson, 'To Allan Macpherson', 3 December 1792, SRO GD80/931/1. The current owners, Mr and Mrs Allan Macpherson-Fletcher, note the house as complete in 1790, but this letter states only the 'whole of the ground Story and Attics were completely finished'.
23 James Macpherson, 'To Caleb Whitefoord', 20 March 1794, BM, ADD, 36,593. The line Macpherson quotes from a Cumberland play has not been located. Professor Robert D. Hume, Pennsylvania State University, suggests Macpherson may just have heard the joke and chose to apply it derogatively to Cumberland. Message to author, 9 March 2015 (email).

2: Ossian and the Gaelic World

1 John Ramsay, *Scotland and Scotsmen in the Eighteenth Century, from the mss. of John Ramsay, esq. of Ochtertyre*, ed. by Alexander Allardyce, 2 vols (Edinburgh and London: William Blackwood and Sons, 1888), I, pp. 545–46.
2 The collecting of Gaelic material, particularly Fionn ballads, gathered pace after the publication of Macpherson's *Ossian* works. Collections made in the second half of the eighteenth century included those by the Rev. James MacLagan (1728–1805) of Blair Atholl; and Ewen MacDiarmid, Rannoch (a manuscript written between 1762 and 1769); Duncan Kennedy, a schoolmaster in Kilbrandon, Argyll, in 1774; Mathew Young, Bishop of Clonfert, in the Scottish Highlands in 1784; Dr Alexander Irvine, Minister of Little Dunkeld, Perth, in 1801. See J. F. Campbell, *Leabhar na Feinne. Heroic Gaelic Ballads collected in Scotland chiefly from 1512 to 1871* (London: Spottiswoode and Co., 1872); Derick Thomson, *Companion to Gaelic Scotland* (Glasgow: Gairm, 1994), p. 82; Anja Gunderloch, *Làmh-sgrìobhainnean Gàidhlig Oilthigh Ghlaschu. The Gaelic Manuscripts of Glasgow University: A Catalogue* (Glasgow: University of Glasgow, 2007).
3 Stone's poem was not a translation but it used the broad theme of 'Bás Fhraoich'.
4 *Scots Magazine*, 18 (1756), pp. 15–17.

5   Derick Thomson, '"Ossian" Macpherson and the Gaelic World of the Eighteenth Century', *Edinburgh University Review*, 40 (1963), p. 9.
6   Moray Watson and Michelle Macleod (eds), *The Edinburgh Companion to the Gaelic Language* (Edinburgh: Edinburgh University Press, 2010), p. 11; Donald E. Meek, 'The Scottish Tradition of Fian Ballads in the Middle Ages', in Cathal Ó Háinle and Donald E. Meek (eds), *Unity in Diversity: Studies in Irish and Scottish Gaelic Language, Literature and History*, (Dublin: School of Irish, Trinity College Dublin, 2004), p. 9.
7   Ibid., p. 10.
8   For a detailed discussion, see Kuno Meyer, *Fianaigecht: Being a collection of hitherto inedited Irish poems and tales relating to Finn and his Fiana, with an English translation* (Dublin: Hodges, Figgis & Co., 1910); Gerard Murphy, *The Ossianic Lore and Romantic Tales of Medieval Ireland* (Dublin: At The Three Candles, 1961); Joseph Falaky Nagy, *The Wisdom of the Outlaw: The Boyhood Deeds of Finn in Gaelic Narrative Tradition* (Berkeley: University of California Press, 1985); James MacKillop, *Fionn mac Cumhaill: Celtic Myth in English Literature* (Syracuse: Syracuse University Press, 1986); Dáithí Ó hÓgáin, *Fionn Mac Cumhaill: Images of a Gaelic Hero* (Dublin: Gill & Macmillan, 1988); and Sharon J. Arbuthnott and Geraldine Parsons (eds), *The Gaelic Finn Tradition* (Dublin: Four Courts Press, 2012).
9   For a detailed consideration of the *Agallamh*, see Aidan Doyle and Kevin Murray (eds), *In Dialogue with the Agallamh. Essays in Honour of Seán Ó Coileáin* (Dublin: Four Courts Press, 2014). See also, Nollaig Ó Muraíle, 'Agallamh na Seanórach', in Pádraig Ó Fiannachta (ed.), *An Fhiannaíocht, Léachtaí Cholm Cille, 25,* (Maynooth: An Sagart, 1995), pp. 96–127.
10 Derick S. Thomson, *The Gaelic Sources of Macpherson's 'Ossian'* (Edinburgh and London: Oliver and Boyd, 1952), p. 11. Macpherson has often been criticised for mixing the two cycles together.
11 Donald Meek has drawn attention to the problematic use of the terms 'ballad' and 'lay' to translate the Gaelic terms 'laoi' and 'duan'. See Donald E. Meek, 'Development and Degeneration in Gaelic Ballad Texts', in Bo Almqvist, Séamas Ó Catháin and Pádraig Ó Héalaí (eds), *The Heroic Process* (Dublin: Glendale Press, 1987), p. 132.
12 Murphy, *Ossianic Lore*, p. 56.
13 Meek, 'Development and Degeneration', pp. 132–33.

14 In Scotland the Fionn ballads are most commonly known as *Duain na Féinne(adh)*. In colloquial Gaelic the *fianna* are known as *Féinn*, *Fèinn* or *Fìnn*, depending on dialect, and also *An Fhéinn* and *Na Fiantaichean*. An individual is known as *Fiantaiche*. See John MacInnes, 'Twentieth-Century Recordings of Scottish Gaelic Heroic Ballads', in Almqvist et. al, *Heroic Process*, p. 103.

15 Donald Meek, 'The Banners of the Fian in Gaelic Ballad Tradition', *Cambridge Medieval Celtic Studies*, 11 (Summer 1986), p. 29.

16 Peadar Ó Conaire, *Na Laoithe Fiannaíochta sa Bhéaloideas* (unpublished MA thesis, University College Galway, 1982), p. 3.

17 Murphy, *Duanaire Finn* III, pp. 204–15; Pádraig Ó Fiannachta, 'The Development of the Debate between Pádraig and Oisín', in Almqvist et. al, *Heroic Process*, pp. 183–205; Síle Ní Mhurchú, 'Agallamh Oisín agus Phádraig: composition and transmission', in Arbuthnot and Parsons (eds), *Gaelic Finn Tradition*, pp. 195–208. For the development of the relationship between Oisín and St Patrick, and the portrayal of a 'tragi-comic Oisín' with a shift from the heroic to the humorous, see David Krause, 'The Hidden Oisín', *Studia Hibernica*, 6 (1966), pp. 7–24.

18 Ó Fiannachta, 'The Development of the Debate', p. 194.

19 Meek, 'Scottish Tradition of Fian Ballads', p. 20.

20 Ibid., p. 14. In Scotland, the ballads and their melodies, dating from the later medieval period, were recorded from the 1940s onwards by members of the University of Edinburgh's School of Scottish Studies. See, MacInnes, 'Twentieth-century Recordings', pp. 101–30.

21 Meek, 'Development and Degeneration', p. 137.

22 Murphy, *Duanaire Finn* III, p. 121.

23 Meek, 'Scottish Tradition of Fian Ballads', p. 17.

24 Meek, 'The Gaelic Ballads of Scotland: Creativity and Adaptation' in Howard Gaskill (ed.), *Ossian Revisited* (Edinburgh: Edinburgh University Press, 1991), pp. 32–35.

25 James Macpherson, 'A Critical Dissertation on the Poems of Ossian' published in *The Works of Ossian, The Son of Fingal* (1765). See Gaskill, *The Poems of Ossian and Related Works* (Edinburgh: Edinburgh University Press, 1996), p. 223. For a discussion of the reaction of scholars in Ireland to such claims, see Clare O'Halloran, *Golden Ages and Barbarous Nations* (Cork: Cork University Press, 2004); Mícheál Mac Craith, '"We know all these poems": The Irish Response to Ossian', in Howard Gaskill (ed.), *The Reception of Ossian in Europe*

(London: Continuum, 2004), pp. 91–108; Lesa Ní Mhunghaile, *Charlotte Brooke's Reliques of Irish Poetry* (Dublin: Irish Manuscripts Commission, 2009), pp. xxxvi–xxxvii.

26 For *The Book of the Dean of Lismore*, see S. Innes and A. Petrina, 'The Sixteenth and Seventeenth Centuries', in Carla Sassi (ed.), *The International Companion to Scottish Poetry* (Glasgow: Scottish Literature International, 2016), pp. 44–45; Martin MacGregor, 'Creation and Compilation: *The Book of the Dean of Lismore* and Literary Culture in Late-Medieval Gaelic Scotland', in Thomas Clancy and Murray Pittock (eds), *The Edinburgh History of Scottish Literature*, 3 vols (Edinburgh, 2007), I, 209–18; Martin MacGregor, 'The view from Fortingall: the worlds of *The Book of the Dean of Lismore*', *Scottish Gaelic Studies*, 22 (2006), pp. 35–85.

27 Watson and Macleod, *Edinburgh Companion*, p. 14. The orthography is the same kind used to write Lowland Scots and was a common way of writing Scottish Gaelic in the Late Middle Ages.

28 Meek, 'Scottish Tradition of Fian Ballads', p. 13. For a detailed consideration of *The Book of the Dean of Lismore*, see Donald E. Meek, 'The corpus of Heroic Verse in *The Book of the Dean of Lismore*' (unpublished Ph.D. thesis, University of Glasgow, 1982).

29 Neil Ross (ed.), *Heroic Poetry from The Book of the Dean of Lismore* (Edinburgh: Scottish Gaelic Texts Society, 1939).

30 Ruairí Ó hUiginn, 'Duanaire Finn: patron and text', in *Duanaire Finn: Reassessments*, ed. by John Carey (London: Irish Texts Society, 2003), pp. 79–106.

31 Meek, 'Scottish Tradition of Fian Ballads', p. 15.

32 Standish Hayes O'Grady, *Catalogue of Irish Manuscripts in the British Library*, 3 vols (London: British Museum, 1926), I, p. 637.

33 Máirtín Ó Briain, 'Some material on Oisín in the Land of Youth' in D. Ó Corráin *et al.* (eds), *Sages, Saints and Storytellers* (Maynooth: An Sagart, 1989), pp. 181–99. There has been some debate regarding the authorship of the ballad. It was first published by the Ossianic Society and the following was stated as a foreword to the text: 'The Council of the Ossianic Society do not hold themselves responsible for the authenticity or antiquity of the following poem; but print it as an interesting specimen of the most *recent* of the Fenian Stories'. See Brian O'Looney (ed.), *Transactions of the Ossianic Society for the year 1856* (Dublin: John O'Daly, 1859), p. 228.

34 Máirtín Ó Briain, 'Micheál Coimín agus Oisín i dTír na nÓg' in

Aingeal Ní Chualáin and Gearóid Denvir (eds), *Macalla* (Gaillimh: Coláiste na hOllscoile, Gaillimh, 1984), pp. 162–63; 164.

35 Seosamh Watson, 'Laoi Chab an Dosáin: Background to a late Ossianic Ballad', *Eighteenth-Century Ireland/Iris an Dá Chultúr*, 5 (1990), pp. 37–44 (p. 37).

36 Gaskill, *Poems of Ossian*, p. 51. In 1760, after the success of *Fragments of Ancient Poetry*, Macpherson toured the Highlands searching for Gaelic manuscripts that would vindicate his claims as to the authenticity of his Ossianic poems. Among the valuable manuscripts he is credited with salvaging were *The Book of the Dean of Lismore* and *The Little Book of Clanranald*. He also took down many Fionn ballads from oral recitation.

37 Mícheál Mac Craith, 'Ionrachas James Macpherson?' in Mícheál Mac Craith and Pádraig Ó Héalaí (eds), *Diasa Díograise. Aistí i gCuimhne ar Mháirtín Ó Briain* (Indreabhán: Cló Iar-Chonnachta, 2009), pp. 121–42.

38 Thomson, *Gaelic Sources*, p. 63.

39 Diarmaid Ó Catháin, 'An Irish Scholar Abroad: Bishop John O'Brien of Cloyne and the Macpherson Controversy' in Patrick O'Flanagan and Cornelius G. Buttimer (eds), *Cork History and Society: Interdisciplinary Essays on the History of an Irish County* (Dublin: Geography Publications, 1993), pp. 499–533.

40 Ibid, p. 511.

41 Henry Mackenzie (ed.), *Report of the Committee of the Highland Society of Scotland: Appointed to inquire into the Nature and Authenticity of the Poems of Ossian* (Edinburgh: Archibald Constable & Co., 1805), pp. 151–54 (p. 152).

42 *Highland Society Report*, pp. 333–34. See also Ní Mhunghaile, *Charlotte Brooke's Reliques*, Part I, pp. 288–93, Part II, pp. 56–64.

43 Ludwig Chr. Stern, 'Die Ossianischen Heldenlieder' in *Zeitschrift für vergleichende Litteraturgeschichte*, 8 (1895), pp. 50–86, 143–74. Translated in *Transactions of the Gaelic Society of Inverness*, 22 (l. 897–98), pp. 257–325.

44 Stern, 'Ossianischen Heldenlieder', p. 268; James Macpherson, *The Poems of Ossian, in the original Gaelic, with a literal translation into Latin by the late Robert Macfarlan*, 3 vols (London: W. Bulmer & Co., 1807).

45 Stern, 'Ossianischen Heldenlieder', pp. 274–75.

46 Derick Thomson, 'James Macpherson – the Gaelic Dimension' in

Fiona Stafford and Howard Gaskill (eds), *From Gaelic to Romantic: Ossianic Translations* (Amsterdam: Rodopi, 1998), p. 21; idem, Thomson, *Gaelic Sources*. See also Mícheál Mac Craith, 'Fingal: Text, Context, Subtext', in Stafford and Gaskill (eds), *From Gaelic to Romantic*, pp. 59–68.

47 Derick Thomson, 'Macpherson's Ossian: Ballads to Epics', *Béaloideas*, pp. 54–55 (1986–87), pp. 243–64 (p. 260).
48 Stern, 'Ossianischen Heldenlieder', pp. 308–10; Thomson, *Gaelic Sources*, pp. 29–31.
49 Thomson, *Gaelic Sources*, p. 14.
50 Thomson, 'James Macpherson – the Gaelic Dimension', p. 22.
51 Thomson, *Gaelic Sources*, p. 47.
52 Ibid., p. 48.
53 Ibid., p. 49.
54 Ibid., p. 14.
55 Ibid., p. 28.
56 Meek, 'Gaelic Ballads of Scotland', p. 40.
57 Reidar Th. Christiansen, *The Vikings and the Viking Wars in Irish and Gaelic Tradition* (Oslo: I kommisjon hos J. Dybwad, 1931); Proinsias Mac Cana, 'The Influence of the Vikings on Celtic Literature', in Brian Ó Cuív (ed.), *The Impact of the Scandinavian Invasions on the Celtic-speaking Peoples c. 800–1100 AD* (Dublin: Dublin Institute for Advanced Studies, 1975), pp. 78–118.
58 Meek, 'Gaelic Ballads of Scotland', p. 47 n. 57.
59 Meek, 'Gaelic Ballads of Scotland', p. 41.
60 Howard Gaskill, 'Ossian in Europe', *Canadian Review of Comparative Literature/Revue Canadienne de Littérature Comparée*, 21:4 (December 1994), pp. 643–78 (p. 658).
61 For a discussion, see Krause, 'The Hidden Oisín', pp. 7–24.
62 Gaskill, *Poems of Ossian*, p. 355.
63 Liam Mc Cóil, 'Ossian', *Oghma* 8 (1996), pp. 20–31.
64 Gaskill, *Poems of Ossian*, p. 356.
65 Meek, 'Gaelic Ballads of Scotland', p. 38.
66 Gaskill, *Poems of Ossian*, p. 398.
67 Ibid., p. 9.
68 Ibid., p. 18.
69 Mc Cóil, 'Ossian', p. 27.
70 Gaskill, *Poems of Ossian*, p. 375.
71 Meek, 'Gaelic Ballads of Scotland', p. 47 n. 57.

72 Derick Thomson, 'Bogus Gaelic Literature', *Transactions of the Gaelic Society of Glasgow*, 5 (1958), pp. 172–88 (p. 177).
73 Donald Meek, 'The Sublime Gael: The Impact of Macpherson's Ossian on Literary Creativity and Cultural Perception in Gaelic Scotland' in *Reception of Ossian in Europe*, ed. by Gaskill, p. 43.

3: Ossian and the State of Translation in the Scottish Enlightenment

1 Gideon Toury, *Descriptive Translation Studies and beyond*, Benjamins Translation Library, 4 (Amsterdam: John Benjamins, 1995), p. 40.
2 Ibid., p. 51.
3 Gauti Kristmannsson, *Literary Diplomacy: The Role of Translation in the Construction of National Literatures in Britain and Germany 1750–1830*, Scottish Studies International 37, vol. 1 (Frankfurt an Main: Peter Lang, 2005), pp. 23–26. Hereafter *LD I*.
4 André Lefevere and Susan Bassnett, *Constructing Cultures: Essays on Literary Translation*, Topics in Translation XI, (Bristol: Multilingual Matters, 1998), pp. 27–28; Henry Mackenzie (ed.), *Report of the Committee of the Highland Society of Scotland, Appointed to Inquire into the Nature and Authenticity of The Poems of Ossian* (Edinburgh and London: Constable *et al.*), p. 185; Derick Thomson, *The Gaelic Sources of Macpherson's 'Ossian'*, Aberdeen University Studies 130 (Edinburgh: Oliver and Boyd, 1952); Donald Meek, 'The Gaelic Ballads of Scotland: Creativity and Adaptation' in Howard Gaskill (ed.), *Ossian Revisited* (Edinburgh: Edinburgh University Press, 1991) pp. 19–48; Fiona Stafford, *The Sublime Savage: A Study of James Macpherson and The Poems of Ossian*, (Edinburgh: Edinburgh University Press, 1988); Howard Gaskill, 'Introduction' in *Ossian Revisited*, pp. 1–18.
5 See *LD I*, pp. 97–108.
6 Toury, p. 45.
7 James Boswell, *Life of Johnson*, ed. R. W. Chapman, revised edn. (Oxford: Oxford University Press, 1980), p. 578.
8 Gauti Kristmannsson, 'The Trial Continues. Ossian in the Court of Literary Appeal' in *Eighteenth Century Scotland*, 24 (2010), pp. 13–16.
9 Kristmannsson, 'The Trial', pp. 14–16.
10 Thomas Curley, *Samuel Johnson, the Ossian Fraud, and the Celtic Revival in Great Britain and Ireland*, (Cambridge: Cambridge University Press, 2009).

11 *LD I*, pp. 21–23 and 40–44.
12 Marshall McLuhan, *The Gutenberg Galaxy: The Making of Typographic Man* (Toronto: University of Toronto Press, 1997 [1962]), p. 199.
13 Michael Cronin, *Translating Ireland* (Cork: Cork University Press, 1996), pp. 10–11.
14 Dante Alighieri, *De vulgari eloquentia*, ed. and trans. Steven Botterill (Cambridge: Cambridge University Press, 1996), p. 57.
15 *Petrarch and Dante. Anti-Dantism, Metaphysics, Tradition*, ed. Zygmunt G. Baranski and Theodore J. Cachey, Jr. (Notre Dame: University of Notre Dame Press, 2009); Kristmannsson, *LD I*, p. 22.
16 *The Oxford Guide to Literature in English Translation*, ed. Peter France (Oxford: Oxford University Press, 2000), p. 45. The situation in Ireland was different again, given the tradition of translation from the Middle Ages onwards. See Kevin Murray (ed.), *Translations from Classical Literature: Imtheachta Aeniasa and Stair Ercuil ocus a Bás*, Irish Texts Society, Seminar Series 17 (London: Irish Texts Society, 2006).
17 Outi Merisalo, 'Translating the Classics into the vernacular in sixteenth-century Italy', *Renaissance Studies*, 29 (2015), pp. 55–77.
18 *Oxford Guide*, p. 46.
19 See for example Lawrence Venuti, *The Translator's Invisibility. A History of Translation*, (London: Routledge, 1995), pp. 41–98.
20 Douglas Robinson (ed.), *Western Translation Theory from Herodotus to Nietzsche* (Manchester: St Jerome Publishing, 2002 [1997]), p. 172. Excerpts from Denham, Cowley, and Dillon can also be found in this reader.
21 Ample evidence can be found in two volumes of Penguin Classics: D. S. Carne-Ross and Kenneth Haynes (eds), *Horace in English* (Harmondsworth: Penguin Books, 1996); and K. W. Gransden (ed.), *Virgil in English* (Harmondsworth: Penguin Books, 1996).
22 *Oxford Guide*, p. 55.
23 *LD I*, pp. 21–23.
24 See for example *Horace in English*.
25 Samuel Johnson, *The Works of Samuel Johnson, LL.D. in Eleven Volumes*, 3 (London: J. Buckland *et al.*, 1787), p. 309, italics in original.
26 Daniel Weissbort and Astradur Eysteinsson (eds), *Translation – Theory and Practice* (Oxford: Oxford University Press, 2006), pp. 174–82.
27 Samuel Johnson, *Dictionary of the English Language*, (London: W. Strahan *et al.*, 1755), p. 1050.
28 Boswell, p. 62.
29 It is oft repeated in the secondary literature, both on paper and the

web, that this was the first poem to bear Johnson's name. In fact, the title page states clearly that the poem is by Juvenal and 'imitated by Samuel Johnson'. en.wikipedia.org/wiki/File:Vanity_of_Human_Wishes.jpg.
30 Venuti, pp. 118–47.
31 On the direct British response, cf. *LD I*, pp. 122–72.
32 See James Macpherson, *The Poems of Ossian and Related Works*, ed. Howard Gaskill (Edinburgh: Edinburgh University Press, 1996), p. 415.
33 Macpherson, *Ossian*, p. 6.
34 Ibid., p. 52.
35 James Macpherson, *An Introduction to the History of Great Britain and Ireland: or, an Inquiry into the Origin, Religion, Future State, Character, Manners, Morality, Amusements, Persons, Manner of Life, Houses, Navigation, Commerce, Language, Government, Kings, General Assemblies, Courts of Justice, and Juries of the Britons, Scots, Irish and Anglo-Saxons*. 3rd rev. edn. [1771] (London: T. Becket, 1773).
36 Macpherson, *Ossian*, p. 412.
37 Cf. George Steiner (ed.), *Homer in English* (Harmondsworth: Penguin Books, 1996); and a list of published English translations: records. viu.ca/~johnstoi/homer/homertranslations.htm.
38 Ibid., p. 108.
39 Sebastian Mitchell, 'Macpherson, Ossian, and Homer's *Iliad*' in *Ossian and National Epic*, in Gerald Bär and Howard Gaskill (eds), Studies in Cultural Sciences, (Frankfurt am Main: Peter Lang, 2012), pp. 55–72, p. 60.
40 Mitchell, p. 60.
41 Gauti Kristmannsson, 'The Subversive Loyalty of Ossian: Politics, Poetry, and Translation in the Eighteenth Century' in *Scotlands* 4.1, 1997, pp. 71–85, p. 83.
42 Mitchell, p. 63.
43 Anon., 'Article I. *The Iliad of* Homer. *Translated by* James Macpherson, *Esq.*' In *The Critical Review*, March, 1773, pp. 161–175. Can be seen here: archive.org/stream/criticalreview012unkngoog#page/n172/mode/2up.
44 James Macpherson, 'Preface' in *The Iliad of Homer*, trans. James Macpherson, 2 vols (London: T. Becket and A. Hondt, 1773), pp. i–xiv.
45 Ibid., pp. xiv–xv.
46 Ibid., p. xv.
47 Ibid., p. xvi.

48 Anne Dacier, 'My Condemnation' in *Western Translation Theory*, pp. 187–90.
49 Alexander Pope, 'Preface' in *The Iliad of Homer*, trans. Alexander Pope, ed. Steven Shankman (Harmondsworth: Penguin Classics, 1996), p. 12.
50 Macpherson, 'Preface', p. xviii.
51 Ibid., p. xviii.
52 Ibid., p. xix.
53 Anon, 'Article I', p. 162.
54 See *LD I*, pp. 97–108.
55 Boswell, p. 579.
56 Boswell, p. 303.
57 Alexander Fraser Tytler, *An Essay on the Principles of Translation* (London: J. M. Dent, n.y. [1791]), p. 105.
58 Venuti, p. 68.
59 Tytler, p. 9.

4: Nostalgic Ossian and the Transcreation of the Scottish Nation

1 Fiona Stafford, *The Sublime Savage: A Study of James Macpherson and the Poems of Ossian* (Edinburgh: Edinburgh University Press, 1988), p. 127.
2 David Hill Radcliffe, 'Ossian and the Genres of Culture', *Studies in Romanticism* 31 (1992), pp. 213–32 (p. 219).
3 Andreas Höfele, 'Der Autor und sein Double: Anmerkungen zur literarischen Fälschung', *Germanisch-Romanische Monatsschriften* 49:1 (1999), pp. 79–101 (p. 84).
4 Tejaswini Niranjana, *Siting Translation: History, Post-Structuralism, and the Colonial Context* (Berkeley: University of California Press, 1992), p. 56.
5 Ibid., p. 55.
6 Ibid., p. 84.
7 Susan Bassnett and Harish Trivedi, *Post-colonial Translation: Theory and Practice* (London: Routledge, 1999), p. 13.
8 Ibid., p. 14.
9 Ibid., p. 10.
10 Richard Bauman and Charles L. Briggs, *Voices of Modernity: Language Ideologies and the Politics of Inequality* (Cambridge: Cambridge University Press, 2003), p. 129.
11 Katie Trumpener, *Bardic Nationalism: The Romantic Novel and the British Empire* (Princeton: Princeton University Press, 1997), p. 75.

ENDNOTES   151

12 Colin Kidd, *Subverting Scotland's Past: Scottish Whig Historians and the Creation of an Anglo-British Identity, 1689-c. 1830* (Cambridge: Cambridge University Press, 1993), p. 245.
13 Dafydd Moore, *Enlightenment and Romance in James Macpherson's The Poems of Ossian: Myth, Genre and Cultural Change* (Aldershot: Ashgate, 2003), p. 98.
14 Howard Gaskill (ed.), *The Poems of Ossian and Related Works* (Edinburgh: Edinburgh University Press, 1996). All references appear parenthetically within the text.
15 Moore, p. 104.
16 Ibid., p. 163.
17 Bauman/Briggs, p. 144; Trumpener, pp. 11ff.
18 Murray Pittock, *The Myth of the Jacobite Clans*, (Edinburgh: Edinburgh University Press, 1999 [1995]), p. 38.
19 Svetlana Boym, *The Future of Nostalgia* (New York: Basic Books, 2001), p. xv.
20 Ibid., p. xvii.
21 Ibid., p. 19.
22 George Steiner, *Nostalgia for the Absolute* (Toronto: Anansi, 1997 [1974]), p. 5.
23 Boym, p. 354.
24 Augustine, *Confessions*, trans. Henry Chadwick (Oxford: Oxford University Press, 2008), p. 11, p. 13.
25 Fiona Stafford, 'Fingal and the Fallen Angels: Macpherson, Milton and Romantic Titanism' in Fiona Stafford and Howard Gaskill (eds), *From Gaelic to Romantic: Ossianic Translations* (Amsterdam: Rodopi, 1998), p. 169.
26 Peter T. Murphy, 'Fool's Gold: The Highland Treasure of Macpherson's Ossian', *ELH* 53 (1986), pp. 567–91 (p. 588).
27 Valentina Bold, 'Ossian and James Macpherson' in Marco Fazzini (ed.), *Alba Literaria: A History of Scottish Literature* (Venezia Mestre: Amos, 2005), p. 193.
28 Murray Pittock, *The Invention of Scotland: The Stuart Myth and the Scottish Identity, 1638 to the present*, (London: Routledge, 1991), p. 75.

5: Landscape and the Sense of Place in the Poems of Ossian

1 Peter Womack, *Improvement and Romance: Constructing the Myth of the Highlands* (Basingstoke: Palgrave and Macmillan, 1989), pp. 78–79.
2 Ibid., p. 79.

3   Howard Gaskill (ed.), *Fragments of Ancient Poetry*, in *The Poems of Ossian and Related Works* (Edinburgh: Edinburgh University Press, 1996). All further in-text citations to the poems are to this edition.

4   For twenty-first-century accounts of the contemporary reception of the poems in Britain, see Dafydd Moore, 'The Reception of the Poems of Ossian in England and Scotland', in *The Reception of Ossian in Europe*, ed. Howard Gaskill (London: Thoemmes Continuum, 2004), pp. 21–39; and Sebastian Mitchell, *Visions of Britain, 1730–1830: Anglo-Scottish Writing and Representation* (Basingstoke: Palgrave Macmillan, 2013), pp. 128–38.

5   See Clare O'Halloran, *Golden Ages and Barbarous Nations: Antiquarian Debate and Cultural Politics in Ireland* (Cork: Cork University Press, 2004), pp. 97–124.

6   See Margaret Rubel, *Savage and Barbarian: Historical Attitudes in the Criticism of Homer and Ossian in Britain 1760–1800* (Amsterdam: North Holland Publishing, 1978), pp. 39–54.

7   See David Hume, 'Of the Authenticity of the Ossian Poems', in *Essays, Moral, Political and Literary*, 2 vols (London: Ward and others, 1875), I, pp. 414–25.

8   See Samuel Johnson, *A Journey to the Western Isles of Scotland* and James Boswell, *The Journal of a Tour to the Hebrides*, ed. Peter Levi (Harmondsworth: Penguin, 1984), pp. 118–19.

9   'Crom-leach' approximates in Gaelic to 'bend/crooked stone'. Macpherson probably took the word from Welsh antiquaries, who used the term 'cromlech' to refer to Neolithic burial cairns. I am grateful to Thomas Clancy for these observations.

10 William Watson states that the earliest Roman mention of the Clyde is Tacitus's *Agricola*, where the river is named 'Clōta', rather than Macpherson's 'Glotta'. Macpherson's etymology is also improbable. Watson suggests that 'Clōta is really the name of a river goddess' and that the Latin and Gaelic terms have a common root: 'clou' (G.), wash; and 'cluo' (L.), purify. See William J. Watson, *The History of the Celtic Place-Names of Scotland* (Edinburgh: Blackwood, 1926), p. 44.

11 For modern discussion of the differences between the first and revised edition of the *Works of Ossian*, see Howard Gaskill, 'Ossian in Europe', *Canadian Review of Comparative Literature*, 21 (1994), 643–78 (pp. 648–59); and Sebastian Mitchell, 'Macpherson, Ossian and Homer's *Iliad*' in *Ossian and the National Epic*, ed. Gerald Bär and Howard Gaskill (Hamburg: Peter Lang, 2012), pp. 55–72 (pp. 61–62).

12 The standard accounts of the editions of Ossian are George F. Black, *Macpherson's Ossian and the Ossianic Controversy: A Contribution Towards a Bibliography* (New York: New York Public Library, 1926); and John J. Dunn, 'Macpherson's Ossian and the Ossianic Controversy: A Supplementary Bibliography', *Bulletin of the New-York Public Library* 75 (1971), pp. 463–73. Paul Barnaby records the European translations of the poems to 2004 in his 'Timeline of Ossian's European Reception', in *The Reception of Ossian in Europe*, ed. Gaskill, pp. xxi–lxviii.

13 Robert Crawford, *The Modern Poet: Poetry, Academia, and Knowledge Since the 1750s* (Oxford: Oxford University Press) p. 53, cited in Dafydd Moore 'Tradition, Memory and Cultural Transmission in the *Poems of Ossian*', *Eighteenth-Century Ireland*, 23 (2008), pp. 75–93 (p. 85).

14 Ibid., p. 85.

15 Hugh Blair, *A Critical Dissertation on the Poetry of Ossian, the Son of Fingal*, in *Works of Ossian*, ed. Gaskill, p. 355.

16 Walter J. Ong, *Orality and Literacy: the Technologizing of the Word* (London: Routledge, 2002), pp. 34–39.

17 Fiona J. Stafford, *The Sublime Savage: A Study of James Macpherson and the Poems of Ossian* (Edinburgh: Edinburgh University Press, 1988), pp. 133–50; and Gaskill, 'Ossian in Europe', pp. 670–73.

18 Nigel Leask, 'Fingalian Topographies: Ossian and the Highland Tour, 1764–1810', *Journal for Eighteenth-Century Studies*, 39 (2016), pp. 183–96. See also Paul Baines, 'Ossianic Geographies: Fingalian Figures on the Scottish Tour, 1760–1830', *Scotlands*, 4 (1997), pp. 44–61; and Eric Gidal's account of the geological and industrial aspects of Ossian's nineteenth-century reception in his *Ossianic Unconformities: Bardic Poetry in the Industrial Age* (Charlottesville: University of Virginia Press, 2015).

19 See Rhiannon Williams, 'Welsh Turner Mountain Scene Revealed to be in Scotland', *Daily Telegraph*, 2 October 2013, read online at www.telegraph.co.uk/culture/art/art-news/10344692/Welsh-Turner-mountain-scene-revealed-to-be-set-in-Scotland.html [accessed 23 January 2015]; and Murdo Macdonald, 'Ossian and Visual Art: Mislaid and Rediscovered, *Journal for Eighteenth-Century Studies*, 39 (2016), pp. 235–48.

20 For recent accounts of the visual interpretation of Ossian, see Murdo Macdonald, 'Ossian and Art: Scotland into Europe via Rome', in *The Reception of Ossian in Europe*, pp. 393–404; and Sebastian Mitchell, 'Celtic Postmodernism: Ossian and Contemporary Art', *Translation and Literature*, 22 (2013), pp. 401–35.

21 See Paul Van Teighem, 'Ossian et l'ossianisme au XVIIIe siècle', *Le Préromantisme*, 1 (1924), pp. 195–287 (p. 281), cited in Gaskill, 'Ossian in Europe', p. 671. See also Robert Rix's contribution to the current volume.

22 For discussion of Goethe and Ossian, see John Hennig, 'Goethe's Translation of Ossian's Songs of Selma', *Journal of English and Germanic Philology*, 45 (1946), pp. 77–81; Hennig, 'Goethe's Translation from Macpherson's Berathon', *Modern Language Review*, 42 (1947), pp. 127–30; and Howard Gaskill 'Ossian and Goethe Reconsidered', in *Goethe and the English-Speaking World: a Cambridge Symposium for His 250th Anniversary*, ed. Nicholas Boyle and John Guthrie (Rochester NY: Camden House, 2002), pp. 47–59. Goethe's contribution to the development of literary German is discussed by Eric A. Blackhall, *The Emergence of German as a Literary Language*, 2nd edn (Ithica: Cornell University Press, 1978), pp. 512–25.

23 See Gerald Bär, 'Ossian by Werther', *Journal for Eighteenth-Century Studies*, 39 (2016), pp. 223–34.

24 Gabriella Hartvig, 'Ossian in Hungary', in *The Reception of Ossian in Europe*, pp. 222–39.

6: Ossian's Impact on the Discovery of Ancient Scandinavian Literature

1 Dafydd Moore, 'General Introduction', in D. Moore (ed.), *Ossian and Ossianism*, vol. 1 (London and New York: Routledge, 2004), p. lix.

2 *The Works of Ossian, the Son of Fingal. Translated from the Galic Language by James Macpherson*, vol. 2 (London: T. Becket and P. A. De Hondt, 1765), pp. 115–16 note.

3 See *The Poems of Ossian, &c. Containing the Poetical Works of J. Macpherson, Esq. … with Notes and Illustrations by Malcolm Laing. Esq. …* (Edinburgh: A. Constable et al., 1805), pp. 151–52 note.

4 P. F. Suhm, *Om Odin og den hedniske gudelære og gudstieneste udi Norden* (Copenhagen: Berling, 1771), pp. 95–96; and *Historie af Danmark*, vol. 1 (Copenhagen: Berling, 1782), pp. 19–23.

5 Finnur Magnússon, *Forsøg til Forklaring over nogle Steder af Ossian, mest vedkommende Skandinaviens Hedenold* (Copenhagen: Skandinaviske Litteraturselskabs Skrifter, 1813).

6 *The Poems of Ossian. Translated by James Macpherson*, rev. ed., vol. 1 (London: W. Strahan and T. Becket, 1773), pp. 7–12.

7 Erik Skjöldebrand, 'Tal, innefattande en undersökning huruvida Ossians Sänger kunna förtjena våre Fornforskares upmarksamhet

jemte en jemnförelse emellem disse Sänger og de gamle Skandin-aviska Barder Qväden', in *Kongl. Vitterhets, Hitstorie och Antiquitets Akademiens Handlinar*, Part VII (Stockholm, 1802).

8   Cleanth Brooks (ed.), *The Correspondence of Thomas Percy and William Shenstone* (New Haven and London: Yale University Press, 1977), pp. 71, 74.

9   Thomas Percy (ed. and trans.), *Five Pieces of Runic Poetry Translated from the Islandic Language* (London: Dodsley, 1763). The preface is not paginated.

10 Paul-Henri Mallet, *Northern Antiquities: or, A Description of the Manners, Customs, Religion and Laws of the Ancient Danes, and Other Northern Nations; Including Those of Our Own Saxon Ancestors*, trans. T. Percy, vol. 1 (London: T. Carnan and Co., 1770), p. xix.

11 'Remarks on Bishop Percy's Preface', in Mallet, *Northern Antiquities*, new edition by I. A. Blackwell (London: Henry G. Bohn, 1847), pp. 22–45.

12 Hugh Blair, *A Critical Dissertation on the Poems of Ossian, the Son of Fingal* […] (London: T. Becket and P. A. De Hondt, 1765), p. 215.

13 Percy, *Five Pieces*, pp. x–xi.

14 Thomas Warton, 'Of the Origin of Romantic Fiction in Europe', in *The History of English Poetry, from the Close of the Eleventh to the Commencement of the Eighteenth Century. To which are Prefixed, Two Dissertations*, vol. 1 (London: J. Dodsley et al., 1774), p. lviii.

15 Ibid., pp. lii–liii.

16 John Pinkerton, *An Enquiry into the History of Scotland Preceding the Reign of Malcolm III. Or The Year 1056*, vol. 1 (London: John Nicols, 1789), p. 389.

17 Johann Gottfried Herder, *Schriften*, ed. K. O. Conrady (Munich: Rowohlt, 1968), p. 238.

18 Percy, *Five Pieces*, p. v.

19 Letter from October 1761, in Brooks, *Correspondence*, p. 124.

20 See Margaret Clunies Ross's *The Norse Muse in Britain 1750–1820* (Trieste: Edizioni Parnaso, 1998) for facsimile reproductions of *Fragments* and *Five Pieces* pp. 60, 62.

21 Percy, *Five Pieces*, p. vi.

22 Letter from Sep. 1761 to Shenstone, in Brooks, *Correspondence*, p. 71.

23 Percy, *Five Pieces*, p. iv.

24 See the updated discussion of Even-Zohar's theories in Philippe Codde, 'Polysystem Theory Revisited: A New Comparative Introduction', *Poetics Today* 24.1 (2003), pp. 91–126.

25 *The Letters of Thomas Gray*, ed. Duncan Tovey, vol. 2 (London: George Bell and Sons, 1904), pp. 146–47.
26 *Poems by Mr. Gray, A New Edition* (London: J. Dodsley, 1768), pp. 72–96, citation on p. 75.
27 Thomas James Mathias, *Runic Odes: Imitated from the Norse Tongue in the Manner of Mr. Gray* (London: T. Payne et al., 1781).
28 Frank Sayers, *Dramatic Sketches of the Ancient Northern Mythology* (London: J. Johnson, 1790).
29 George Allan, *Life of Sir Walter Scott: with Critical Notices of his Writings* (Edinburgh: T. Ireland Jnr, 1835 [1832]), p. 87.
30 Walter Scott, 'Introductory Remarks on Popular Poetry, and on Various Collections of Ballads of Britain, particularly Those of Scotland', in *Minstrelsy of the Scottish Border: Consisting of Historical and Romantic Ballads*, vol. 1 (Edinburgh: Longman et al., 1821), p. 74.
31 Walter Scott, *The Lay of the Last Minstrel: A Poem*, 4th edn (London: Longman et al., 1806), p. 326.
32 Scott recalls his composition of the poem in the 'Introduction' to *Lord of the Isles* (Edinburgh: A. and C. Black, 1857), pp. 16–17.
33 Walter Scott, *Harold the Dauntless*, in *Norse Romanticism: Themes in British Literature, 1760–1830*, ed. Robert W. Rix, A Romantic Circles Electronic Edition (2012), www.rc.umd.edu/editions/norse/index.html.
34 John Gibson Lockhart, *Memoirs of the Life of Sir Walter Scott*, vol. 3 (Edinburgh: R. Cadell, 1837), p. 190.
35 George Barry, *History of the Orkney Islands* (Edinburgh: Archibald, Constable & Co. 1805), pp. 489–95.
36 See, for example, advertisement [following the list of contents] in *Report of the Committee of the Highland Society of Scotland, appointed to enquire into the nature and authenticity of the poems of Ossian* (Edinburgh: Archibald Constable and Co., 1805).
37 For a reception history of Ossian in Scandinavia, see Gauti Kristmannsson, 'Ossian in the North', *Translation and Literature* 22 (2013), pp. 361–82.
38 Charlotte Christensen, 'Ossian-illustrationer i Danmark', *Fund og Forskning* 19 (1972), p. 10.
39 See Itamar Even-Zohar, *Papers in Culture Research* (2010), pp. 48–50. Ebook at www.tau.ac.il/~itamarez/works/books/EZ-CR-2005_2010.pdf.
40 See Gersternberg's article from *Briefe über die Merkwürdigkeiten der Litteratur* (1766), repr. in Wolf Gerhard Schmidt, *James Macphersons*

Ossian, zeitgenössische Diskurse und die Frühphase der deutschen Rezeption, vol. 4 (Berlin: Walter de Gruyter, 2003), pp. 623–24.
41 Ibid., vol. 1 (2004), pp. 527–42.
42 For an analysis of *Gedicht* in relation to Gersternberg's cultural 'in-between' identity, see Anne-Bitt Gerecke, *Transkulturalität als literarisches Programm: Heinrich Wilhelm von Gerstenbergs Poetik und Poesie* (Göttingen: Vandenhoeck & Ruprecht, 2002).
43 Quoted in Wolf Gerhard Schmidt, *Homer des Nordens und Mutter der Romantik: James Macphersons Ossian und seine Rezeption in der deutschsprachigen Literatur*, vol. 1 (Berlin: Walter de Gruyter, 2003), p. 519. Unless otherwise indicated, all translations are my own.
44 F. G. Klopstock, *Oden und Epigramme* (Leipzig: Philipp Reclam jun., 1945), pp. 142–43.
45 See Sandro Jung, 'The Reception and Reworking of Ossian in *Hermanns Schlacht*' in Howard Gaskill (ed.), *The Reception of Ossian in Europe* (London; New York: Thoemmes Continuum, 2004), pp. 143–55.
46 Letter from Ewald to P. F. Suhm, 9 Aug. 1780, in *Johannes Ewalds Samlede Skrifter*, vol. 4 (Copenhagen: Gyldendal, 1969), p. 375.
47 *Samtlige Skrifter*, I, 1780, p. xxxi. To read *Ossian*, Ewald taught himself English, which was an unusual language to undertake in Denmark at the time.
48 Citation from *Bidrag til den Oehlenschlägeriske litteraturs historie*, vol. 1. (Copenhagen: Samfundet til den danske litteraturs fremme, 1868), pp. 14–16.
49 For a discussion of Oehlenschläger's use of Norse metres, see Ida Falbe-Hansen, *Oehlenschlägers nordiske digtning og andre afhandlinger* (Copenhagen, Ascheschou, 1921), pp. 70–77.
50 Adam Oehlenschläger, *Poetiske Skrifter*, ed. H. Topsøe-Jensen, vol. 1 (Copenhagen: Gad, 1926), pp. 121–22.
51 F. J. Billeskov Jansen, 'Inledning', *Oehlenschläger Æstetiske Skrifter 1800–1812* (Copenhagen: Oehlenschläger Selskabet, 1980), p. xxiii.
52 'Blomster fra den nordiske Oldtid', *Bidrag*, p. 259.
53 'Forsøg til besvarelse af de ved Kiøbenhavns Universitet fremsatte Prisspøgsmaal', *Æstetiske skrifter 1800–1812*, ed F. J. Billeskov Jansen (Copenhagen: Oehlenschlägerselskabet, 1980), p. 19.
54 Adam Oehlenshläger, *Digte* (Copenhagen: F. R. Brummers Forlag, 1803 [date on title page]), pp. 75–82. The translation used in the following is by Claus Bratt Østergaard, in *European Romanticism: A Reader*, ed. Stephen Prickett (London: Continuum, 2010), pp. 437–43.

55 Adam Oehlenshläger, *Tale i Anledning af Thorvaldsens Hjemkomst til Fædrelandet, holden ved Festen den 16de October 1819* (Copenhagen, 1819), pp. 42–43. Translation from Kira Kofoed, 'Norse Mythology in Thorvaldsen's art', trans. David Possen, Thorvaldsen Museum Archives, arkivet.thorvaldsensmuseum.dk/articles/norse-mythology.
56 Steen Steensen Blicher, *Udvalgte værker*, vol. 3 (Copenhagen: Gyldendal / Blicher Selskabet, 1983), pp. 269–80.
57 *Steen Steensen Blicher* (1840), in *Udvalgte værker*, vol. 1 (Copenhagen: Gyldendal / Blicher Selskabet, 1982), p. 10.
58 Steen Steensen Blicher, *Ossian's Digte*, vol. 1 (Copenhagen: Den Wahlske Boghandling, 1847), p. 247. The ambiguity is shared in Gaelic: Lochlin is derived from Lochlann, the Gaelic word for Scandinavia, but the precise nature of where it referred to has never been properly identified (though it is usually taken to be Norway in that instance).

7: The Sigificance of James Macpherson's *Ossian* for Visual Artists

1 See Murdo Macdonald and Eric Shanes, 'Turner and Ossian's "The Traveller"', *Turner Society News*, Autumn 2013, pp. 4–7. Also, Murdo Macdonald, 'Found at Last: Turner's Lost Ossian Work', *Scottish Art News*, 21, Spring 2014, pp. 16–19.
2 For more detailed discussion of the French response to *Ossian*, see Murdo Macdonald, '*Ossian* and Art: Scotland into Europe via Rome', in Howard Gaskill (ed.), *The Reception of Ossian in Europe*, vol. v, Athlone Critical Traditions Series (London: Continuum, 2004). For wider context see Timothy Wilson-Smith, *Napoleon and his Artists* (London: Constable, 1996).
3 In doing so it complements and updates my chapter 'Ossian and Art: Scotland into Europe via Rome'.
4 The exhibition subsequently toured to New York, Chicago, and Montreal.
5 Calum Colvin, 2002, *Ossian: Fragments of Ancient Poetry / Oisein: Bloighean de Sheann Bhàrdachd* at the Scottish National Portrait Gallery.
6 See also, Calum Colvin, 2012, 'Ossian – An Epic Visual Journey' in Gerald Bar and Howard Gaskill (eds), *Ossian and National Epic* (Frankfurt: Peter Lang, 2012) pp. 291–313.
7 For a discussion of this see Murdo Macdonald, *Scottish Art* (London: Thames and Hudson, 2000), especially chapter four, 'Classicism and Celticism'.

8   John Gage, 'Turner and Stourhead: The Making of a Classicist?' *Art Quarterly*, 37, 1974, p. 87, n. 51. For the positive identification of Turner's Ossian work see Murdo Macdonald and Eric Shanes, 'Turner and Ossian's "The Traveller"', *Turner Society News*, Autumn 2013, pp. 4–7.
9   Sebastian Mitchell, *Visions of Britain* (Basingstoke: Palgrave Macmillan, 2013).
10 Howard Gaskill (ed.), *The Reception of Ossian in Europe*, vol. v, Athlone Critical Traditions Series (London: Continuum, 2004).
11 See, for example, Murdo Macdonald, 'Art and the Scottish Highlands: An Ossianic Perspective' in F. Ogee and M. Geracht (eds), *Interfaces, Image, Texte, Language*, No. 27, *Ossian Then And Now* (Paris: Université Paris Diderot, and Worcester, Mass: College of the Holy Cross, 2008).
12 Sebastian Mitchell, 'Celtic Postmodernism: Ossian and Contemporary Art' *Translation and Literature* 22, 2013, pp. 401–35.
13 Gayle Chong Kwan, *The Obsidian Isle* (Glasgow: Graphical House, 2011). This catalogue includes essays by, *inter alia*, Murdo Macdonald and Fiona Stafford.
14 Geoff MacEwan, *Temora* (Artist's Book, 2010).
15 Alexander Stoddart, *Cabinet Works and Studies* (Edinburgh: Bourne Fine Art, 2010).
16 For Shaw and Colvin's *Ossian* work considered together see Murdo Macdonald, 'Art as an Expression of Northernness: the Highlands of Scotland', *Visual Culture in Britain*, vol. 11, no. 3, November 2010, pp. 355–71.
17 *Uinneag Dhan Àird an Iar: Ath-lorg Ealain na Gàidhealtachd / Window to the West: the Rediscovery of Highland Art*, an exhibition held at the City Art Centre, Edinburgh, from 20 November 2010 to 6 March 2011, curated by Murdo Macdonald and Arthur Watson. See also Murdo Macdonald *et al.*, *Rethinking Highland Art: The Visual Significance of Gaelic Culture/Sealladh as ùr air Ealain na Gàidhealtachd: Brìgh Lèirsinn ann an Dualchas nan Gàidheal* (Edinburgh: Royal Scottish Academy, 2013).
18 Duncan Macmillan, 'Scottish Printmakers in the Eighteenth Century', in Geoffrey Bertram, *The Etchings of John Clerk of Eldin* (Thurloxton: Enterprise Editions, 2012).
19 Martin Myrone, *Bodybuilding: Reforming Masculinities in British Art 1750–1810* (New Haven and London: Yale University Press, 2006).
20 Sebastian Mitchell, 'Ossian and Ossianic Parallelism in James Barry's Works', *Eighteenth-Century Ireland* 23, 2008, pp. 94–120.

21 Joep Leerssen, 'The Bard's Garb: Ossian's Dress Sense' in Gerald Bar & Howard Gaskill (eds), *Ossian and National Epic* (Frankfurt: Peter Lang, 2012), pp. 277–89.
22 Calum Colvin, 'Ossian – An Epic Visual Journey' in Gerald Bar and Howard Gaskill, op. cit., pp. 291–312.
23 Henry Okun, 'Ossian in Painting', *Journal of the Warburg and Courtauld Institutes* vol. 30, 1967, pp. 327–56.
24 (i) Hannah Hohl and Hélène Toussaint, *Ossian* (Paris: Musées Nationaux, 1974). (ii) Hannah Hohl and Hélène Toussaint, *Ossian und die Kunst um 1800* (Munich: Prestel, 1974). Both are catalogues of the closely related exhibitions at Grand Palais, Paris (15 February to 15 April, 1974), and Kunsthalle, Hamburg (8 May to 26 June, 1974).
25 Werner Spies, 'The Nordic Homer and Romanticism', written in 1974 and reprinted in Spies, W., *Focus on Art* (New York: Rizzoli, 1982), pp. 17–20.
26 William St Clair, *The Reading Nation in the Romantic Period* (Cambridge: Cambridge University Press, 2004).
27 Dafydd Moore, 'The Reception of *Ossian* in England and Scotland', in Howard Gaskill (ed.), *The Reception of Ossian in Europe* (London: Continuum, 2004), pp. 21–39; 39.
28 William Stukeley, 1763, *A Letter from Dr Stukeley to Mr Macpherson on his Publication of Fingal and Temora. With a Print of Cathmor's Shield*, London: printed by R. Hett, sold by J. Baillie. Reprinted in Dafydd Moore (ed.), *Ossian and Ossianism: Volume III: Critical Writings* (London: Routledge, 2004), pp. 105–13.
29 Robert Huish, *The historical gallery of celebrated men ... exhibiting a series of authentic portraits by artists of the first celebrity, accompanied by biogr. sketches and observations* (London: Thomas Kelly, 1830). Entry on 'John Bacon', pp. 1–2.
30 Thanks to Helen Smailes of the National Galleries of Scotland for that interesting speculation.
31 Huish, *The historical gallery of celebrated men ...*
32 The British Museum date of '1753 (circa)' is wrong, and probably a typographical error because it is inconsistent with the Museum's other holdings of Pine's work, which date in the main from the 1760s and the 1770s.
33 A copy can be found in the British Museum.
34 For more on Barry's contribution see Murdo Macdonald, 2004, op. cit.; and Sebastian Mitchell, S., 2008, op. cit.
35 See Macdonald, 2004, op. cit., p. 398.

36 Murdo Macdonald, 'Art as an Expression of Northernness: the Highlands of Scotland', *Visual Culture in Britain*, vol. 11, no. 3, November 2010, pp. 355–71 (p. 363).
37 Murdo Macdonald, 'The Visual Preconditions of Celtic Revival Art in Scotland', *Journal of the Scottish Society for Art History*, vol. 13, *Highlands* issue, 2008–2009, pp. 16–21 (p. 16).
38 Dawson Turner (ed.), *The Literary Correspondence of John Pinkerton*, 2 vols (London: Colburn and Bentley, 1830), vol. II, p. 92. Quoted in Sam Smiles, *The Image of Antiquity: Ancient Britain and the Romantic Imagination*, (New Haven and London: Yale University Press, 1994), p. 69. Quoted in Mitchell, 2014, *op. cit.*, p. 103.
39 Ewen Cameron, 1776, *The Fingal of Ossian, An Ancient Galic Poem in Six Books Translated from the Galic by J. Macpherson and Rendered into Heroic Verse by E. Cameron*. See Sebastian Mitchell, 'Ossian and Ossianic Parallelism in James Barry's Works', *Eighteenth-Century Ireland* 23, 2008, pp. 94–120 (pp. 104–05).
40 Perth and Kinross Museums.
41 Musée des Arts Decoratifs, Paris.
42 Robert Rosenblum, *Transformations in Late Eighteenth Century Art* (Princeton: Princeton University Press, 1967), pp. 46–49.
43 Luigi Zandomeneghi, engr. Felice Zuliani, 'Ossian invita al canto la mesta Malvina' in *I Canti di Ossian pensieri d'un Anonimo, disegnati, et incise a Contorno* (Venezia: Giuseppe Battaggia, 1817).
44 Fernando Mazzocca, 'La Fortuna Figurativa di Ossian in Italia Negli Anni Della Restaurazione', in Gennaro Barbarisi e Guilo Carnazzi (eds), *Aspetti dell'Opera e della Fortuna di Melchiorre Cesarotti*, 2 vols (Milano: Cisalpino, 2002), pp. 835–55. Zandomeneghi's Ossian and Malvina work is reproduced on page 847, and is also reproduced on the cover. See also Murdo Macdonald, 2013 'Italy and the Response to Ossian in Visual Art', at www.ossianet.it/wp-content/uploads/2014/08/MM-Padua-Paper-edited.pdf.
45 Camillo Guerra, 1825, 'Ossian e Malvina', Napoli, Museo Nazionale di Capodamonte. See Mazzocca, op. cit., p. 854.
46 Giacomo Trécourt, 1846, 'Ossian che canta a Malvina le gesta di Carthon', Brescia, Civici Musei d'Arte e Storia. See Mazzocca, op. cit., p. 853.
47 Guiseppe De Nigris, 1859, 'Ossian e Malvina', Caserta, Palazzo Reale. See Mazzocca, op. cit., p. 855.
48 Guildhall, Totnes, Devon, England. For a short biography of Brockedon see Lise Wilkinson 'William Brockedon, F.R.S. (1787–1854)', Notes

and Records of the Royal Society of London, vol. 26, no. 1 (June 1971), pp. 65–72.
49 For more on this see Murdo Macdonald, (in press) 'James Macpherson's Ossian and European Art' for *Scottish Studies International*.
50 Mary Potter, *Poetry of Nature* (London: Caslon, 1789).
51 See Colm Ó Baoill (ed.), *Bàrdachd Shìlis na Ceapaich* (Edinburgh: Scottish Gaelic Texts Society, 1972).
52 See Colm Ó Baoill (ed.), *Màiri nighean Alasdair Ruaidh: Song-maker of Skye and Berneray* (Glasgow: Scottish Gaelic Texts Society, 2014).
53 For general context see Murdo Macdonald, 'Anima Celtica: embodying the soul of the nation in 1890s Edinburgh', in T. Cusack and S. Bhreathnach-Lynch (eds), *Art, Nation and Gender: Ethnic Landscapes, Myths and Mother-Figures* (Aldershot: Ashgate, 2003). For specific identification of the figure with Ella Carmichael see Murdo Macdonald, 'The Visual Dimension of *Carmina Gadelica*' in D. U. Stiubhart (ed.), *The Life and Legacy of Alexander Carmichael* (Port of Ness: The Islands Book Trust, 2008), pp. 135–45.
54 But see, e.g., Macdonald, 2004, op. cit.
55 Robert Rosenblum, *Modern Painting and the Northern Romantic Tradition* (London: Thames & Hudson, 1975), p. 41.
56 Statens Museum for Kunst, Copenhagen.
57 Colin J. Bailey, 'George Augustus Wallis in Italy', in *Scotland and Italy* (Edinburgh: Scottish Society for Art History, 1989), pp. 28–58 (p. 39).
58 Mitchell B. Frank, *Central European Drawings from the National Gallery of Canada* (Ottowa: National Gallery of Canada, 2007), pp. 98–99.
59 Ibid., p. 98.
60 Okun, op. cit., pp. 341–42.
61 Toledo Museum of Art, Ohio, USA. Oil on canvas.
62 For this dating see Anne Macleod, *From an Antique Land* (Edinburgh: Birlinn, 2012), p. 76. One of these certificates is on public display in the West Highland Museum in Fort William. The certificate itself was printed from a wood engraving by Luke Clennell (1781–1840). It is regarded as one of his finest pieces.
63 New York: Ezra Sargeant.

8: Macpherson's *Iliad* and the Logic of Literary Primitivism

1 Cited in Thomas Bailey Saunders, *The Life and Letters of James Macpherson* (London and New York: S. Sonnenschein & Co., 1894), pp. 220–21.

2   Hume, *Letters*, ed. J. Y. T. Grieg, 2 vols, (Oxford: Oxford University Press, 1932), II, p. 180; Mason and Walpole in Walpole, *Correspondence*, ed. W. S. Lewis *et al.* (Oxford and Yale: Yale University Press, 1955), XVIII, p. 64, p. 71.

3   George Steiner, *Homer in English* (London: Penguin, 1996); David Hopkins, 'Homer', in David Hopkins and Charles Martindale (eds), *The Oxford History of Classical Reception in English Literature, vol. 3 (1660-1790)* (Oxford: Oxford University Press, 2012), pp. 165-96.

4   Sebastian Mitchell, 'Macpherson, Ossian, and Homer's *Iliad*' in Howard Gaskill and Gerald Bar (eds), *Ossian and National Epic* (Frankfurt am Main: Peter Lang, 2012), pp. 55-71 (p. 55).

5   James Macpherson, *The Iliad of Homer translated by James Macpherson Esq.*, 2 vols, (London: T. Becket and P. A. De Hondt, 1773), I, p. xix. Future references are to volume and page and appear parenthetically in the text.

6   The challenges of translating Greek measures into English were well recognised. See David Fairer, 'Lyric and Elegy' in *Oxford History of Classical Reception in English Literature volume 3*, p. 520.

7   Alexander Pope, *The Iliad of Homer, Translated by Mr Pope*, 2nd edn, 6 vols (London: B. Lintot, 1720). Future reference are to this edition and appear, giving book and line number, parenthetically in the text.

8   John Dryden, *Fables Ancient and Modern* (London: J. Tonson, 1700), p. 189.

9   Adam Potkay, 'Virtue and Manners in Macpherson's *Poems of Ossian*' *PMLA* 107 (1992), pp. 120-31 (p. 124).

10 Paul deGategno, *James Macpherson* (Boston: Twayne, 1987), p. 79.

11 Hopkins, 2012, p. 184.

12 Noting the errors and inconsistencies in Macpherson's handling of classical paratexts and their translations, Mitchell suggests that 'a general sense of correspondence' rather than 'scholarly exactitude' is the aim (2012, p. 56). What seems to be the case in this 'general sense' is that, whatever Macpherson's later strictures on the subject, he is taking it for granted that Pope provides an adequate insight into Homer.

13 Thomas Blackwell, *An Enquiry into the Life and Writings of Homer* (London: np, 1735), pp. 72-73.

14 Kathryn Temple, *Scandal Nation: Law and Authorship in Britain, 1750-1832* (Ithaca: Cornell University Press, 2003), p. 97; Margaret Russett, *Fictions and Fakes: Forging Romantic Authenticity, 1760-1845*

(Cambridge: Cambridge University Press, 2006), p. 4. For the seminal importance of Macpherson's combination of primitive poet and scholarly apparatus, see also Robert Crawford, *The Modern Poet: Poetry, Academia, and Knowledge Since the 1750s* (Oxford: Oxford University Press) p. 53.

15 Daniel Webb [?], *Fingal Reclaimed* (1763) in Dafydd Moore (ed.), *Ossian and Ossianism* (London, 2004), III, p. 82.

16 See, for example, *The Critical Review* 12 (December 1761), pp. 405–18 and 13 (January 1762) pp. 45–53; and *The Monthly Review* 26 (January 1762) pp. 41–57 and 27 (February 1762) pp. 130–41. These and other such documents are reprinted in volume 3 of Moore's *Ossian and Ossianism* (2004).

17 Hopkins, 2012, p. 188.

18 Hopkins, *Conversing with Antiquity: English Poets and the Classics, from Shakespeare to Pope* (Oxford: Oxford University Press, 2010), p. 36, p. 30.

19 Mitchell, 2012, p. 61.

20 For this wider historiographical context, see Nicholas Philipson, 'The Scottish Enlightenment' in R. Porter and M. Teich (eds), *The Scottish Enlightenment in National Context* (Cambridge: Cambridge University Press, 1981), pp. 19–40; Colin Kidd, *Subverting Scotland's Past: Scottish Whig Historians and the Creation of an Anglo-British Identity, 1689-c.1830* (Cambridge: Cambridge University Press, 1993); Karen O'Brien, *Narratives of Enlightenment: Cosmopolitan History From Voltaire to Gibbon* (Cambridge: Cambridge University Press, 1997).

21 Donald Foerster, *Homer in English Criticism: The Historical Approach in the Eighteenth Century* (New Haven and London: Yale University Press, 1947), p. 118.

22 See, for example, O'Brien, '"These Nations Newton Made his Own": Poetry, Knowledge, and British Imperial Globalisation' in Daniel Carey and Lynn Festa (eds), *The Postcolonial Enlightenment: Eighteenth-Century Colonialism and Postcolonial Theory* (Oxford: Oxford University Press, 2009).

23 See the introduction to Hopkins, *Conversing with Antiquity* (pp. 1–36) for a succinct survey of the field in these terms.

9: Principles, Prejudices, and the Politics of James Macpherson's Historical Writing

1 Karen O'Brien, *Narratives of Enlightenment: Cosmopolitan History from Voltaire to Gibbon* (Cambridge: Cambridge University Press,

1997); Noelle Gallagher, *Historical Literatures: Writing About the Past in England, 1660–1740* (Manchester: Manchester University Press, 2012); Mark Salber Phillips, *Society and Sentiment: Genres of Historical Writing in Britain, 1740–1820* (Princeton: Princeton University Press, 2000); and J. G. A. Pocock, *Barbarism and Religion: Volume Two – Narratives of Civil Government* (Cambridge: Cambridge University Press, 1999).

2   See Ian Haywood, *The Making of History: A Study of the Literary Forgeries of James Macpherson and Thomas Chatterton in Relation to Eighteenth-Century Ideas of Fiction and History* (London: Associated University Press, 1986).

3   James Macpherson, *A Short History of the Opposition during the Last Session of Parliament* (London: T. Cadell, 1779), hereafter *Short History*; and James Macpherson, *The History and Management of the East-India Company, from its Origin in 1600 to the Present Times* (London: T. Cadell, 1779).

4   James Macpherson, *The History of Great Britain, from the Restoration, to the Accession of the House of Hannover*, 2 vols (London: W. Strahan and T. Cadell, 1775), hereafter *History*.

5   See Rebecca Bullard, *The Politics of Discourse, 1674–1725: Secret History Narratives* (London: Pickering and Chatto, 2009), pp. 185–86.

6   Lionel Grossman, 'Anecdote and History', *History and Theory* 42.2 (May 2003), pp. 143–68.

7   James Macpherson, *Original Papers: Containing the Secret History of Great Britain, from the Restoration, to the Accession of the House of Hannover*, 2 vols, (London: W. Strahan and T. Cadell, 1775). Hereafter *Original Papers*. Compare Steven Pincus, *England's Glorious Revolution 1688–1689: A Brief History with Documents* (Boston: Bedford St Martin's, 2006).

8   Footnotes were controversial, being regarded as a benefit by some scholars and as an anathema to others. See also Nigel Leask, *Robert Burns and Pastoral: Poetry and Improvement in Late Eighteenth-Century Scotland* (Oxford: Oxford University Press, 2010).

9   David Hume, 'To William Strahan' [August 1770], *The Letters of David Hume*, ed. J. Y. T. Greig, 3 vols, (Oxford: Clarendon Press, 1932), II, p. 230. The letter is prompted by Robertson's commencement of his *History of America* and several other histories then 'on the stocks'.

10 James Macpherson, *The Rights of Great Britain Asserted against the Claims of America: being an Answer to the Declaration of the General Congress* (London: T. Cadell, 1776). See also Kathleen Wilson, *The*

Sense of the People: Politics, Culture and Imperialism in England, 1715–1785 (Cambridge: Cambridge University Press, 1995), p. 241.
11 Pocock, *Barbarism and Religion*, p. 257. For this context see John Brewer, *Party Ideology and Popular Politics at the Accession of George III* (Cambridge: Cambridge University Press, 1976); and Stephen Conway, *The British Isles and the War of American Independence* (Oxford: Clarendon, 2000).
12 See Catherine Macaulay, *The History of England from the Accession of James I to that of the Brunswick Line*, 4 vols (London: Edward and Charles Dilly, 1769–71); Edmund Burke, *Thoughts on the Cause of the Present Discontents* (London: J. Dodsley, 1770); and *The History of American Taxation* (London: J. Dodsley, 1775). References in this essay are taken from *Writings and Speeches of Edmund Burke*, Gen. ed. Paul Langford, 8 vols (Oxford: Clarendon, 1981–2015).
13 See Burke, *Writings and Speeches*, II, pp. 270–79, 314–18. See also Robert W Jones, *Literature, Gender and Politics in Britain during the War for America, 1770–1785* (Cambridge: Cambridge University Press, 2011), chapter 1.
14 Deidre Shauna Lynch, *The Economy of Character: Novels, Market Culture, and the Business of Inner Meaning* (Chicago: Chicago University Press, 1998), introduction.
15 Dafydd Moore, 'James Macpherson and Celtic Whiggism', *Eighteenth-Century Life*, 30, (2005), pp. 1–24; and Murray G. H. Pittock, *Poetry and Jacobite Politics in Eighteenth-Century Britain and Ireland* (Cambridge: Cambridge University Press, 1995).
16 James Macpherson, *The History of Great Britain, from the Restoration, to the Accession of the House of Hannover*, 2 vols (Dublin: J. Exshaw, D. Chamberlain, J. Potts, and seven others), I, p. 513.
17 See David Hume, 'Of the Study of History' in *Essays Moral, Political and Literary*, ed. Eugene F. Miller (Indianapolis: LibertyClassics, 1985), pp. 563–68.
18 Burke, *Writings and Speeches*, II, p. 453.
19 See Mark Salber Phillips, *On Historical Distance* (New Haven: Yale University Press, 2013).
20 See G. J. Barker-Benfield, *The Culture of Sensibility: Sex and Society in Eighteenth-Century Britain* (Chicago: University of Chicago Press, 1992); and John Mullan, *Sentiment and Sociability: The Language of Feeling in the Eighteenth Century* (Oxford: Clarendon Press, 1988).
21 Philips, *Society and Sentiment*, pp. 40–42.
22 Pocock, *Barbarism and Religion*, pp. 177–98.

23 Charles Polhill, *Reflections on a Pamphlet, entitled, A Short History of Opposition* (Sevenoaks: G. Stout, 1779).
24 Dafydd Moore, 'James Macpherson and William Faulkner: A Sensibility of Defeat' in Fiona Stafford and Howard Gaskill (eds), *From Gaelic to Romantic: Ossianic Translations* (Amsterdam: Rodopi, 1998), pp. 164–82.

Further Reading

There has been an upsurge in interest in Macpherson and *Ossian* since the mid-1980s. The following list identifies some key initial resources, representative readings, and starting points for further investigation. It is highly selective. The bibliography noted below is recommended for a more detailed descriptive and thematic bibliography.

Bibliography

Moore, Dafydd, 'James Macpherson' in *Oxford Bibliographies in British and Irish Literature*. www.oxfordbibliographies.com/view/document/obo-9780199846719/obo-9780199846719-0066.xml

Editions

Gaskill, Howard (ed.), *The Poems of Ossian and Related Works* (Edinburgh: University of Edinburgh Press, 1996) – A standard modern edition also containing Hugh Blair's *Critical Dissertation on the Poems of Ossian*.

Moore, Dafydd (ed.), *Ossian and Ossianism*, 4 vols, (London and New York: Routledge, 2004) – Four volumes of *Ossian* and *Ossian*-related primary sources (including the critical and creative response to the poems) and a wide-ranging introduction. Facsimile text of the poems themselves highlights effects of notes on reading experience.

Books devoted to Macpherson

Gaskill, Howard (ed.), *Ossian Revisited* (Edinburgh: University of Edinburgh Press, 1991) – A collection of ten essays covering a variety of aspects of Macpherson's Scottish Enlightenment context and reception.

Gaskill, Howard (ed.), *The Reception of Ossian in Europe* (London: Continuum, 2004) – Twenty essays recounting *Ossian*'s impact in fifteen different parts of Europe and its influence in art, music, and literary criticism. Also contains a valuable timeline of responses across Europe.

Moore, Dafydd, *Enlightenment and Romance in the Poems of Ossian* (Burlington and Aldershot: Ashgate, 2003) – Book-length study of the central themes of Ossian – the sentimental, the sublime, the cult of defeat – through the lens of genre.

'Macpherson's Ossian', *Scotlands* 4.1 Special Issue (1997)

Stafford, Fiona, *The Sublime Savage: A Study of James Macpherson and the Poems of Ossian* (Edinburgh: Edinburgh University Press, 1987) – Seminal biography and bedrock of modern Macpherson revisionism.

Stafford, Fiona, and Howard Gaskill (eds), *From Gaelic to Romantic: Ossianic Translations* (Amsterdam: Rodopi, 1998) – Seventeen essays on various aspects of Ossian.

Thomson, Derick, *The Gaelic Sources of Macpherson's Ossian* (Edinburgh: Aberdeen University Press, 1952).

Chapters/Articles

Gibbons, Luke, 'The Sympathetic Bond: Ossian, Celticism and Colonialism' in Terence Brown (ed.), *Celticism* (Amsterdam: Rodopi, 1996).

Potkay, Adam, 'Virtue and Manners in Macpherson's *Poems of Ossian*', *PMLA* 107 (1992), pp. 120–30.

Sher, Richard, '"Those Scotch Imposters and their Cabal": Ossian and the Scottish Enlightenment' in Roger Emerson (ed.), *Man and Nature: Proceedings of the Canadian Society for Eighteenth-Century Studies* (London, Ontario: Canadian Society for Eighteenth-Century Studies, 1982), pp. 55–63.

Stafford, Fiona, 'Romantic Macpherson' in Murray Pittock (ed.), *The Edinburgh Companion to Scottish Romanticism* (Edinburgh: Edinburgh University Press, 2011).

Significant treatment in broader studies

Davis, Leith, *Acts of Union: Scotland and the Literary Negotiation of the British Nation 1707–1830* (Stanford: Cambridge University Press, 1998).

Haywood, Ian, *The Making of History: A Study of the Literary Forgeries of James Macpherson and Thomas Chatterton in relation to Eighteenth-Century Ideas of History and Fiction* (Rutherford, NJ: Fairleigh Dickinson University Press, 1987).

McGann, Jerome, *The Poetics of Sensibility: A Revolution in Literary Style* (Oxford: Oxford University Press, 1996).

Mitchell, Sebastian, *Visions of Britain 1730–1830: Anglo-Scottish Writing and Representation* (Basingstoke: Palgrave, 2013).

Pittock, Murray, *Scottish and Irish Romanticism* (Oxford: Oxford University Press, 2008).

Simpson, Kenneth, *The Protean Scot: The Crisis of Identity in Eighteenth-Century Scottish Literature* (Aberdeen: Aberdeen University Press, 1988).

Shields, Juliet, *Sentimental Literature and Anglo-Scottish Identity, 1745–1820* (Cambridge: Cambridge University Press, 2010).

Trumpener, Katie, *Bardic Nationalism: The Romantic Novel and the British Empire* (Princeton: Princeton University Press, 1997).

Weinbrot, Howard, *Britannia's Issue: The Rise of British Literature from Dryden to Ossian* (Cambridge: Cambridge University Press, 1993).

Womack, Peter, *Improvement and Romance: Constructing the Myth of the Highlands* (Basingstoke: Macmillan, 1989).

Notes on Contributors

Paul J. deGategno is Professor of English at the Pennsylvania State University, Brandywine. Author of *James Macpherson* (1989), *Ivanhoe: The Mask of Chivalry* (1994), and *The Critical Companion to Jonathan Swift* (2006), he is currently working on Macpherson's government pamphlets.

Robert W. Jones is a Senior Lecturer in Eighteenth-Century Literature at University of Leeds. His most recent book is *Literature, Gender and Politics in Britain during the War for America 1770–1785* (2011). With Martyn J. Powell (Aberystwyth), he is currently leading a Leverhulme-funded project on Richard Brinsley Sheridan's political career and cultural involvements.

Gauti Kristmannsson is Professor of Translation Studies at the University of Iceland. Having studied English at the University of Iceland, Scottish literature at Edinburgh University, and translation studies at Johannes Gutenberg-University in Mainz/Germersheim, he has published on Scottish and German literature and translation studies, translated scholarly works and poetry, and written on Icelandic contemporary literature.

Cordula Lemke is Professor of English Literature at Freie Universität Berlin. Author of *Wandel in der Erfahrung: Die Konstruktion von Welt in den Romanen von Virginia Woolf und Jeanette Winterson* (2004), she coedited *Joseph Conrad (1857–1924)* (2007) and *Weeds and Viruses: Ecopolitics and the Demands of Theory* (2016), has published on gender studies, postcolonial studies and nineteenth- to twenty-first-century literature, and is currently working on a book project on Scottish hospitality.

NOTES ON CONTRIBUTORS

Murdo Macdonald is Professor of History of Scottish Art at Dundee University. Author of *Scottish Art* in Thames and Hudson's World of Art series, he was made an honorary member of the Royal Scottish Academy in 2009 and an honorary fellow of the Association for Scottish Literary Studies in 2016.

Sebastian Mitchell is Senior Lecturer in English Literature at Birmingham University. Having written widely on eighteenth- and early nineteenth-century literature and art, his *Visions of Britain, 1730–1830: Anglo-Scottish Writing and Representation* (2013) was shortlisted for the Saltire Society research book of the year. He has edited a special *Journal for Eighteenth-Century Studies* issue on Ossian. His transhistorical study of the literature of idealism, *Utopia and its Discontents*, will be published in 2017.

Dafydd Moore is Professor of Eighteenth-Century Literature at the University of Plymouth. He has published widely on Macpherson and Ossian, including *Enlightenment and Romance in the Poems of Ossian* (2003) and *Ossian and Ossianism* in four volumes (2004).

Lesa Ní Mhunghaile lectures in Irish at the National University of Ireland, Galway, and has published on various aspects of Gaelic scribal culture and interaction between Protestant antiquarians and Gaelic scribes during the eighteenth century. Her books include *Ré Órga na nGael: Joseph Cooper Walker (1761–1810)* (2013), recipient of a 2014 American Conference for Irish Studies book award, and *Rí na Gréine: Aistí i gcuimhne ar An Seabhac* (2015), co-edited with Ríonach uí Ógáin and Deirdre Ní Loingsigh.

Robert W. Rix is Associate Professor at Copenhagen University, publishing on eighteenth-century politics, book history, nationalism and antiquarianism, *William Blake and the Cultures of Radical Christianity* appearing in 2007. Having published on late eighteenth- and early nineteenth-century British reception of Nordic legend and mythology and anthologising original texts (*Norse Romanticism: Themes in British Literature 1760–1830* [2012]), he published, on earlier periods, *The Barbarian North in Medieval Imagination: Ethnicity, Legend, and Literature* (2015).

Index

Aberdeen University, 1
Abildgaard, Nicolai, 102
 Blind Ossian Singing (painting), 99
 Fingal Sees the Ghosts of his Forefathers by Moonlight (painting), 85
 Ossian Sings His Swan Song (painting), 85
Act of Proscription (1747), 100
Act of Union (1707), 130
Adam, 61
'Agallamh na Seanórach' ('The Colloquy of the Ancients'), 27, 28, 30
Agallamh Oisin agus Phadraig, 29
America, 17–18, 22, 103, 104, 131
'An Ionmhuinn', 33
An Leabhar Mòr / The Great Book of Gaelic, 94
analepsis, 72
Anderson, Alexander, 104
Angliota, 30
Anglo-Scottish cultural relations, 7
Anne, Queen, 130
'archipelagic' ('four nations') approach, 8, 9

'Ard Aigneach Goll' ('*The Praise of Goll*'), 33
Arminius, 87
Arnold, Matthew, 46
astrological approach, 98
authorship, 41

Bacon, John, *Head of Ossian* (sculpture), 98
Badenoch, 26
Bailey, Colin, 103
Balavil (Belville), 6, 98
Baldwin, Henry, 20
Balgowan, 15
ballads *see* Fionn ballads
Bar, Gerald and Gaskill, Howard, *Ossian and the National Epic*, eds., 95
Baratti, Antonio, 97, 98, 99
Bardengebrull, 87
bardic tradition, 62–63, 66 *see also* female bards
Barry, George, *History of the Orkney Islands*, 85
Barry, James, 95
 The Progress of Human Culture (mural), 98, 99
Barthes, Roland, 'Death of the Author', 41

Bartholin, Thomas, 83
  Antiquitatum Danicarum de causis contempta a Danis adhuc gentilibus mortis (Danish Antiquities about the Pagan Danes' Disdain of Death), 80
'Bás Chonlaoich' ('The Death of Conlaoch'), 33, 34
'Bás Fhraoich' ('Fraoch's Death'), 27
Basire, James, 99
Bassnett, Susan and Trivedi, Harish, 53
'The Battle of Lora', 33
Bauman, Richard and Briggs, Charles, 55
Becket, Thomas, 20, 21
Bellay, Joachim du, 42
Benfield, Paul, 21
Berrathon, 74, 97, 100
Bible, 40, 41, 42
Blackwell, I. A., 79
Blackwell, Thomas the Younger, *Enquiry into the Life and Writings of Homer*, 113
Blair, Hugh
  Critical Dissertation on the Poetry of Ossian, the Son of Fingal, 71
  on *Fragments*, 3, 4, 15, 16, 66
  on Homer, 105
  influence, 31, 70
  and Johnson, 7
  on Ossian, 35
  St Clair on, 96
  and translation, 46
Blake, William, 98, 99
Blicher, Steen Steensen, 90, 91
  Digte (Poems), 90
  E Bindstouw, 90
  Jyllandsrejse i sex Dogn (Travels in Jutland over Six Days), 90
blindness, 62, 63
Book of Leinster, 28
Book of the Dean of Lismore, 30, 32, 33, 145n36
Boswell, James, 4, 50, 139n12
Boutcher, W., 43
Boym, Svetlana, 56, 57
Bragi, 87
Brockedon, William, *Ossian Relating the Fate of Oscar to Malvina* (painting), 101
Brooke, Charlotte, *Reliques of Irish Poetry*, 32
'Bruidhean Chaorthainn' ('The Rowan-tree Dwelling'), 32
Burgoyne, John, 131
Burke, Edward, 131
  History of American Taxation, 125
  Thoughts on the Cause of the Present Discontents, 121, 122
Burns, Robert, 98
Bute, Lord, 18

Calmar, 71, 72
Camelford, Cornwall, 5
Cameron, Ewen, 48, 100
Canova, Antonio, 100
Carlyle, Alexander, 139n12
Carmichael, Ella, 102
Carmichael, Stewart, 100
Carstens, Asmus Jacob, 85
  Fingal and the Spirit of Loda (painting), 103
  Fingal Battling Loda (painting), 86

'Carthon', 33, 34, 69
'Cath Finntrágha' ('*The Battle of Ventry*'), 28, 31, 34
'Cath Gabhra' ('*The Battle of Gabhra*'), 28
'Cath Ríogh na Sorcha' ('*The Battle with the King of Sorcha*'), 29
Catholicism, 123, 128, 132
Celtic culture, 77–78, 80
Celtic Revival, 95
Cesarotti, Melchiorre, 101
  Poesie di Ossian, trans., 97, 99, 102
Cesarotti Project, University of Padua, 100
Charles II, King, 122, 123, 124, 125
chivalry, 37
Chong Kwan, Gayle, 94
Christian VIII, Crown Prince of Denmark, 86
Christianity, 34, 41, 42, 57–61, 84
Cicero, 41
City Art Centre Edinburgh, 94
Classical Gaelic, 27
classicism, 76, 94, 102
Clessámmor, 33, 69
'Clutha' or 'Cluäth' (Clyde), 69
Coade, Eleanor, 98
Coimín, Micheál, 30, 31
Colvin, Calum, 94, 95
  Ossian: Fragments of Ancient Poetry / Oisein: Bloighean de Sheann Bhardachd (exhibition), 93
'The Complaint of Harold', 80
'Cona' (Glencoe), 69, 71, 72, 73
Conchobar mac Nessa, King, 28
Conlaoch, 33
'contributionist' argument, 8

Conway, Henry S., 18
Copenhagen, 76
Cordiner, Charles
  Antiquities and Scenery in the North of Scotland, 99
  Cascade near Carril (painting), 99, 100, 103
Cotman, John Sell, 74, 99
Cowper, William, 116
Crawford, Robert, 6, 7, 16, 70
Cromla, 68, 71, 72
Cronin, Michael, 42
Crugal, 114, 115
Cuchullin (Cú Chulainn), 28, 33, 55, 58–62, 67, 68, 71–72
Culloden, 1, 100

Dacier, Anne, 49
Dante, *De vulgari eloquentia*, 42
De Nigris, Guiseppe, 101
'The Death Song of Regnar Lodbrog', 80
deGategno, Paul, 4, 110
Denis, Michael, 86, 87
Denmark, 69, 77, 78, 86, 88, 91
Dillon, Wentworth, 44
Dryden, John, 43, 44–45, 51, 106, 108–09, 112, 113
'Duan a' Ghairbh', 33
'Duan na n-Inghinn' ('*The Ballad of the Maiden*'), 33
Duanaire Finn (*The Poem Book of Fionn*), 29, 30, 35, 35, 37
Duncan, John, 95
  Anima Celtica (illustration), 101, 102
Dunscaich, Isle of Skye, 68

'The Earl of Orkney and the King of Norway's Daughter', 85

'Eas Ruaidh' ('*Assaroe*'), 29, 32
East India Company, 5, 18, 19, 21, 22, 24
Echtrae Chonnlai, 30
Edinburgh Review, 2
Edinburgh, University of, 2, 15
engravings, 92, 96, 97, 104
Enlightenment, 52, 54, 60, 64, 117
Ernest, Max, 96
etchings, 97, 98
Even-Zohar, Itamar, 82
Ewald, Johannes
    Balders Dod (The Death of Balder), 87, 88
    Rolf Krake, 87

female bards, 101, 102 *see also* Malvina
Ferdiad, 34
Ferguson, Adam, 2, 4
fianna warriors, 27, 28, 29, 30, 36, 37
Fiannaigheacht see Fionn ballads
figurative painting, 92, 103
Fingal Regained (pamphlet), 114
'Fingal's visit to Norway', 33
Fionn ballads (*Fiannaigheacht*), 26, 27–28, 30, 31, 32, 35, 37–38, 64
Flaxman, John, 101
Fletcher, Archibald, 26, 27, 33
Flitcroft, Henry, 94
Foerster, Donald, 117
folklore, 84, 90
'four nations' ('archipelagic') approach, 8, 9
Fox, Charles James, 131
Francia, François Louis Thomas, 74
Frank, Mitchell, 103

Fraser-Mackintosh, Charles, *Antiquarian Notes*, 6
Fuseli, Henry, 98

Gaelic language, 42, 69
Gaelic literature, 2, 3, 7, 8, 141n2
    heroic, 26, 27–31
    Macpherson and, 31–38
Gage, John, 94
Garrick, David, 20, 139n12
Gaskill, Howard, 73
    The Reception of Ossian in Europe, ed., 93, 95
genre, 7, 31, 43, 45, 55, 86, 128
George III, King, 6
Gérard, François, 92
Germany, 75, 76, 77–78, 80, 118
Gerstenberg, Heinrich Wilhelm von, *Gedicht eines Skalden* (Poem of a Skald), 86
Gibbon, Edward, *Decline and Fall of the Roman Empire*, 121
Girodet, Anne-Louis, *Ossian Receiving the Ghosts of French Heroes* (painting), 92, 93
Girtin, Thomas, 74, 99, 103
Goethe, Johann Wolfgang von, 96
    Die Leiden des jungen Werthers (*The Sorrows of Young Werther*), 74, 75
Goldsmith, Oliver, 120
Gothic tradition, 39, 76, 78, 79–82, 87, 91
Grafton, Duke of, 19, 20
Graham of Balgowan, 2
Grand Palais, Paris, *Ossian* exhibition, 95
Gray, Thomas
    'The Descent of Odin', 83
    'The Fatal Sisters', 83, 85

Grenville, George, 18
Griffiths, Ralph, 21
Guerra, Camillo, 101
'La guerre ou la descente de Dearg files de Diric Roi de Lochlin' (*The war of the descent of Dearg, son of Diric, King of Lochlin*'), 32

Hapsburg Empire, 75
Harald Fairhair, King of Norway, 78
Harald III, King, 80
Harold, Edmund von, *Die Gedichte Ossian*, trans., 89
Hartvig, Gabriella, 75
Harvey, Elizabeth, *Malvina lamenting the Death of Oscar* (painting), 100
Hastings, Warren, 5, 23, 24
Herder, Johann Gottfried, 118
   Auszug aus einem Briefwechsel uber Ossian und die Lieder alter Volker (Extract from a Correspondence about Ossian and the Songs of Ancient Peoples), 78
   Iduna, oder Apfel der Verjungung (Iduna, or the Apple of Rejuvenation), 80
heroic couplets, 44, 45, 47, 48
Highland Society of Scotland, 15, 32, 104
historicism, 7, 117, 120, 122
Hoare, Henry, 94
Hoare, Richard Colt, 93, 94
Hole, Richard, 48
   Arthur; or, the Northern Enchantment, 84
   Poetical Translation of Fingal, 84
Home, John, 15
   Douglas (play), 2
Homer
   epic poetry, 9, 66
   Iliad, 57
   translations, 5, 46, 47, 48–51, 105–18
Hopkins, David, 106, 112, 116
Horace, 41, 42
   Ars poetica, 44
Hume, David
   character in, 122
   The History of England, 5
   A History of Great Britain, 119, 120
   on Homer, 105
   on *Ossian*, 4, 66
   women readers, 125
Hungary, 75

Icelandic texts, 76
identity, 9, 62–63
Immram Brain, 30
income, 24, 25
India, 4, 5, 19, 22, 23
Ingres, Jean-Auguste-Dominique, 92
'Inistore' (Orkney), 69
Interfaces – Image, Texte, Language (journal), 94
Invertromie, 25
Ireland
   ballad tradition, 29, 30
   Gaelic tradition, 27, 54
   Macpherson and, 7, 8, 66
   manuscript culture, 29
   translation, 42, 148n16
   Viking invasion, 34

'Is fada anocht a n-Oil Finn'
    ('*Time passes wearily in Elphin tonight*'), 29
Italy, 43, 97, 102

Jacobite Rising 1745, 1
Jacobitism, 55, 102, 130
James VII and II, King, 124, 125, 126–29, 130, 132
Jamieson, Robert, 84
Jenkinson, Charles, 18, 19
Jerningham, Edward
    The Rise and Progress of the Scandinavian Poetry, 83
Johnson, Samuel
    Dictionary of the English Language, 45
    Irene, 46
    London, 46
    and *Ossian*, 3, 7, 39, 40, 67
    Redford on, 21
    on translation, 45, 46, 50, 51
    The Vanity of Human Wishes, 46
    A Voyage to Abyssinia, 45
Johnstone, George, 4, 17–18
Journal des Scavans, 31
Journal of the Warburg and Courtauld Institutes, 95
Jutland, 69, 89, 90, 91
Juvenal, *Satires*, 46

Kauffmann, Angelica, 98, 99
Keating, Geoffrey, 34
Kennedy, Duncan, 32
Keppel, Augustus, 131
Kerrigan, John, 9
Kidd, Colin, *Subverting Scotland's Past*, 54
King's College, Aberdeen, 1
Kingussie, 1, 6, 25
Klopstock, Friedrich Gottlieb, 86, 87
    Hermanns Schlacht (Hermann's Battle), 87
    'Der Hügel und der Hain' (The Hill and the Grove), 87
    'Unsere Sprache' (Our Language), 87
Knox, Robert, *Races of Men*, 80
Knytlinga saga, 80
Koch, Joseph Anton, 99, 102, 103
Krafft, Johann Peter, 102
Kunsthalle, Hamburg, *Ossian* exhibition, 95, 96

'Lá dhúinne ar Sliabh Fuaid' ('*One day on Sliabh Foy*'), 31
Lahde, C. F. W., 91
Laing, Malcolm, 77
Lake Lego, Ulster, 68
landscape and place, 65–75, 92, 99
    'Claudian', 94
    and English artists 73, 74, 92
'Laoi Chab an Dosáin' ('*The Ballad of the Mouth of the Tuft*'), 31
'Laoi Mheargaigh' ('Laoi Mhná Mheargaigh') ('*The Ballad of Meargach*') ('*The Ballad of Meargach's wife*'), 31
'Laoi Oisín ar Thír na nÓg' ('*Oisin's lay concerning the Land of Youth*'), 30
laoi(dh) (dan or *duan)* (narrative poems), 28

'Laoidh an Mhoighre Bhoirb' ('Cath Rìgh na Sorcha' or 'Eas Ruadh'), 32
'Laoidh an Tailleoir' (*The Ballad of the Tailor*), 28
'Laoidh Dhiarmaid', 29
'Laoidh Fhraoich', 29
'Laoidh Mhaghnuis', 33
'last of the race' motif, 62, 63
Lathmon, 37
Latin, 41, 42, 43, 44, 45, 49, 77, 113 *see also* Virgil
Leask, Nigel, 73
Leerssen, Joep, 95
Lefevere, André, *Constructing Cultures*, 39
literalism in translation, 48, 49–50, 51
literary primitivism, 105, 107, 112, 113, 115, 117–18
The Little Book of Clanranald, 145n36
Loch Lomond, 74
Lockhart, John, *Life of Scott*, 85
Loda or Loden (Odin) 77
'Longes Mac nUislenn' (*The Exile of the Sons of Uisneach*), 28
Lorrain, Claude, 94
Louis XIV, King, 128
Low, George, 85
Luäth, 68
Lucan, 81
Lynch, Deidre Shauna, 122

mac Cumhaill, Fionn, 27
Mac Domhnaill, Captain Somhairle, 30
mac Ronáin, Caoilte, 28
Macartney, Lord George, 22, 23
Macaulay, Catherine, 121
Macdonald, Flora, 102
MacDonald, Keith Norman, *In Defence of Macpherson's Ossian*, 101
Macdonald, Murdo, 73
MacEwan, Geoff, 94
MacGann, Jerome, 6
MacGregor, Duncan, 30
MacGregor, Sir James, 30
Macintosh, Anne, 102
MacIntyre, Lieutenant Colonel John, 24
Mackintosh of Borlum, 6
MacLagan, James, 33, 34
Maclaren, Alexander, 101
Maclean, J. N. M., 19, 20, 22
Macleod, Captain Alexander, 19
MacMhurchaidh, Uilleam, 34
Macmillan, Duncan
  Painting in Scotland: The Golden Age, 95
  Scottish Art, 95
MacNicol, Donald, 27
Macpherson, Andrew (father JM), 1
Macpherson, Colonel Allan of Blairgowrie, 21
Macpherson, Ewan of Cluny (uncle JM), 1
Macpherson, James
  bequest, 3, 4
  birth, 1
  Cathlin of Clutha, 100
  Cath-Loda, 97
  correspondence, 14–25
  death, 1, 6
  'The Death of Cuchullin: A Poem', 68

Macpherson, James (*cont.*)
  education, 1, 2
  Fingal, An Ancient Epic Poem in Six Books; Together with Several Other Poems, Composed by Ossian the Son of Fingal, 3, 16, 31, 32, 33, 34, 55, 46, 47, 48, 53, 54, 56–72, 92, 97, 106, 113, 114, 117
  Fragments of Ancient Poetry Collected in the Highlands of Scotland, 2, 3, 15, 35–36, 60, 62, 65, 66, 67, 78, 81
  as government writer, 5, 17, 19–20
  The Highlander, 2
  historical writing, 119–33
  The History and Management of the East India Company, from its origins in 1600 to the present time, 5, 21, 119
  The History of Great Britain, from the Restoration, to the Accession of the House of Hannover, 5, 119, 121, 122–29
  The Hunter (epic poem), 2
  The Iliad of Homer in prose, 5, 47, 105–18
  An Introduction to the History of Great Britain and Ireland, 4, 5, 19, 47
  on Irish claims, 29
  as member of parliament, 5
  Original Papers: Containing the Secret History of Great Britain, from the Restoration, to the Accession of the House of Hannover, 5, 120
  The Poems of Ossian, 3, 6, 7, 8, 9, 26–51, 62–64, 74, 82, 85
  political journalism 19, 20
  Rights of Great Britain asserted against the claims of America: Being An Answer to the Declaration of the General Congress, 5, 6
  Short History of the Opposition during the Last Session of Parliament, 6, 20, 119, 121, 122, 130–33
  Temora: An Ancient Epic Poem in Eight Books; Together with Several Other Poems, Composed by Ossian the Son of Fingal, 3, 66, 67, 70, 77, 89, 97, 113, 113, 118
  translations of Gaelic language, 31–34, 35
  'The War of Caros', 74
  Works of Ossian, 70
Macpherson, John, 5, 18, 19, 20, 22, 24
Macpherson, Reverend John of Sleat, *Critical Dissertations on the Origins, Antiquities, of the Caledonians*, 19
Magnússon, Finnur, 78, 86
Mallet, Paul-Henri
  Introduction a l'histoire du Danemarch ou l'on traite de la religion, des moeurs, des lois, et des usages des anciens Danois (Introduction to the History of Denmark, or Discussion of the

Religion, Laws and Manners of the Ancient Danes), 77
Monumens de la mythologie et de la poesie des Celtes, et particulierement des anciens Scandinaves (Monuments of the Mythology and the Poetry of the Celts, in Particular the Ancient Scandinavians), 77
Northern Antiquities, 79
Malvina, 97, 100–02
manuscript tradition, 27, 28–30
Marischal College, Aberdeen, 1
Marshal, William of Gent, 39
Marshall, P. J., 22
Mason, William, 105
Mathias, Thomas James, *Runic Odes: Imitated from the Norse Tongue in the Manner of Mr. Gray*, 83
Mazzocca, Fernando, 100, 101
McElroy, George, 19, 20
McLuhan, Marshall, 41
Meek, Donald, 30, 34, 35, 37
Memoire de M. de C. a Messieurs les Auteurs Du Journal des Scavans (anon), 31
metre, 31, 44, 108
Milton, John, *Paradise Lost*, 57, 58, 59, 61
Mitchell, Sebastian, 48, 95, 106, 107, 109, 112, 117, 163n12
  'Celtic Postmodernism: Ossian and Contemporary Art', 94
Mohammed Ali, Nawab of Arcot, 5, 19, 21, 22, 23

'Moighre Borb', 33
Monmouth Rebellion 1685, 126
Monument at Sandwick (engraving), 99
Moore, Dafydd, 55, 70, 96
Morison, Roderick (An Clàrsair Dall, The Blind Harper), 63
Mortimer, John Hamilton, 100
Morven, 68, 90
Murdoch, John, 96
Myrone, Martin, *Bodybuilding: Reforming Masculinities in British Art 1750–1810*, 95

Napoleon, 92
Nasmyth, Alexander, 98
National Gallery of Canada, 103
national identity, 52–53, 55
neoclassicism, 7, 92
Newman, Francis, 46
Ní Mhunghaile, Lesa, 3
Nighean Alasdair Ruaidh, Màiri, 102
Niranjana, Tejaswini, 53
Normand, Tom, 94
Norse-inspired poetry, 82, 83–90, 91
Norse literature, 68, 76, 78–82
Norse mythology, 76, 77, 80, 86
North, Lord Frederick, 6, 19, 20, 22, 24, 119
Northern Isles, 85
nostalgia, 36, 55, 56–64, 74

Ó Catháin, Niall Gruama, 30
Ó Dochartaigh, Aodh, 30
Ó Gormáin, Muiris, 31
Ó Neachtain, Seán, 30
O'Brien, John, Bishop of Cloyne, 31

Odin, 77, 78, 84, 86, 90
Oehlenschläger, Adam
    'Guldhornene' (The Golden Horns), 89
    Langelands-Reise (Journey to Langeland), 88
O'Flaherty, Roderick, 34
oglachas (syllabic verse), 28
O'Grady, Standish Hayes, 30
Oisín (Oiséan), 27, 28–31, 34, 35, 36–37
Okun, Henry, 95, 99
Ong, Walter, 72
Opitz, Martin, 42
oral tradition, 27, 28, 29, 72
Orkney, 69, 78
Ossian Then and Now conference, 94
Oxford Guide to Literature in English Translation, 44
Oxford History of Classical Reception in English Literature, 106

parataxis, 72
paratexts, 39, 46, 55, 67, 70, 73
Passow, Anna Catharina von, *Den uventede Forlibelse eller Cupido Philosoph* (Unexpected Love, or Cupid the Philosopher), 88
Peacock, Thomas Love, *Fiolfar*, 84
Percy, Thomas
    Five Pieces of Runic Poetry Translated from the Islandic Language, 78, 79, 79–82
    Reliques of Ancient English Poetry, 82

Petrarch, 42
Pine, Robert Edge, *Calliope*, 98
Pinkerton, John, 80, 100
Pittock, Murray, 9, 55
Pléiade poets, France, 42
Pocock, J. G. A., 120
Polwhele, Richard
    'Ossian Departing to His Fathers: Imitated from Macpherson's Ossian', 83
    Poems Chiefly by Gentlemen of Devonshire and Cornwall, ed., 83
Pope, Alexander Rev
    collection of, 26
Pope, Alexander
    Messiah, 45
    translation of *Iliad*, 44, 45, 49, 109–16
postcolonialism, 52, 53–54
Potkay, Adam, 110
Potter, Mary, *Poetry of Nature*, ed., 101
Pram, Christen, *Frode and Fingal*, 88
primitivism, 105, 107, 112, 113
print culture, 40, 41, 42, 81, 83, 87, 95
Priolo, Paolo, 96
pseudotranslation, 39–41

racialism, 80
Raitts, 6, 25
Ramsay, Allan, 98
Rawes, Alan and Carruthers, Gerard, *English Romanticism and Celtic Nationalism* eds 9
Redford, Bruce, 21, 22
Reformation, 29, 41
Renaissance, 41, 42, 43

Restoration, 132
rewriting, 43, 44, 45, 48, 53–54
Reynolds, Joshua, 98
rhythmical prose, 31
Richardson, Samuel, 122, 128
Robertson, William
    History of America, 120
    History of Scotland, 120
Romantic Nationalism, 91
Romanticism, 6, 8, 9, 16, 74
Rose, Robert Traill, 101
Rosenblum, Robert,
    Transformations in Late Eighteenth Century Art, 100
Rousseau, Jean-Jacques, 55
Rudhraigheacht (Ulster cycle), 27, 28, 34
Runciman, Alexander, 93, 95, 97, 98, 99
rune script, 82
Runge, Philipp Otto, 98
Russet, Margaret, 113
Ruthven, 2

Sammes, Aylett, 79
Saunders, Thomas Bailey, 6, 7, 8, 14, 15, 19, 20, 21
Saxo Grammaticus, *Gesta Danorum* (The Deeds of the Danes), 87
Sayers, Frank
    'The Descent of Frea', 83
    Dramatic Sketches of the Ancient Northern Mythology, 83
Scandinavian literature, 76–91
    Celtic and Germanic culture, 77–78
    Gothic tradition in Britain, 78, 79–82

Norse-inspired poetry, 82, 83–90, 91
Schmidt, Wolfgang, *'Homer des Nordens' und 'Mutter der Romantik': James Macphersons 'Ossian' und seine Rezeption in der deutschsprachigen Literatur*, 8
Scott, Walter
    Harold the Dauntless, 84, 85
    The Lay of the Last Minstrel, 84
    The Pirate, 85
Scottish Celtic Revival, 101–02
Scottish Enlightenment, 10, 16
Scottish Highlands, 65, 66, 67
Scottish National Portrait Gallery, Edinburgh, 93
Scottish nationalism, 40, 42, 52, 54, 55, 74, 75
sculpture, 98, 101
'secretary hand', 30
Sentimentalism, 55, 80, 128–29
Shaw, Norman, 94
Shelburne, Lord, 139n12
Shenstone, William, 81
Sheringham, Robert, 79
Shetland Islands, 85
Sìleas na Ceapaich, 102
Skáldaspillir, Eyvindr
    Hakonarmaal, 89
skaldic poetry, 78, 79, 80, 86, 87, 89
Skjöldebrand, Erik, 78
'Sliabh nam Ban Fionn', 33
Smart, John Semple, 7, 8
Smollett, Tobias, *The Complete History of England*, 120
Society of Antiquaries of Scotland, 93
'The Songs of Selma', 74

Sophocles, *Sofonisba*, 42
Sotheby, William, 47
Spies, Werner, 95, 96
St Augustine, 57
St Clair, William, *The Reading Nation in the Romantic Period*, 96
St Jerome, 41
St Patrick, 34
stadial historiography, 66, 117
Staël, Germaine de, *Corinne*, 103
Stafford, Fiona, 4, 9, 15, 73
Stafford, Fiona and Gaskill, Howard, *From Gaelic to Romantic*, eds., 9
Stamp Act (1765), 18
Steiner, George, 57
  Homer in English, ed., 47, 106
Stern, Ludwig Chr., 32, 33
Sterne, Laurence 128
Stoddart, Alexander, 94
Stone, Jerome, 27, 33
Stourhead, 94
Strahan, William, 20, 139n11, 139n12
Stukeley, William, 97, 98
Suhm, Peter Frederik, 78
'Suireadh Oisein air Eamhair Aluinn' ('*Oisin's Courtship*'), 33
'Suirghe Ghuill', 30
Swaran, 61, 67, 69, 71, 72
Sweden, 78, 86
Symbolism, 102

Tacitus, 121
  Germania, 87
'Táin Bó Cúailnge' ('*The Cattle Raid of Cooley*'), 28, 34
tartan, 99, 100
Taylor, Isaac, 92, 97
'Teanntachd Mhòr na Fèinne' ('*The Fian's great distress*'), 33
Temple, Kathryn, 113
Temple, William, 79
Thompson, D. S., *The Gaelic Sources of Macpherson's Ossian*, 7
Thomson, Derick, 28, 33, 34
Thorlaug, 86
Thorvaldsen, Bertel, 89
Tír na nÓg, 30
Tiresias, 63
Tolkien, J. R. R, 102
'Tóraigheacht Dhiarmada agus Ghráinne' ('*The Pursuit of Diarmaid and Grainne*'), 28
Torfæus, Thormod, 83
  Orcades, 85
Toury, Gideon, *Descriptive Translation Studies and beyond*, 39–40
Townshend, Thomas, 131
'transcreation', 53, 54, 55, 60, 64
translation, 39–51
  translation theory, 11, 41–42, 45
Translation Studies, 53
Treaty of Ryswick (1697), 128
Trécourt, Giacomo, 101
Trevor-Roper, Hugh, 19, 20
Trissino, Gian Giorgio, 42
Trumbull, John
  The Declaration of Independence (painting), 103
  Lamderg and Gelchossa (painting), 104

Trumpener, Katie, 54, 55
Turner, J. M. W.
   Aeneas and the Sibyl, Lake Avernus (painting), 94
   Ben Lomond Mountains, Scotland: The Traveller – Vide Ossian's War of Caros (painting), 92
   The Golden Bough (painting), 94
   and *Ossian*, 74, 92, 93, 94, 99
   Staffa, Fingal's Cave (painting), 94
Tytler, Alexander Fraser, *Essay on the Principles of Translation*, 51

Ulaidh, 28
Ulster, 67–68
Ulster cycle see *Rudhraigheacht*
Union of Parliaments (1707), 52

Van Teigham, Paul, *Ossian en France*, 8
Venuti, Lawrence, 44, 51
   The Translator's Invisibility, 46
vernacular poetry, popularity of, 76, 77
vernacularisation, 41, 42
Vikings, 34, 80, 84
Virgil
   Aeneid, 57, 113
   and visual art, 93
visual arts, 92–104
   American dimension 103, 104
   Nordic mythology, 85, 86

scholarship on, 95–96
and Scottish Highlands, 94, 95
Vulgate Bible, 41

Wale, Samuel, 92, 96, 97, 99
Walker, William, 100
Wallis, George Augustus, 99, 103
Walpole, Horace, 105
   The Castle of Otranto, 39
Warton, Thomas, *The History of English Poetry*, 80
Watson, William, 152n10
West, Benjamin, 104
Whitefoord, Caleb, 20, 139n12
William III, King, 124, 127, 129, 130
Wodrow, John, 48
Womack, Peter, *Improvement and Romance: Constructing the Myth of the Highlands*, 65
Woodfall, H. S., 20–21
Woodfall, William, 20
Worm, Ole, *Runir: seu Danica literatura antiquissima, vulgo Gothica dicta luci reddita* (Runes: or the Most Ancient Danish Letters, Popularly Called Gothic, Brought to Light), 82

Zandomeneghi, Luigi, 100, 102
   Ossian invita al canto la mesta Malvina (illustration), 101
   tomb of Titian (sculpture), 101

www.ingramcontent.com/pod-product-compliance
Lightning Source LLC
Chambersburg PA
CBHW070825250426
43671CB00036B/2072